THE STRUGGLE
FOR PUBLIC EDUCATION

THE STRUGGLE FOR PUBLIC EDUCATION

Ten Themes in American Educational History

**Donald Parkerson
and
Jo Ann Parkerson**

ROWMAN & LITTLEFIELD
Lanham • Boulder • New York • London

Published by Rowman & Littlefield
A wholly owned subsidiary of The Rowman & Littlefield Publishing Group, Inc.
4501 Forbes Boulevard, Suite 200, Lanham, Maryland 20706
www.rowman.com

Unit A, Whitacre Mews, 26-34 Stannary Street, London SE11 4AB

Copyright © 2017 by Rowman & Littlefield

All rights reserved. No part of this book may be reproduced in any form or by any electronic or mechanical means, including information storage and retrieval systems, without written permission from the publisher, except by a reviewer who may quote passages in a review.

British Library Cataloguing in Publication Information Available

Library of Congress Cataloging-in-Publication Data Available

ISBN: 978-1-4758-3019-4 (cloth : alk. paper)
ISBN: 978-1-4758-3020-0 (pbk. : alk. paper)
ISBN: 978-1-4758-3021-7 (electronic)

∞ ™ The paper used in this publication meets the minimum requirements of American National Standard for Information Sciences—Permanence of Paper for Printed Library Materials, ANSI/NISO Z39.48-1992.

Printed in the United States of America

To Public Education—
The Cornerstone of American Democracy

CONTENTS

Preface	vii
Acknowledgments	xi
Introduction	xiii

1. The Authoritarian and Democratic Schools of Education: The Philosophical Debate — 1
2. The Structure and Organization of American Schools: The States Seize Control — 13
3. Consolidation and Its Discontents: From Intimacy to Bureaucracy — 29
4. The Struggle for Diversity: The Emergence of a Multicultural Consciousness — 45
5. The Curriculum: From Religious to Secular and Comprehensive — 63
6. Instruction: From Memorization to Comprehension — 77
7. Discipline in the Classroom: From Corporal Punishment to Preventative Techniques — 91
8. Moral Education: From Virtue Centered to Cognitive Moral Development — 109
9. Testing and Assessment: From Recitation to Standardized Assessment — 127
10. Rights and Responsibilities of Teachers and Students: From *in loco parentis* to Individual Rights — 143

Conclusion: The Complexity of Change in American Education	161
References	177
Index	187
About the Authors	199

PREFACE

Two powerful schools of educational thought have challenged one another for the heart and soul of American education. The sometimes bitter rivalry between the authoritarian and democratic visions of education has been shaped by powerful economic, social, political, and cultural forces and is expressed in virtually every aspect of American educational history.

The authoritarian school of education is rooted in a number of educational philosophies including perennialism, essentialism, and behaviorism. It is derived in part from the educational writings of John Locke in the late 1600s as well as a number of modern educators such as Mortimer Adler, Theodore Sizer, William James, and B. F. Skinner.

Authoritarian school advocates typically favor an educational system that emphasizes the products of education. For these educators, the facts represent the centerpiece of the curriculum and therefore, the subject-centered, teacher-focused approach is preferred. Moreover, convergent thinking is promoted since the mastery of a specific "body of knowledge" is seen as the goal of education. This "inside the box" thinking encourages the use of objective tests—often multiple-choice standardized tests.

As a result, authoritarian educators have embraced programs such as the No Child Left Behind Act, end-of-grade, high-stakes testing, mastery learning, and various forms of programmed learning. Moreover, they often have preferred a STEM-oriented curriculum—science, technology, engineering, and math—over one centered in the humanities and social sciences.

Finally, authoritarian school advocates often have embraced the corporate business model for the organization of schools. Over time, they have advocated for state control of local school districts, school and administrative consolidation, professionalization, quantitative assessment of teachers, greater "productivity" of students, as well as vocational education.

Clearly, the authoritarian school of education has been influential over the policies of education in America. But not all educators agree with this approach. In fact, the dialogue between advocates of the authoritarian school and those of the democratic school of education has provided a context to help us understand the sometimes erratic development of our educational system.

The democratic school of education (sometimes referred to as the "non-authoritarian school") is quite different. It is drawn in part from the writings of Jean-Jacques Rousseau in the mid 1700s, but it is also rooted in the modern philosophies of pragmatism, progressivism, humanism, constructionism, and postmodernism. Moreover, it is represented by philosopher/educators such as John Dewey, Johann Pestalozzi, Jean Piaget, Michael Apple, and Michel Foucault.

Democratic educators typically reject the authoritarian idea that education is primarily the acquisition of a body of knowledge—the products of learning. Rather, they embrace the process of learning itself. Here, an experience-centered or student-centered curriculum is favored where learning is achieved through a dialogue between the student and the teacher.

Democratic reformers typically promote thinking that is "outside the box"—divergent thinking. Here, students are encouraged to offer unique and creative solutions, often to important social problems. Finally, democratic educators have traditionally supported local control of schools and vigorous community involvement in education and generally have opposed school consolidation.

In recent years, democratic educators have also opposed the No Child Left Behind Act as well as crude school and national comparisons of test scores. They also have opposed the exclusive use of standardized, multiple-choice examinations and most forms of high-stakes testing. Rather, they favor teacher-created essay examinations, research papers, portfolios, group projects, and discussions as the basis of student assessment.

And yet, there is more to this story. This book situates this important educational conflict in the context of the ten major themes in American education. These include the structure and organization of schools; the struggle for diversity, curriculum and instruction, discipline, and moral education; testing and assessment; and the rights and responsibilities of both teachers and students.

By understanding the struggle between these two powerful philosophical educational schools and how each have responded to economic, social, political, and cultural change, we can better appreciate the apparent, never-ending debate over the direction of American public education.

ACKNOWLEDGMENTS

We wish to thank our family, friends, and colleagues for their support and encouragement, especially, Cindy Ripperger; Gonzalo Soruco; Ken Wilburn; Bill Grobe; Chris Oakley, chair of the History Department; and William Downs, dean, Thomas Harriot College of Art and Sciences, East Carolina University. We appreciate the generous endorsement of our book by Marjorie Ringler and Charles Coble. Also thank you to associate editor Carlie Wall, Hannah Fisher, and the entire production staff, who have been extremely helpful.

Finally, a special thank you to Tom Koerner, vice president and editorial director of education at Rowman & Littlefield Publishers, who provided formative and essential feedback for this book. Thanks Tom!

INTRODUCTION

American educational history is complex. It is rooted in a past that reaches from antiquity, with the contributions of the Greeks and Romans through the philosophers of the European Enlightenment to American educators who have made their own unique contributions to this history. These include an open and forgiving system of learning, free or inexpensive primary and secondary education, and a decentralized organization that has supported learning both culturally and financially.

As we have seen, however, American educational history has been a monumental struggle between two powerful schools of educational thought: the authoritarian and the democratic. In addition to their underlying philosophical perspectives, the policies promoted by each of these schools have been influenced by dramatic economic, social, political, and cultural changes throughout American history.

By placing this struggle in the context of the ten major educational themes presented here, we hope that you will be in a better position to make sense of the complex world of education today.

In chapter 1, we begin our story by revisiting the two primary schools of educational thought—the authoritarian and the democratic. By understanding the interplay between these two schools in the context of the historical forces shaping the history of our nation, we can better understand how the basic thematic elements of educational history have unfolded over the years.

In chapter 2, we turn to the ongoing struggle to control American public education. Here we see those who favor local control of schools representing an early form of the democratic position and those who favored state control as an important element of the authoritarian position.

This chapter traces the changing structure and organization of American public schools from the uneven educational experiments of the colonies to the common school of the early nineteenth century to the graded schools at the turn of the twentieth century and finally to the large consolidated schools of today.

As we shall see, early American schools, from the colonial period through the early nineteenth century, were locally controlled. Moreover, the quality of these schools varied greatly. Some communities in New England and New York, for example, provided their children with a good, basic education. Others in the middle colonies such as Pennsylvania and New Jersey often relied on the church to furnish an education for their children. Still others, in rural and frontier regions, were less impressive, and children in these communities often had no access to schools whatsoever.

In the South, communities typically embraced private schools and tutors. As a result, only the rich were able to receive an education. Poor whites and African American slaves, of course, had no access at all. Wealthy planters and merchants, on the other hand, often employed tutors and governesses to educate their children and prepare them for secondary and university education either in the North or abroad.

During the American Revolution and early Republic, however, there were some important changes in our attitudes toward education. These changes were slow in coming, however, and were defined by a combination of early federal involvement and then abandonment, general state apathy, and continued local control.

The federal government, under the Articles of Confederation, took some interest in schools and provided generous land grants to communities for education under the Northwest Ordinance of 1787. This important federal directive stated clearly that "knowledge being necessary to good government and the happiness of mankind, schools and the means of education shall forever be encouraged." In addition, founding fathers such as Benjamin Franklin, Thomas Jefferson, Benjamin Rush, and many others used their influence to promote education at all levels (Parkerson and Parkerson 2001).

With the ratification of the U.S. Constitution in 1789 and the adoption of the Tenth Amendment in 1793, however, direct federal support essentially ended. The Tenth Amendment to the U.S. Constitution clearly expressed America's commitment to federalism—that is, the shared power between the federal government and the states. It stated that "the powers not delegated to the United States by the Constitution . . . are reserved to the states." What this meant for education was simple—since there was no mention of schooling in the U.S. Constitution itself, states and not the federal government were now responsible for education (Parkerson and Parkerson 2001).

And yet, the states were curiously silent regarding education during the early years of the Republic. State legislators typically ignored calls for the development of an educational system and deferred to religious and private institutions to control their schools as they had done during the colonial era. This uneven form of education would persist into the first decades of the nineteenth century.

However, as male suffrage expanded during these years and as the market revolution swept across young America, individuals and groups began to recognize the importance of free public education for their children. This grassroots democratic support encouraged state leaders to act. Among those promoting public education were workingmen, small-business owners, and a new class of commercial farmers. This critical combination of grassroots support and idealistic political leadership helped to launch the common school movement of the early nineteenth century.

By the middle of the century, individual states began to wrest control of education from local communities. This process took some time and involved important constitutional mandates from the states, a legislative crusade led by authoritarian reformers, and critical support from the courts that validated the states' authority over education.

Over the next hundred years, states, driven by this authoritarian vision of education, gradually assumed some of the funding of the schools, consolidated their control over the schools, and expanded their authority over the structure and direction of public education.

These changes were dramatic. The locally funded "democratic" schools as well as religious and private institutions of the early Republic gradually disappeared during this period, replaced by public school systems that were funded and controlled administratively by the states and some larger municipalities.

The administrative centralization and physical consolidation of schools began in the late nineteenth century. It represented an important victory for authoritarian educators of the period who sought to both improve education and save money for the taxpayers.

Many authoritarian educators had become enchanted with the success of corporate America during the late nineteenth century and were convinced that the corporate-business model of organization was appropriate for schools. They argued that a top-down, hierarchical administration as well as the adoption of merit-based promotion standards for teachers would move education into a bright future. Moreover, through physical consolidation of facilities, they could achieve substantial savings.

While democratic child-centered progressives were skeptical, they gradually accepted some of these reforms. Many assumed correctly that larger consolidated schools would help attract professionally trained teachers but perhaps naively felt that these savings would allow schools to purchase better equipment and books and establish more up-to-date facilities for their students. In short, while most reformers of this period saw consolidation as a plus for education, this clearly was a major victory for authoritarian reformers.

The transformation of schools during a period—what we have called "the Consolidation Century" had three distinct components or phases, as we discuss in chapter 3. The first was the high school movement that gained momentum in the late nineteenth and early twentieth centuries. High schools provided the basic template of consolidated schools that would follow (Parkerson and Parkerson 2015).

The second phase was the primary-school-consolidation movement that closed thousands of rural schools and consolidated them into larger "campus-like" institutions. Paralleling this was the urban consolidation movement that embraced a model of business efficiency through both administrative centralization and teacher professionalization.

The third phase of school consolidation was what might be called "desegregation consolidation" where thousands of all-black schools were closed, and African American children were bused to larger, predominately white institutions. While this represented the beginning of the end of school segregation, it was also a major shift toward even greater white cultural hegemony in education. This has had a lasting negative impact on African American children throughout the nation.

By the end of the consolidation century, the educational landscape of America was radically altered. On the eve of World War I there were over 270,000 schools throughout the country, while today there are fewer than half that many, about 100,000. The one-room schoolhouses of America had a similar fate; peaking at about 150,000 in the early twentieth century, today they are virtually nonexistent (Parkerson and Parkerson 2015).

Local school districts also disappeared during the consolidation century. As late as 1917, there were about 130,000 school boards throughout the nation providing local input into educational policy. Today, however, larger centralized boards have all but replaced them—with only about 20,000 boards remaining. These changes have had a dramatic impact on virtually every element of the educational village.

In chapter 4, we turn our attention to the struggle for diversity in public education. As we shall see, this battle was a painful reminder that American public education was built on the values and assumption of a white, male-dominated, "pan-Protestant" nation and often failed to adapt to our rapidly changing multicultural society.

While both democratic and authoritarian reformers eventually reached a consensus regarding the importance of diversity in schools, the struggle to admit women, African Americans, and immigrants into schools was hard fought over many years and typically was led by democratic reformers. Indeed the struggle continues today in many communities throughout America.

The parochial nature of education during our colonial period is well documented. Schools were designed to meet the needs of the local community or members of their church. Others simply were not welcome. Moreover, these schools were designed for white boys, and young girls typically were not admitted.

With the emergence of the common school in the early to mid-nineteenth century, change seemed possible. The idealistic goal of the common school was to provide an education that was "within the reach of all." But that objective was not achieved (Parkerson and Parkerson 1998).

In fact, the "original sin" of early public schools—and one that continues to plague the nation—was their failure to embrace the diverse cultures and religions of our nation's newest citizens—ethnic and Roman Catholic children from Europe and, of course, African Americans, who were brought to this country as slaves.

As the nineteenth century progressed, young women eventually were allowed into the schools in most communities, though there were limitations. Courses in math and science, for example, often were denied to women, and not until the twentieth century were women admitted to colleges throughout the nation.

The experiences of African Americans were much more difficult. The American Civil War (1861–1865) and the ratification of the Thirteenth Amendment of the U.S. Constitution ended slavery but certainly not bigotry, segregation, or exclusion from schools. The federal government established the Freedmen Bureau schools, during the early years of Reconstruction in 1866, to provide young black children and adults with free public education. This experiment, though successful, was short-lived, and by the end of the nineteenth century, the Supreme Court had validated the discriminatory policies of Jim Crow with its infamous *Plessy v. Ferguson* decision in 1896.

As a result, for nearly half a century, black children in America were forced to rely on local churches and private philanthropy for their education. And while the situation in northern states was somewhat better, segregation in its many ugly forms persisted throughout this period.

Following years of bitter civil rights struggle that mobilized the black community and democratic reformers throughout the country, progress was made. Through legislation, court decisions (most notably *Brown v. Board of Education* in 1954), organizations such as the NAACP, and the direct action by the people themselves, public education gradually became more inclusive for African American children.

And yet the struggle continues. As our nation becomes more diverse as a result of immigration from Latin America, Asia, and more recently, the Middle East, the doors of our schools remain only partly open. Opposition to bilingual education and consistent calls for English-only instruction continues to obstruct equal educational opportunities for immigrant children.

Moreover, the consolidated mega-schools of today, vigorously supported by authoritarian educators, have been shown to be inadequate for the needs of poor, immigrant, and black children. Clearly, we have made progress, but there is much more to do (Parkerson and Parkerson 2015).

In chapters 5 and 6, we examine the dramatic changes in both the curriculum and classroom instruction of American public schools and trace the important elements in that transformation. As we have seen, during the early colonial period, religion was the centerpiece of the curriculum for Puritans, Anglicans, and Roman Catholics alike. In communities from the Far North to the Deep South, these schools promoted their particular vision of faith. Reading the Bible and memorizing a catechism was the centerpiece of their curriculum, and there was little emphasis on math, science, or the humanities.

Following the American Revolution in the late eighteenth century, and as the market economy spread across the nation in the nineteenth century, democratic reformers helped to fundamentally transform the curriculum of schools. While religion continued to have an important role, it gradually took on less of a sectarian focus. A kind of pan-Protestantism replaced specific references to a particular religious denomination so common during the colonial era and the early Republic.

Moreover, as America grew from a small collection of colonies to a modern nation, public schools embraced a more authoritarian vision of education by developing a curriculum that emphasized national unity through the reading and memorizing of patriotic poems, stories, and myths. Similarly, as the economy of young America was transformed during this period, and the market revolution touched nearly every corner of the nation, common schools responded by promoting secular values of hard work, determination, persistence, and punctuality (Parkerson and Parkerson 2008).

At the same time, a rigorous classical form of education was being promoted by democratic educators in the new high schools of the nation. These high schools were a kind of "Peoples College" and helped to prepare a small but talented group of students with the skills that would allow them to succeed in college or enter the professions.

By the early twentieth century, however, the needs of the nation were changing, and the curriculum of our schools was transformed once again. Young America, once a rural, agricultural, and homogeneous country, had now matured into an urban, industrial, and multicultural nation. By the first decades of the twentieth century, there was a growing movement to change the curriculum.

In response to these changes, authoritarian educators promoted a vocational curriculum to prepare students both as trained workers with skills for the workplace and as corporate managers who understood the complex world of business. In addition, the enormous influx of immigrants during these years signaled to authoritarian educators that there was a need to accommodate and assimilate millions of these new arrivals into American society.

These changes triggered a furious debate over the direction of the curriculum and, once again, represented the classic struggle between the authoritarian and democratic visions of education.

Eventually, an uneasy compromise was reached with the publication of the National Education Association's *Cardinal Principles* in 1918. Vocational training and academic tracking programs, promoted by authoritarian reformers, became an important element of the new curriculum. At the same time, new creative methods of instruction, favored by democratic educators, also were embraced as part of this compromise. Moreover, the new curriculum promoted student health, physical activity, civics education, and the development of an ethical character (*Cardinal Principles* 1918).

However, this compromise eventually collapsed as the nation descended first into World War II and then into a bitter cold war. Now, as the survival of the free world appeared to be in jeopardy, authoritarian reformers promoted a "back to basics" curriculum to compete with our "mortal" enemies. For their part, democratic progressives responded with new innovative approaches to both the curriculum and instruction during the 1960s and 1970s.

Nevertheless, the resolve of authoritarian educators was renewed with the publication of the infamous report *A Nation at Risk* in 1983, which helped to move American public schools, once again, toward a "back to basics," business-oriented, and vocational curriculum with new measures of standardized assessment for both students and teachers.

The recent demise of the No Child Left Behind Act as well as persistent questions regarding the validity of high-stakes standardized testing has signaled a shift both in public opinion and among educational reformers toward a more democratic vision. But only by understanding the fierce debate between authoritarian and democratic education can these curricular changes be understood.

As the curriculum of American schools was transformed during these years, so was classroom instruction. While these changes were complex, the essential change in instruction involved a shift from an authoritarian focus on memorization and recitation to a more democratic approach centering on comprehension and understanding of the material. This is the focus of chapter 6.

From the early colonial period through the nineteenth century, the primary method of instruction was memorization and recitation. A lack of reading materials plagued these early schools, and standardized readers typically were not available. Having students memorize passages from the Bible or a book provided by the teacher and then recite them in front of the teacher was the essence of early instruction.

A second reason for the persistence of these instructional methods was the entertainment of the community. In an era before organized sports or virtually any form of mass entertainment, the recitations of young boys and girls were a welcome diversion. Spelling bees and math contests at the local school also were exciting events supported by many members of the community.

But gradually things began to change. Democratic educators recognized that simply reciting a passage from a book or reeling off the multiplication "times tables" did not mean that the students understood what they had memorized. These educators of the late nineteenth and early twentieth centuries rejected the routine use of memorization—though that practice would continue to be a part of classroom instruction for some time.

Building on the work of Rousseau, Pestalozzi, and others, democratic educators promoted a new progressive form of instruction. John Dewey, for example, recommended that students "learn by doing" through cooperative experiences. He argued that these experiences were the gateway to knowledge. Later, Kilpatrick's Project Method built on Dewey's progressive vision, encouraging students to understand the interconnectedness of society through cooperative group work.

By the 1930s, basal readers such as the Dick and Jane series were introduced into classrooms throughout the nation. These readers were scientifically designed by educators to match students' developmental levels. Rather than reading, memorizing, and then reciting material they did not understand, students now were better able to comprehend the passages they read. This allowed students to perceive reading as a tool rather than as simply an incomprehensible passage to recite to the teacher.

While some of these and other innovations were rejected by authoritarian advocates, the influence of progressive, democratic educators was central to the growth of education and instruction. Today, comprehension in reading and understanding the principles of math and science (rather than simply computations) has become the cornerstone of modern classroom instruction.

In chapter 7, we turn to the changes in classroom discipline over the years. As with other aspects of public education, discipline reflected the changing norms of American society. And yet, over the years, teachers have employed a variety of techniques to maintain order in the classroom. As a result, discipline has evolved from various forms of physical, corporal punishment favored by authoritarian educators of the colonial era and early Republic to an assortment of psychological techniques, behavior modification, and preventative disciplinary techniques embraced by democratic educators.

During the American colonial era our attitudes toward the discipline of children were rooted in the Judeo-Christian idea of original sin. Children were seen as "stained" at birth, and it was felt that only through severe discipline could they be wrested from the "delusions of Satan." In short, the biblical imperative "Spare the rod and spoil the child" had a profound effect on our attitudes toward children and their discipline.

In the eighteenth century, the writings of visionaries such as John Locke and, later, Jean-Jacques Rousseau as well as the liberating spiritual ideas of the First Great Awakening gradually began to change our attitudes toward discipline. By the nineteenth century, new democratic methods of punishment gradually emerged that focused less on physical abuse and more on preventing misbehavior in the first place.

By the early twentieth century, as the corporate/business model of education was embraced by many school systems, however, a new form of authoritarian "industrial discipline" was seen as the solution for unruly children. This approach became very popular in large school systems that were experiencing rapid population growth due to immigration and consolidation. Students sat at desks that were bolted to the floor and were required to remain silent with their feet flat on the floor and hands folded until the teacher clapped her hands to signal the beginning of the school day.

While elements of industrial discipline would persist, by the middle of the twentieth century new preventive techniques also were introduced by democratic educational reformers. Some recommended the subtle manipulation of the student's work environment. Others promoted nonverbal methods of communication, while others suggested the use of rewards to promote discipline.

In short, the transformation of discipline in the classroom has been a reflection of changes in American society since the colonial period. As with other aspects of American educational history, teachers have adapted to these changes, and today they are having a positive impact on the behavior of their students.

Just as disciplinary techniques in America were transformed over the years, there were parallel changes in moral-character education as well. This is the focus of chapter 8. As we have seen, during the American colonial era, the authoritarian vision of education embraced religion as the basis of the curriculum, instructional methods, and disciplinary techniques of schools. Central to their education, moreover, were the moral lessons promoted through books such as *The New England Primer* with its Shorter Catechism, The Lord's Prayer, The Creed, and other religious tracts.

Memorization and recitation of these passages and prayers not only served as the basis of reading instruction but also provided the centerpiece of moral education. The family, of course, continued to be the primary authority of moral values, while members of the community also were expected to monitor and promote those values.

With the emergence of the common school in the nineteenth century, however, moral education began to change. The family, community, and church, of course, would continue their important functions in developing and maintaining values among children, but now the common school also would play an important role.

But common school teachers had to deal with the realities of the developing meritocratic society, a central part of the market revolution and the American Revolution. The new mindset among Americans—especially young Americans—was the rejection of traditional "deference" and obedience to individuals simply because of their position at birth or through inheritance. No longer would children be expected to "obey" simply because of an individual's social status within society (Parkerson and Parkerson 2001).

To attend to these dramatic changes, democratic educators embraced the concept of the "virtuous balanced curriculum" as the basis of instruction and moral education. This meant addressing not only the student's intellectual growth but also his or her moral development. While this was not a new idea, it found urgency in our emerging egalitarian society.

Religion also would continue to play a role in classroom instruction, but now the centerpiece of ethical training shifted to a more secular-oriented, democratic approach that emphasized the importance of both God *and* Country. These values, moreover, were promoted by "virtuous teachers," often young women.

Armed with copies of McGuffey *Readers*, generations of these young, virtuous teachers not only taught their students the basics of reading, writing, and arithmetic, but they also instructed them in the lessons of individual responsibility and the importance of the community. And yet, older students also were introduced to the values of nationalism through the more traditional authoritarian methods of memorizing and then reciting to the teacher patriotic poems and passages.

By the beginning of the twentieth century, as young America matured into a large, diverse, industrial nation, however, the lessons of the McGuffey *Readers* seemed quaint and old-fashioned. Educators from both ends of the ideological spectrum challenged the simple moral teachings of the nineteenth century.

Democratic progressives such as John Dewey maintained that the moral codes of the earlier era were too rigid and argued that students must develop a "social intelligence" that would help them face the moral dilemmas of the new century. Authoritarian businessmen reformers, on the other hand, rejected the "relativism" of Dewey and others, and suggested that students needed an unambiguous character education that focused on a set of absolute moral principles.

This debate over the proper form of moral education has raged over the years among different groups with remarkably similar positions to those developed at the turn of the twentieth century. Today neo-progressives democratic educators favor a moral education based on "values clarification" or "cognitive-based values development." Each of these approaches pays homage to earlier democratic progressive ideas, especially their recognition of moral relativism. Neo-conservative authoritarians, on the other hand, continue to promote a form of moral absolutism through literature, integrated into the curriculum, such as William Bennett's popular *The Book of Virtues*.

While most educators today recognize the need for some form of moral education, the furious debate over the direction and content of that education continues. This has led many school administrators to avoid any form of moral education altogether. And yet, American students need a moral compass, and a compromise of sorts is desperately needed.

In chapter 9, we turn to testing and assessment. As we shall see, since the early colonial period, some form of testing and assessment has been an important part of the American educational experience. What has changed, however, is the form of that assessment.

Schools throughout the colonies used traditional authoritarian methods of memorization and recitation as the centerpiece of their assessment of student progress. Young men who did not have the opportunity to go to school, on the other hand, often served as an apprentice in a trade where they were tested by members of the artisan guild to certify their knowledge and skills. Young women, on the other hand, often deprived of a formal education, learned these values in the family kitchen or garden, instructed by their mothers, aunts, and sisters.

While memorization and recitation would persist well into the nineteenth century, the "bee" also became an important form of community assessment of students. While these gatherings clearly were a form of community entertainment, they also served as an important form of assessment of both students and teachers.

Beginning in the mid-nineteenth century and slowly developing in the decades that followed, the in-class, written examination emerged. Designed by democratic educators and based on the curriculum presented in local classrooms, this form of assessment continues to be an important part of the educational experience—complete with the dreaded "report card."

By the beginning of the twentieth century, however, the standardized exam slowly made its way into the classrooms of America. These exams, vigorously promoted by authoritarian educators, have gradually competed with the "in class" exam as the primary method of student assessment.

Today, educators find themselves in a difficult position. On the one hand, we recognize the need for student assessment. On the other hand, many teachers have become overwhelmed by the sheer number of standardized exams that are required of our students.

The powerful testing establishment has promoted these standardized exams as an essential component of quality education, and many politicians and some educators and administrators have enthusiastically accepted these assumptions. Test preparation and test taking, however, can be time-consuming and costly. Moreover, many democratic reformers have pointed out that, as a result, "teaching to the test" has become a dark classroom reality.

As the pendulum of educational reform swings away from our collective infatuation with standardized assessment, we may now be able to reach a new compromise. Perhaps with the limited use of standardized exams and greater emphasis placed on more democratically oriented, teacher-created, in-class exams, we can return authority to classroom teachers and create a more "user friendly" educational experience.

In chapter 10, we examine the struggle for human rights and civil rights of students and teachers in public schools. Like other aspects of American education, this struggle has reflected the changes in American society as a whole. Discrimination against female students and teachers, African Americans, immigrants, the poor, the handicapped, the sick, and the LGBTQ community has been the dark backdrop of public education for over two centuries.

During the colonial era and well into the nineteenth and early twentieth centuries, progress against these forms of discrimination was virtually nonexistent. In fact, only in the final decades of the last century was real progress achieved. This success was accomplished as the result of steady, democratic, grassroots efforts on the part of individuals and groups within society, coupled with favorable court rulings.

As to the question of a student's constitutional rights, in general, it is clear that throughout much of our educational history, there were few provisions. American education was built on the authoritarian premise that educators were *in loco parentis*—in place of parents. As a result, teachers and administrators often treated students of all ages as children. And despite the fact that these "children" often were American citizens, they clearly were deprived of their basic constitutional rights.

As we have seen, corporal punishment was a common practice in schools from the colonial era through the early twentieth century and continues in some communities today. Moreover, until recently, students have had no access to their personal school records; they have had no due process when accused of a crime, and they have had no protection from unlawful search and seizure. And of course, students typically have had little or no freedom of speech.

As with the struggle for human rights and civil rights, the great democratic effort to achieve basic constitutional and legal rights for students and teachers has been long and hard. Like other changes, these require a rethinking of traditional authoritarian policies and laws that have been part of our culture for many years. And while progress has been made, we want more!

We demand greater protection from discrimination as our society becomes more culturally, ethnically, and racially diverse. And we demand basic constitutional rights for every staff member, teacher, administrator, and student in American public schools.

The transformation of American public schools over the years has been dramatic and involved a complex struggle between authoritarian and democratic educators played out against the backdrop of dramatic economic, social, political, and cultural change. The structure, organization, and control of schools have changed; the composition of the student body has changed; the curriculum, methods of instruction, and moral education have changed; the professionalism and expectations of teachers have changed; the assessment and testing of students has changed; and the rights and responsibilities of students and teachers have changed as well.

The one thing that has not changed is the simple act of teaching—that basic human connection between teachers and students. As we begin our incredible journey through America's educational history, this will remain our central focus.

I

THE AUTHORITARIAN AND DEMOCRATIC SCHOOLS OF EDUCATION

The Philosophical Debate

In the preface, we saw that America's educational system has been a monumental struggle between two powerful schools of thought—the authoritarian and the democratic. These two "schools" have embraced unique philosophical perspectives on education; they tend to view students very differently; they see learning and therefore instruction in very different ways; they favor distinct approaches to curriculum and moral education; and each has its own position regarding testing and assessment.

This struggle between the advocates of each of these schools is sometimes quiet, sometimes vocal, and sometimes contentious; but it is always present. It reflects the current political climate of the nation, region, and community; it echoes existing economic conditions; and it is structured by the changing demographics of the nation.

Understanding the debate between these two schools of education is sometimes challenging. Neither perspective is completely unique—indeed both the authoritarian and democratic schools have a great deal in common—advocates of each, for example, are committed to the education of American students.

And yet distinguishing between these two schools can be useful. It helps us understand that changes in educational philosophy and policy are not random—though sometimes they appear that way. It also helps us

Figure 1.1. Authoritarian and democratic educational reformers have very different visions as to the proper direction of American education. Courtesy of iStock by Getty Images, credit rawpixel.

understand why progress in the development of education in general is sometimes maddening slow.

Above all, this struggle reminds us that our educational history is a central piece of our nation's past—not an incidental element of it. It is embedded in virtually every aspect of American history, and its story is our story. Moreover, as educators, we are the stewards of that history.

THE AUTHORITARIAN SCHOOL

The authoritarian school of education is rooted in a number of educational philosophies including perennialism, essentialism, and behaviorism. It is also informed by the writings of John Locke in the late 1600s as well as more contemporary figures such as Mortimer Adler, Theodore Sizer, William James, and B. F. Skinner.

Locke's ideas have come to define the authoritarian school of education. He believed that young men, and by inference young women, were blank slates (*tabula rasa*), and therefore it was the job of the teacher, governess, or tutor to provide them with information, insights, and values to help them to succeed in life and promote national prosperity.

In his path-breaking work *Some Thoughts Concerning Education*, published in the early 1700s, Locke argued that children were malleable, and as a result, he favored a form of education that developed rational attitudes. His suggested method of instruction centered on the development of a healthy body and a virtuous character. Locke also promoted a form of scientific education that focused on geography, astronomy, and anatomy, but also recommended that all young men receive some vocational training (Locke 1705).

Although Locke centered his attention on the education of the nobility, his work has served as the basis of education for all students in every socioeconomic class. In fact, his approach is often seen as the beginning of "bourgeois" or middle-class education where training for a future occupation was essential. Finally, while Locke did not address the education of women, most scholars, including his contemporary Mary Astell, argued that women, like men, had the ability to become rational and virtuous (Astell 1700).

Locke's "thoughts" clearly revolutionized our ideas regarding education. And although his influence is immense and cannot easily be pigeonholed into one educational philosophy, conservative perennialists within the authoritarian school typically see his work as providing the foundation of their perspective.

Mortimer Adler is a good example of this philosophy. Adler, of course, is a more contemporary advocate of the authoritarian school and has consistently argued that all students must be exposed to a standardized curriculum. Like other conservative perennialists, Adler has recommended a standardized "Great Books" approach as well as mastery learning (Adler, Fadiman, and Goetz 1990).

Adler argued that since nature was constant, the curriculum should be invariable and unchanging as well. In his *Paideia Proposal*, for example, he argued that all students must be exposed to a curriculum that would help develop their intellect. Factual knowledge was the basis of his proposed curriculum and was best taught through direct instruction (Adler 1982).

While Mortimer Adler represents the perennialist wing of the authoritarian school, Theodore Sizer is an advocate of the essential schools movement. This educational perspective has reemerged in recent years as an expression of the demands of the business community and has become an important component of the authoritarian approach.

Sizer's influential *Horace's Compromise* was first published in 1984, just a year after the infamous report *A Nation at Risk* that we will discuss later in this book. As the report did, Sizer criticized American education of the late 1970s and early 1980s as "fostering a rising tide of mediocrity." As a result, he favored a "stripped down" version of education that would provide an essential core of knowledge for students. This "back to basics" approach has become a central component of the authoritarian school (Sizer 1984).

Another important element of the authoritarian school is represented by the behaviorists—especially in their advocacy of extensive standardized testing and school comparisons. Behaviorism is rooted in the writings of William James, John Watson, B. F. Skinner, and others.

William James, for example, was the first to establish the concept of "stimulus-response" in learning. He argued that children learned by developing "habits" in response to external stimulation. His classic work on this subject was presented in his *Principles of Psychology* published in 1890 (James 1890).

James demonstrated his ideas with an experiment involving a candle and a baby. When the baby reached for the candle's flame as a normal reflex, she would burn her hand and, as a result, would learn to never do that again because the consequences were too painful. For James, this demonstrated that all learning was a product of stimulus and response (James 1890).

Other behavior psychologists of this era, such as John Watson, carried on this tradition and held that through vigorous training, linked to testing, all students could learn. In fact, Watson rejected much of the prevailing literature on eugenics at the time by arguing that the environment was more important than heredity in learning and achievement. These findings appealed to many teachers and broadened the appeal of behaviorism (Watson 1924).

Finally, B. F. Skinner developed the behaviorist approach even further by arguing that students could learn more quickly when they were given rewards for successful completion of tests. Early on, Skinner's experiments with rats demonstrated that when rodents were given rewards for successfully completing a task, their "learning" improved greatly. Eventually, Skinner expanded this research with humans and initiated what has been called "programmed learning" (Skinner 1951).

Although this concept had been developed earlier by a number of psychologists, including A. A. Lumsdaine, Skinner's "linear programming" methods have proven to be very popular among authoritarian educators and have reinforced the growth and acceptance of standardized testing in education (Lumsdaine 1947; Skinner 1954).

John Locke, Mortimer Adler, Theodore Sizer, and behaviorists such as William James, John Watson, B. F. Skinner, and a number of others have come to define the pedagogy of the authoritarian school of education. Each of these philosopher/educators has advocated for curricular and instructional reforms such as scientific education, vocational education, a standardized curriculum focused on great books, mastery learning, essential schools, and Common Core. Others have championed a stimulus-response form of learning, programmed learning, and standardized testing.

But in addition to these curricular and instructional reformers are a number of other authoritarian educators who have advocated for changes in the organizational structure and general approach to education. These include early twentieth-century businessmen reformers such as, Elwood Cubberley, Andrew Draper, Nicholas Murray Butler, and William Rainey Harper as well as advocates of scientific management such as Frederick Winslow Taylor and John Franklin Bobbitt.

By the end of the nineteenth century, American schools were experiencing a dramatic period of growth as our successful market and industrial revolutions drew millions of immigrants to this country from all over the world. Cities grew rapidly and so did our schools. Educators not only were forced to scramble in order to deal with this unprecedented increase in the number of students, but they also recognized the growing needs of what has been called the "credential-based society."

Businessmen reformers of the authoritarian school offered a number of solutions to these "problems." These included the professionalization of teachers through further education and assessment and the consolidation of schools, administrations, and local boards of education, as well as the assumption of power by the states over local schools.

Elwood Cubberley, the famed authoritarian educator, would celebrate the growing consolidation movement of this period as a victory in one of the great battles against ignorance and what he called the "dog in the manger"—local control of education. Like other businessmen reformers of this era, he favored—among other things—state control of education, a standardized curriculum, and the rapid assimilation of immigrant children (Cubberley 1919, 134).

Nicholas Murray Butler, founder of Teachers College, Columbia University, and later, president of Columbia University, was a central figure in the reorganization and consolidation of New York Schools along the lines of the business model. Butler, an authoritarian reformer, also promoted the expansion of teacher education and assessment along with a system of promotion based on "merit" rather than seniority. Finally as part of his so-called Butler Plan, local school boards were replaced with a centralized board of superintendents drawn from the city at large rather than the local neighborhood school districts (Parkerson and Parkerson 2015).

The Butler Plan became the template for the school consolidation movement of the twentieth century and was embraced by a powerful cadre of educators throughout the nation. In addition to Nicholas Butler, other leading lights of this movement included Andrew Draper and William Rainey Harper. These businessmen reformers knew each other well; they went to the same schools and often worked together. They served on the same academic panels at conferences, and they shared a vision of efficiency, productivity, and order as a reflection of the corporate business model.

Directly related to the businessmen reformers of the authoritarian school were the advocates of scientific management. These "efficiency experts"—as they were often called—sought to improve the efficiency and productivity of industrial production. And as a central part of the new emerging corporate ethos, their ideas were also seen as appropriate for the schools of America.

The leading light in the promotion of scientific management was Frederick Winslow Taylor—affectionately known as "speedy Taylor." Taylor's most important work, *Scientific Management*, was published in 1911 at the onset of the school consolidation movement in America. His primary thesis was that through his "time study" techniques, profits would skyrocket through increased productivity (Parkerson and Parkerson 2015).

These time studies, moreover, would demonstrate the "natural laziness" of workers who typically engaged in what he called "systematic soldiering." Testifying before the House of Representatives, Taylor noted that "the average workingman believes it is his best interest . . . to go slow instead of going fast, to restrict output instead of turning out as large a day's work as is practicable" (Taylor 1911, 9).

Many authoritarian businessmen reformers of this period saw a parallel between Taylor's "workers" and American teachers who were "mechanical and dull." Improving the "productivity" of teachers through education, assessment, and administrative control was one of the keys to their reform agenda.

The other important element of improving schools based on the business model was school and administrative consolidation tied directly to the overall reorganization of schools. As consolidation swept through the country in the early years of the twentieth century, authoritarian educators such as Franklin Bobbitt turned their attention to the "productive school" (Bobbitt 1912).

Bobbitt's plan for the growing Gary, Indiana, school system was built on a number of "scientific principles" that included increasing the "efficiency of the laborer, i.e. the pupil" as well as the efficiency of "the product," that is, the curriculum and instruction. In fact, as one advocate of this approach noted, by increasing the efficiency of schools, "the amount of output and the value to the capitalist" would be increased (Callahan 1962, 48).

Bobbitt's "platoon system" employed at the Gary schools was enthusiastically embraced by many administrators and educators. It centered on the idea that higher productivity was good for teachers, students, and the community, and it set the stage for the standardization of schools for the next half-century.

Conclusion: The Authoritarian School

In short, authoritarian school advocates typically favored an educational system that emphasized the products of education. For these educators, the facts represented the centerpiece of the curriculum and, therefore, the subject-centered, teacher-focused approach to instruction was preferred.

Moreover, they promoted convergent thinking since the mastery of a specific "body of knowledge" was the primary goal of education. This "inside the box" thinking encouraged the use of objective tests—often multiple-choice, standardized tests. Students were expected to furnish exact solutions to math and science problems, precise definitions of words, and fixed answers to questions in the humanities and social sciences.

Educators who embraced the authoritarian approach have traditionally supported programs such as the No Child Left Behind Act, end-of-grade, high-stakes testing, mastery learning, and various forms of programmed learning. Moreover, they typically preferred a STEM-oriented curriculum—science, technology, engineering, and math—over one centered in the humanities and social sciences.

Finally, authoritarian school advocates often embraced organizational policies that were associated with the corporate business model. State control of local school districts, school and administrative consolidation, professionalization and assessment of teachers, standardization of school architecture, and greater "productivity" of teachers and students as well as vocational education were central components of this approach.

The authoritarian school of education is powerful, and over the years it has had a great deal of influence over educational policies of schools in America. Despite its power and influence, however, not all educators subscribe to it. In fact, it is the ongoing debate between authoritarian and democratic school educators that has provided an important historical context to understand the sometimes contentious development of our educational system.

THE DEMOCRATIC SCHOOL

The democratic school of education (sometimes referred to as the "non-authoritarian school") is drawn in part from the writings of Jean-Jacques Rousseau in the mid-1700s but is also rooted in the contemporary philosophies of pragmatism, progressivism, humanism, constructionism, and postmodernism. It is represented by such diverse philosopher/educators as John Dewey, Johann Pestalozzi, Jean Piaget, and Michel Foucault.

While John Locke is credited with being the leading light of the authoritarian school, Jean-Jacques Rousseau ("Jean" is pronounced similarly to "John") is often associated with the democratic school of education. Unlike Locke, who perceived children coming to school as blank slates, Rousseau argued that each child had an innate sense of goodness and entered the classroom with experiences and ideas—though undeveloped. The job of the democratic teacher, therefore, was to build on those experiences and allow students to learn at their own pace in a nurturing atmosphere.

In his classic novel *Emile*, Rousseau wrote, "God makes all things good; man meddles with them and they become evil." Although he was influenced by John Locke, Rousseau modified Locke's ideas and argued that education should be child centered, that is, built on the experiences of the child and not simply directed from the outside by the teacher, governess, or tutor. In short, learning should be a dialogue between the student and teacher (Rousseau 1974).

Rousseau argued further that learning—especially among young children—should be based on experiences and children's need to know and understand. Forcing the child to learn to read was not very effective. In his novel *Emile*, for example, the main character received several invitations to parties but was unable to read them. And since he could not find anyone in the household to read the invitations to him, he was forced to learn to read—and he did.

A contemporary of Rousseau, Johann Pestalozzi, established the important humanist principle of the democratic school of education. Like Rousseau, Pestalozzi presented his educational ideas in the form of a novel with the main character, Gertrude, as the innovative, humanistic teacher. Gertrude used everyday items to teach her class. She might begin a lesson in mathematics by having students count the number of steps from one end of the classroom to the other or learn multiplication by counting the number of panes in a window and then the number of windows to determine the total number of window panes in the classroom (Pestalozzi 1894).

Even more importantly was Gertrude's nurturing love for her students. For Pestalozzi, the "first instruction of the child" was "the business of the senses ... of the mother." Through her boundless love, Gertrude was able to bond with each of her students and help them learn. Pestalozzi's humanistic vision of education, then, set the stage for early childhood education adopted by Charles Mayo's "infant schools," Fredrick Froebel's kindergartens, as well as Maria Montessori's schools (Pestalozzi 1781, 1894; Montessori 1912).

Closely related to humanism was the educational philosophy of constructivism. While humanism centers on the nurturing of young students in order to promote individual development, constructivism focuses on developing hands-on activities for students to "construct" their own frames of thought in order to develop critical-thinking skills. Learning essentially is derived from within and students typically perform experiments of various kinds with little input as to the "correct" results of the experiment.

Although Jean Piaget was not an educator as such, his work as a clinical psychologist helped him understand child's play as an essential component of learning. Rather than perceiving these activities as frivolous and unimportant, Piaget argued that play and exploration were central components of cognitive development (Piaget 1926).

Constructivism as first identified by Piaget has had a dramatic impact on education. Museum public education, for example, where patrons have hands-on experiences to learn science, technology, or history, is directly related to his ideas. Similarly, work by other scholars in this area has promoted collaborative learning through a form of social constructivism. Finally, computer programs such as Logo and a number of gaming programs have been developed as an expression of constructivism (Demetriou, Shayer, and Efklides 1992).

While humanists and constructivists were focused on individual learning and development, pragmatists/progressives of the democratic school were concerned with the relationship between the individual and society and the role of the school. Scholars such as John Dewey argued that modern society had become fragmented because of industrialism, social stratification (the growing gap between rich and poor), and unrestrained individualism.

The role of the school, he argued, was to help students understand the essential interconnections between members of the community and the workforce. To that end, Dewey favored an "open classroom" environment where cooperation rather than competition was the basis of instruction (Dewey 1889; 1916).

In his famous University of Chicago lab school, established with his wife and colleague Alice Chipman Dewey, young students worked together in a cooperative-learning environment on projects such as preparing a meal. Later, they might establish a (simulated) grocery store and learn math lessons by making change and paying bills. Through cooperation rather than competition, students better understood the limits of their own individualism and recognized the interconnectivity of society and the economy (Dewey 1916).

In recent years, a new postmodernist perspective has emerged among some democratic educators. Though very controversial, postmodernism is a method of understanding "the pathologies of the modern world." These pathologies include the degradation of the environment and the ascendency of what President Eisenhower called the "military industrial complex" and its development of weapons of mass destruction. Postmodernists argue that our exuberant embrace of "science and progress" as the answer to all our problems, has in itself become a problem (Kurth 1999).

The primary direction of educational postmodernists, however, is to understand power relationships within society. Scholars such as Michel Foucault, Stanley Fish, and others argue that institutions of government, culture, and the schools have marginalized groups of people such as women, workers, people of color, religious minorities, and people from other nations generally.

They argue that our understanding of our world is not objective but, rather, is based on the values of the dominant culture. As a result, minority groups and people from other cultures are often marginalized. Postmodernist educators argue that the authoritarian curriculum in schools has typically focused on the great works of literature as well as the great men in history. This focus tends to virtually exclude the intellectual, historical, and cultural contributions of other groups and individuals from our diverse society (Foucault 1977; Fish 1994).

Conclusion: The Democratic School

Democratic educators then, typically reject the idea that education is primarily the acquisition of a body of knowledge—the products of learning. Rather, they embrace the process of learning itself. Here, an experience-centered or student-centered curriculum is favored where learning is achieved through a dialogue between students and the teacher. Whereas lectures and workbooks are the primary tools of the authoritarian teacher, democratic teachers focus on discussions and projects.

In the spirit of progressivism and pragmatism, democratic teachers promote thinking that is "outside the box"—divergent thinking. In this way, students are encouraged to offer unique and creative solutions to problems. Moreover, postmodernist educators recognize that in our diverse, multicultural society, education must include the contributions of women, people of color, working people, the poor, and immigrants.

Democratic teachers typically have opposed the No Child Left Behind Act and end-of-grade tests. They also are opposed to the exclusive use of standardized, multiple-choice examinations, most forms of high-stakes testing, and school comparisons. Rather, they favor teacher-created essay examinations, research papers, portfolios, group projects, and formal discussions as the basis of student assessment.

Authoritarian Versus Democratic

It is the tension between these two archetypical schools of education that has helped to define the history of our field. By examining this tension in a historical context, we can better understand the critical challenges facing education today. As we have pointed out, however, this is a fluid model. There is occasional overlap in these philosophies, and educators tend to bristle at the idea of being pigeonholed into one or another school of thought. Nevertheless, we feel that this approach to understand educational history is useful.

As we examine the important themes of American educational history presented in this book, we should continually reflect on the dramatic tensions between the authoritarian and democratic perspectives of education. By doing so, you will be able to better understand the development of American education and your place in it.

In chapter 2, we continue this epic story by examining the changing structure and organization of American public schools—from the educational experiments of the colonies to the growing efforts of local grassroots groups that created the common school (public school) movement to our modern consolidated educational institutions of today.

2

THE STRUCTURE AND ORGANIZATION OF AMERICAN SCHOOLS

The States Seize Control

The structure and organization of the American school has changed dramatically over the years. Early colonial schools were locally controlled, and more often than not, they had a distinctly religious focus. Although these schools varied from one religion to another and from region to region in the New World, their common characteristic was local control.

NEW ENGLAND SCHOOLS

The Puritans of the Massachusetts Bay Colony of New England were the most assertive in this regard and they created a system of nearly universal primary education in the colony. In 1642, Puritan leaders enacted the first education law in the colonies. This law became the "gold standard" of education, and for the next two centuries, it served as a model for other communities throughout the North and into the West.

Puritan leaders were concerned that the children of their colony were not receiving an adequate education at home. Town leaders set out to determine whether Puritan children were learning to "read and understand the principles of religion" (Hillway 1964, 20).

Figure 2.1. Locally supported one-room schoolhouses such as the one depicted here, began to disappear as states assumed control over education. Courtesy of iStock by Getty Images, credit Kenneth Keifer.

As expected, they found that their children had not received an adequate education, and as a result, they passed as series of educational measures including the first compulsory education law in the colonies in 1647. The act, sometimes referred to the "Old Deluder Law," was designed to teach children to read the Bible and thus thwart the "delusions of Satan." Towns of at least fifty households were required to appoint teachers and "provide for his wages." The law went on to mandate that larger towns of one hundred households would "provide a (Latin) grammar school to fit youths for the university" (Hillway 1964).

These educational measures gradually were adopted by other New England colonies over the next century and would provide a model for communities in New York and what is now the upper Midwest until the eve of the American Revolution. The idea of compulsory education for both primary and secondary students clearly was revolutionary.

SCHOOLS IN THE MIDDLE COLONIES

But the educational history of New England was unique among the American colonies. Other sections of the country had a very different experience. The middle colonies of New York, New Jersey, and Pennsylvania, for example, were much more diversified than Puritan New England. And since there was no dominant common culture or religion in these colonies, settlers often turned to their church to provide an education for their children.

New York, for example, had originally been settled and controlled by the Dutch in the 1600s until the colony was seized by the British. The open settlement policies of the Dutch had attracted thousands of colonists representing a variety of ethnic groups and religions. In fact, one contemporary observer of this period noted that in New York City alone, at least eighteen different languages were spoken (Cohen 1974).

New Jersey had a similar history and it, too, had a rich ethnic and religious heritage. But Pennsylvania was the most diverse colony of all. William Penn, the colony's wealthy and influential founder had envisioned Pennsylvania as a refuge for people who had been the victims of religious persecution. His "Holy Experiment" as it has been called, guaranteed religious freedom by the "Great Law" of the 1680s. Over the next half-century thousands of colonial "dissenters," as well as migrants from all over Europe, flocked to Pennsylvania to worship as they pleased. By the eve of the American Revolution in 1776, then, literally hundreds of ethnic and religious communities had been settled in the middle colonies. Each of these groups, moreover, had their own schools (Bronner 1962).

The Dutch, for example, established "catechism" primary schools throughout New York and New Jersey and, later, a handful of "secondary" schools using the Latin school model of classical training. The Quakers established their religious schools throughout Pennsylvania and were the first to accept women and African Americans. And while their focus was on religion, they also introduced some secular subjects such as geography and arithmetic (Bronner 1962).

In Roman Catholic settlements of the middle colonies, and later in Maryland where their numbers were significant, religious education also was the norm. These schools placed special emphasis on memorizing the Roman Catholic Catechism in preparation for the first communion.

Finally, there were numerous self-contained religious settlements throughout the middle colonies, such as the Moravians in Pennsylvania. These settlers placed great emphasis on compulsory primary schooling for all their members, including women. Students were taught by individuals from the community of faith and were instructed in basic reading, arithmetic, and religion.

In short, the rich ethnic and religious heritage of the middle colonies created a tapestry of religiously dominated schools at the local-community level. Some were exceptional and helped their congregants learn to read and attain a basic understanding of the morals and values that were important to the community. Other schools were poor. Sometimes they would disappear with the death of a "virtuous" teacher; others never were able to establish themselves during the colonial era.

SCHOOLS IN THE SOUTHERN COLONIES

The southern colonies also were ethnically and religiously diverse and, in addition, had millions of African American slaves as an important part of their population. Welsh and English settlers were common from Virginia to South Carolina, while in the southern piedmont and coastal plain of North Carolina, there were large settlements of Scots Highlanders and Scotch Irish. The South also had isolated communities of German and Swiss farmers and, as mentioned above, there was a sizable Roman Catholic population in the coastal communities around Baltimore. Locally controlled religious education was common in these regions.

In other areas of the South there were strong ties to Anglicanism, and as a result, these communities adopted educational policies similar to that of England with a *laissez-faire* (hands off) approach to education.

This meant that relatively expensive private schools, academies, and in-home tutoring were commonplace for the children of the wealthy. For others, there were a handful of dame schools (taught by local women) and a few charity schools serving the needs of the very poor. As in other colonial communities, apprenticeship was an important form of education for the marginally poor, while most whites and virtually all African American slaves (and all but a handful of black freedmen) were excluded.

This two-tiered approach to education in the South guaranteed that sons and daughters of wealthy and midlevel planters and merchants would receive an education, but it virtually excluded the majority of white yeoman farming children and slaves. In short, the vast majority of southern children had little access to formal education other than apprenticeship, community dame schools, charity schools, or family and friends.

By the eve of the American Revolution then, virtually every form of educational experiment had been established. From New England's free, compulsory, primary, and secondary schools, to the diverse religious schools of the middle colonies, to the South's tradition of in-home tutoring and private academies, to the apprenticeship system from New England to Georgia—the colonies had tried it all.

THE COMMON SCHOOL

While these diverse educational experiments seemed to make sense during the colonial era, they were wholly inadequate for the needs of a new nation for a number of reasons. Following the American Revolution, there was a growing sense, especially among democratic reformers, that young Americans desperately needed an educational system that would help unite the former colonies into a strong nation and help students develop both their civic responsibility and patriotism.

Similarly, as the market revolution of the early 1800s fundamentally transformed the American economy, it became clear that young men and women needed to develop the skills and values of competition, persistence, and hard work in order to succeed. Moreover, in this new nation, schools needed to be open to every young American, not just the lucky few (the rich) who were able to afford an education.

But change was slow. Despite the fact that many Americans saw the colonial forms of education as inadequate, there was little action to create a new system. The federal government under the Articles of Confederation had taken some interest in schools by providing generous land grants to communities for education under the Northwest Ordinance of 1787.

As we have seen, this important federal directive stated clearly that "knowledge being necessary to good government and the happiness of mankind, schools and the means of education shall forever be encouraged." In addition, founding fathers such as Benjamin Franklin, Thomas Jefferson, Benjamin Rush, and many others used their influence to promote education at all levels (Parkerson and Parkerson 2001).

Jefferson, for example, saw universal education, as a sure defense against power-hungry politicians. In fact, in 1789 he introduced a bill into the Virginia Legislature to establish schools in the state to "guard the sacred rights and liberties of their fellow citizens." He went on to note that "at these schools all the free children, male and female . . . shall be entitled to receive tuition gratis" (Hillway 1964, 20).

With the ratification of the U.S. Constitution in 1789 and the adoption of the Tenth Amendment in 1793, however, direct federal aid to schools came to an abrupt end. The Tenth Amendment to the Constitution shifted some important authority to the states, noting that "powers not delegated to the United States by the Constitution . . . are reserved to the states." In short, since there was no mention of schooling in the U.S. Constitution itself, states and not the federal government were responsible for education (Parkerson and Parkerson 2001).

And yet, state legislators typically ignored calls for the development of an educational system and typically deferred to religious and private institutions to provide education as they had done during the colonial era. This "system" of education would persist into the first decades of the nineteenth century.

As male suffrage expanded during these years and as the market revolution swept across young America, individuals and groups began to recognize the importance of education for their children. A grassroots democratic movement gradually developed to encourage state leaders to act. Among those promoting public education were workingmen, small business owners, and a new class of commercial farmers.

Workingmen's Support of Public Education

Workers of young America were among the first to call for a system of universal education for their children. They realized that only through education could their children succeed in the new market economy. As early as 1829, the New York City mechanics and workers petitioned the state to create such a system. In the next few years, other workingmen's organizations made similar requests of their state legislatures. In Pennsylvania, for example, workingmen petitioned their leaders in the early 1830s to establish an "equal and general system of education" (Noble 1955, 170).

Small-Business Support of Public Education

Small-business owners throughout the nation also supported universal public education, but for a different set of reasons. For them, education would help establish new standards of discipline for their workers. Moreover, these businessmen recognized that the values of hard work and punctuality—that were routinely being promoted in schools—would help them recruit more efficient employees and help them grow their businesses.

Commercial Farmers' Support of Public Education

In addition to workingmen's groups and small-business owners in the cities of young America, a new class of commercial farmers in the nation's heartland also provided support for universal public education. As these farmers became more business oriented in the wake of the market revolution, many began to recognize that a solid education for their children was necessary for their success. Along with these other groups, their support was essential for the development of the common school (Parkerson and Parkerson 1998).

The critical combination of grassroots support and idealistic democratic progressive leadership from all political parties helped to launch the common school movement of the early nineteenth century. Local communities supported these schools through a variety of monetary sources including property taxes and charitable contributions as well as through construction and maintenance work contributed by local members of the community.

Early State Funding

States also contributed to the development of these schools in a variety of ways, though their support was limited to say the least. Delaware, for example, used marriage and tavern licensing fees as their primary source of funding. North Carolina and Rhode Island, on the other hand, used fees derived from liquor and auction licenses to support education. Other states used a variety of funds derived from intestate estates and proceeds from various fines to support schools. All in all, these early efforts were extremely modest, with political leaders typically avoiding direct taxation of the citizenry (Randall 1871).

But by the second quarter of the nineteenth century, however, support for the common school reached a kind of critical mass and states began to seriously address issues of both funding and administrative control of education.

Over the next half-century, however, states, influences by authoritarian reformers, would assume control and partial funding of schools from local communities through constitutional mandates, a vigorous legislative crusade, and finally, affirmation by the courts.

THE CONSTITUTIONAL MANDATE

In the first half of the nineteenth century, authoritarian reformers in many states began to reconsider their positions on education and revised their constitutions to provide more support for schools. There was, of course, a great deal of variation in these efforts, but generally these states created permanent school funds to support education and set the stage for state control of schools.

A good example of this growing commitment to education can be seen in Connecticut's state constitution of 1818. In article 8, section 1, it stated, "There shall always be free public elementary and secondary schools in the state." In addition, Connecticut provided for the creation of a school fund that "shall remain a perpetual fund . . . for the support and encouraging of public schools" (www.clib.org).

LEGISLATIVE ACTION

As states assumed control of public education through their constitutional mandates, legislators influenced by authoritarian reformers also moved aggressively to expand their authority over local schools. Northern states led the way in these matters with Massachusetts and New York providing a model of state jurisdiction in education (Parkerson and Parkerson 2015).

As we have seen, Massachusetts had played an important role in the development of public education since the colonial period. In 1835, it moved aggressively to provide state oversight and administrative control of schools in the state with the creation of the Massachusetts Board of Education. Two years later, the commission appointed Horace Mann as secretary of the board (Parkerson and Parkerson 2001).

Horace Mann was not an educator as such, but he was committed to universal education in the state and had the political savvy to garner public and private support for a centralized public school system. His editorship of *The Common School Journal*, his lobbying of the legislature, and his persuasive annual reports on education positioned him as a national leader in public education, convincing political figures in other states to consider centralizing their educational systems as well (Parkerson and Parkerson 2001).

Although New York did not have the charismatic leadership of Horace Mann, the state was committed to both expanding education and creating a powerful centralized school administration. In 1854, after years of struggle, New York established its own Department of Public Instruction with an independent superintendent as its head. The superintendent had "visitation" power and was allowed to assess the curriculum, discipline, and general administration of local schools throughout the state (Randall 1871).

Following the lead of Massachusetts and New York, other states such as those in the Midwest also instituted measures for the oversight and centralization of education. Indiana's constitution of 1851, section 8, for example, charged the legislature to create a state superintendent of public instruction "whose method of selection, tenure, duties and compensation; shall be prescribed by law" (www.law.indiana.edu).

As expected, the legislative actions of these and other states during these years were met with fierce opposition from local communities. Local school trustees, town commissioners, and members of local school boards often were outraged by these actions, arguing that their authority had been usurped by the states, restricting their basic democratic rights. In conjunction with democratic reformers, they filed petitions with their legislative leaders, they criticized these policies in the press—alleging nepotism and corruption by state officials, and they often threatened legal action. But the tide of change was unstoppable.

THE COURTS VALIDATE STATE CONTROL

As the struggle between local democratic and state authoritarian reformers raged, the courts silenced the arguments with a number of important landmark decisions. In fact, as Ellwood Cubberley wrote in the early years of the twentieth century, the court's actions "helped in the continual enlargement of the sphere of the state in education [and] the development of a positive policy of state unification and authority" (Cubberley and Elliot 1915, 153).

There were a number of key decisions by the courts that validated the legislative actions of states regarding the control of education. Perhaps the most well-known of these was the Kalamazoo Decision of 1874. In this landmark case, the state court ruled that the Kalamazoo Board of Education (with the authority of the state of Michigan) had the right to establish a public high school in the city at taxpayers' expense. The case was appealed to the State Supreme Court and Justice Thomas M. Cooley upheld the decision and essentially settled the question of control of public schools (www.education.stateuniversity.com/pages2579/AppendixIII).

In another important court case, *State ex rel. Clark v. Haworth*, the Indiana court agreed with a directive by the state legislature that allowed the State Board of Education to select textbooks for all local districts of the state. It ruled that education was a matter of "state and not of local jurisdiction" and that "the authority over schools and school affairs is not necessarily a distributive one, to be exercised by local instrumentalities, but on the contrary, it is a central power residing in the legislature of the state" (Cubberley and Elliot 1915, 154).

By the end of the nineteenth century, the structure and organization of the American public schools had changed dramatically. Local schools were now firmly under the control of centralized departments of public instruction, controlled by the states and, in some cases, larger municipalities. And over the next half-century, states would gradually assume some school funding, consolidate their control, and expand their authority over the structure and direction of education. Clearly, the authoritarian vision of centralized state control had prevailed.

THE ROLE OF THE FEDERAL GOVERNMENT

And yet, as the state's grip on local schools tightened, a new player in the struggle to control America's public schools emerged. That player was the U.S. government. Actually, the federal government has had an indirect role in the development of education for the last 250 years.

As we have seen, as early as 1787, under the provisions of the Northwest Ordinance, Congress granted land to territories, which later would become states, for educational use. As a result of this and other provisions, over the years, the U.S. government has awarded states more than 132,000,000 acres of land to support public education. The sale of these lands by the states endowed communities with capital to build schools, employ teachers, and "kick start" the common school movement of the early nineteenth century (Cubberley 1919, 59).

While the ratification of the U.S. Constitution and the passage of the Tenth Amendment in 1793 transferred power to the states in matters of education, the federal government would quietly continue its support over the years.

However, it wasn't until the Reconstruction period, following the American Civil War, that the federal government reasserted it presence in education with the creation of the original Department of Education in 1867. This agency was created specifically to attend to the needs of the Freedmen Bureau schools in the South.

These schools helped to provide a basic education to thousands of former black slaves and poor whites at a time when education was unavailable to them. In many communities throughout the South, these Freedmen Bureau schools represented their first public schools.

In addition, the Department of Education was given the responsibility of "collecting such statistics and facts as shall show the condition and progress of education" in the United States. Although the department was soon downgraded to the status of "Office" within the Department of Interior, it continued to collect statistics and issue educational reports to Congress for the next seventy years (Parkerson and Parkerson 2008).

In 1939, the Office of Education was reassigned to the Federal Security Agency, a New Deal program—later to be called the Department of Health, Education, and Welfare. The Office of Education continued its work in obscurity for the next four decades until 1979, when it achieved full departmental status within the presidential cabinet as the Department of Education.

FUNDING, ADVOCACY, AND RESEARCH

Today, the Department of Education maintains its tradition of indirect support of education by focusing on funding, advocacy, and research. For example, it earmarks funds (with the approval of Congress) for specific purposes such as bilingual education and vocational training, as well as for programs such as antidrug education and Head Start, a preschool program for low-income children.

As an advocate for education, the department works through its secretary to promote new educational policies such as school choice, charter schools, and vouchers. Also, working with the president of the United States, it has helped promote policies as outlined in *A Nation at Risk* under President Reagan, mandatory national reading examinations under President Clinton, No Child Left Behind under President Bush, and the Every Student Succeeds Act under President Obama.

The Department of Education also is involved with educational research. It coordinates the activities of six regional resource centers that serve states throughout the nation. It also coordinates the work of ten regional educational laboratories that sponsor seminars, workshops, and conferences to help educators learn of cutting-edge research in the field (Parkerson and Parkerson 2008).

Associates in each of the regional resource centers conduct educational research and develop new curricular approaches to teaching. The Southeast Regional Center, for example, focuses on early childhood education while the Midwest Regional Center focuses on math and science (Parkerson and Parkerson 2008).

Finally, the department maintains a number of centers, clearinghouses, and regional assistance centers. These organizations disseminate research findings and provide technical assistance for educators. The Eisenhower Regional Mathematics and Science Education Consortia, for example, distributes instructional materials and provides networking opportunities for teachers. The Equity Assistance Center, on the other hand, assists schools to achieve important equity goals (Parkerson and Parkerson 2008).

The Funding of American Public Education

The organization and control of American schools has indeed changed over the years. From the locally controlled private and religious schools of colonial America through the secular community and neighborhood common schools governed by members of local towns and districts, to the growing state involvement in education, and finally to the developing role of the federal government, the structure of American education has changed dramatically.

The history of the funding of American schools, however, is a different story. Although local communities have lost a great deal of control over the administration, curriculum, and instructional methods in their schools, they continue to provide the lion's share of their funding.

As we have seen, colonial-era schools typically were funded entirely by their own communities. The central, theocratic government of the Massachusetts Bay Colony, for example, passed legislation to assure that Puritan children were receiving a quality education in the 1640s, but required that the towns of the colony pay for the construction of the schools and salaries of their teachers.

In the middle colonies, local communities were also on their own when it came to funding of schools. And as a result, rather than taxing their citizens, they deferred to either private academies or religious institutions to provide education. Towns and neighborhoods within small cities might provide a small stipend to a "virtuous woman" to teach in a primary "dame" school, but more often than not, those funds came from a prosperous merchant or mill owner.

In the South, private schools and plantation tutors provided a basic education for the children of the wealthy, while religious institutions might establish a pauper school for indigent children and sometimes free blacks. Here again, funding was derived from private sources and not through taxation.

With the emergence of the common school in the early years of the nineteenth century, the funding of schools began to change. Local communities influenced by democratic reformers at the grassroots level began to recognize the need to educate their children. As a result, citizens from small towns, districts, and city neighborhoods often contributed their own labor to build and maintain local schoolhouses or to hire a schoolteacher.

Later, some communities used a form of property tax to fund these schools.

Delos Hackley, a commercial farmer in Genesee County, New York, like many of his neighbors, felt a strong obligation to his community and to its children. He recorded in his diary in the spring of 1862 that "the old schoolhouse burned down." And over the next eight months Delos attended to his normal duties of farming but also found time to "draw timber to the schoolhouse" and in early June he "went to Batavia after timber [and then] worked on the schoolhouse." Delos and others worked on the schoolhouse until it was completed just in time for the school term in the fall of 1862 (Parkerson and Parkerson 1998, 51).

Later Delos was "put in [as] school trustee" and served in that capacity for a number of years. He collected the school tax from the small towns surrounding Batavia, New York, and also was involved in hiring a new schoolteacher, Miss Carpenter. In order to lure her to Batavia, however, he and another commercial farmer agreed to subsidize her salary out of their own pockets. It was this sort of democratic community-level commitment that made the common school such a success (Parkerson and Parkerson 1998, 52).

As states slowly took control of common schools during the nineteenth century, however, funding also changed. States gradually assumed more school funding, and today they contribute between 10 percent (New Hampshire) and 90 percent (Hawaii) of their state's education budget. On average, about half of the funding for education comes from the states. Much of the balance, of course, is paid by local communities through property taxes.

Property taxes are a mix of revenues derived from real estate taxes—including taxes on land and the buildings on that land, such as commercial structures, factories, and of course, homes. In addition, personal property taxes include taxes on automobiles, furniture in homes, commercial inventories, machinery in factories, and livestock on farms.

These taxes are a stable source of income because they are fixed, and the item taxed cannot be easily moved to avoid taxation. On the other hand, property is often assessed unevenly, and sometimes tax assessors are pressured by politicians to keep their assessments as low as possible. These low assessments are a two-edged sword. On the one hand, they help to attract new businesses to the community, but on the other hand, they negatively affect the quality of schools in some districts (Parkerson and Parkerson 2008).

Then, there is the question of "rich and poor communities." Wealthy and middle-class communities often have more revenues to attract better teachers through higher salaries, to construct better facilities, and to purchase more learning materials including books, software, and computers. Per-pupil expenditures in poor states such as Mississippi, for example, are about one half those of New York or New Jersey. Similarly, urban areas within states are typically wealthier than rural communities. This disparity remains a problem for schools (Yudof, Kirp, and Levin 1992).

Finally, the federal government also has a funding role in public education. Although it has enormous indirect power to advocate for specific reforms in education, it only contributes about 7 percent of the total education budget. While this represents a small fraction of total expenditures, these funds can be helpful, especially for specific programs such as lunch subsidies and Head Start.

CONCLUSION

The structure, organization, and funding of American public schools clearly has changed over the years. The locally controlled and funded schools of the colonial era and the common schools of the early national period gradually disappeared during the nineteenth century as states assumed administrative control over public education.

That process was complex and involved three stages. The first was the constitutional-mandate phase where state constitutions were rewritten to both support education and control schools through administrative supervision.

The legislative phase was the next step. Empowered by their constitutional mandates, state legislatures throughout young America, with the support of authoritarian educational reforms, set out to establish an administrative apparatus such as departments of public instruction.

In addition, they selected state supervisors of public schools and eventually gave them full administrative discretion over hiring and firing of teachers, curriculum, and instructional techniques. Moreover, local boards of education often were replaced by state boards that answered directly to the superintendent.

While members of local democratic communities often were outraged by what they saw as an authoritarian assumption of power by the state, the courts vigorously supported these actions. The process of state control over local schools was nearly complete.

Local communities had lost a great deal of their traditional power with regard to the education of their children, but many submitted quietly to the new school systems because the states also assumed a portion of funding for their schools. Local communities would of course continue to provide the lion's share of funding for education but "the sting" of state control was somewhat eased.

More recently, the federal government has begun to help finance specific programs in the public schools, contributing about 7 percent of local budgets. The price tag for this support, however, can be significant. Compliance with federal directives, constantly changing policies, and onerous paperwork associated with the educational bureaucracy has impacted both administrators and teachers over the last few decades. Nevertheless in this cash-starved educational environment, federal funds are welcomed.

In chapter 4, we turn to the growing educational bureaucracy at both the state and federal level. As we shall see, the hard-fought state control over local schools during the nineteenth century was matched by an aggressive consolidation of schools during the first half of the twentieth century. This consolidation and its attendant growth in educational bureaucracy has had a dramatic impact on education, often negatively impacting teachers, students, and the educational village (Parkerson and Parkerson 2015).

3

CONSOLIDATION AND ITS DISCONTENTS

From Intimacy to Bureaucracy

As states assumed control of education during the nineteenth century, there was also a structural transformation of public schools themselves. This involved a change from the intimate town, village, and neighborhood schools of the nineteenth and early twentieth centuries to the large consolidated, bureaucratic schools of today. This move from the local intimacy of schools to the regional isolation of consolidated schools today has dramatically affected children throughout the nation.

From the early colonial era, through the late nineteenth century, schools were small and intimate. Teachers knew their students and students their teachers. The school was not only the center of learning but also was the heart of the community itself. It was here that democracy worked, where citizens had a sense of control over the direction of the school. The school was a place where the values of the community were transferred from one generation to the next and where there was a collective sense of pride in the success of the school and its children.

But while schools remained small, and communities maintained control during these years, they were far from perfect. Ellwood Cubberley, a prominent authoritarian educator at the turn of the twentieth century, once noted that local communities often had a "dog in the manger" spirit regarding their schools. This attitude was reflected in school funding that sometimes bordered on stinginess. Similarly, they often demonstrated

Figure 3.1. As a result of consolidation, large schools such as this became more common by the middle of the twentieth century. Courtesy of iStock by Getty Images, credit CynthiaAnnF.

parochial policies of exclusion, discrimination, and intolerance (Parkerson and Parkerson 2015, 1).

Much of this criticism was justified. Early on, communities often refused to adequately support education for their children. Of course, there were democratic progressives within these communities that were committed to the improvement of their schools, and they contributed both their time and their money to make this happen. Delos Hackley of Batavia, New York, introduced in the previous chapter, was one of the many individuals who helped their local common schools become successful.

But many community members saw schools as "someone else's responsibility" and refused to support public education. It was for this reason that many of the "Little Red Schoolhouses" romanticized in the literature, often were little more than converted barns or shacks—and weren't even painted red! Many lacked basic educational materials such as books, blackboards and chalk, as well as pencils and paper.

The parochial nature of local communities also led to exclusion and discrimination of individuals based on gender, ethnicity, religion, and of course, race. From New England's rocky shore to the savannahs of Georgia, the struggle for inclusion was difficult and hard fought. Young women were routinely barred from public schools through much of the colonial era and well into the nineteenth century.

Irish Catholics and German-speaking immigrants were similarly excluded from public schools during most of the nineteenth century, and if these children did attend local public school they were often scorned or ridiculed as a result of their culture, dress, or beliefs. And of course, exclusion based on race was commonplace until recently in American history. Only through a vigorous civil rights movement linked to progressive legislation and enlightened court decisions has this form of discrimination been diminished.

By the end of the nineteenth century, the structure of public schools began to change. As we have seen, by then, states and municipalities had assumed control of public education through constitutional provisions, legislative actions, and favorable court mandates. Authoritarian educators initiated the process of administrative centralization of education as well as the physical consolidation of the schools themselves.

These "businessmen reformers" had become fascinated with the dramatic growth and economic success of business corporations during the late nineteenth century—sometimes called the "corporate revolution"—and as a result, they became convinced that the modern corporation was the most appropriate model of school organization.

Consolidated schools based on the corporate model, they argued, would be more productive in terms of learning and would save the taxpayers' money. By centralizing the administrative control of schools, moreover, they claimed that education would become more professionally oriented. In short, by closing small, local community schools in favor of larger, centralized facilities, children would receive a better education at a much lower cost.

Child-centered "democratic progressives," on the other hand, reluctantly embraced consolidation but for different reasons. They felt that these new consolidated schools would attract better, more qualified teachers for their students and that cost savings derived from these larger facilities also would mean better resources and more diverse curricular offerings.

The century-long school consolidation process had a number of distinct phases. The first was the high school movement of the late nineteenth and early twentieth centuries. The second phase was the rural and urban school consolidation of the early to mid-twentieth century and the third was what we have called the "desegregation consolidation" movement of the late twentieth century (Parkerson and Parkerson 2015).

THE HIGH SCHOOL MOVEMENT

While the high school was not a "consolidated school" in the traditional sense, these institutions provided the model for other primary and secondary consolidated schools of the twentieth century. With their centralized regional location, departmentalized learning environment, specialized teaching staff, and complex administrative bureaucracy, high schools were the prototype of the new American consolidated school.

There were only a handful of high schools in the first half of the nineteenth century. The English High School of Boston was established in 1821 and a few others shortly thereafter. Sons of merchants, planters, professionals, and proprietors often attended these high schools before they went on to university study. But it wasn't until after the American Civil War that secondary education seemed important to everyday Americans.

As the market revolution swept across the nation in the early to mid-nineteenth century, the demand for greater educational credentials grew dramatically. While the primary education of the common school was seen as sufficient for young America, high schools had now become a necessity in our maturing society and economy. By the 1870s, the number of high schools in America had grown to nearly seven thousand (Reese 2005).

And yet these schools were still not designed for the vast majority of American children. They continued to provide sons of upper-middle-class families with a sort of "terminal degree" that would prepare them for leadership positions in business, the military, and education. Standards were high, and the curriculum was classical in nature—emphasizing the mastery of Greek and Latin. And some graduates would go on to college or university study (Reese 2005; Parkerson and Parkerson 2015, 28).

By the 1920s, however, the high school had been transformed. As the nation became more diverse as a result of rapid immigration and as businesses demanded greater educational credentials from their workers, a debate raged as to the proper direction of education—especially secondary education.

While democratic progressive educators continued to favor the classical high school, authoritarian businessmen reformers wanted a more open, vocational system that would train greater numbers of students for the booming economy. This debate raged for over two decades and was framed by two important educational reports: the *Report of the Committee of Ten* in 1892 and the *Cardinal Principles of Secondary Education* in 1918.

The *Report of the Committee of Ten* generally was supported by child-centered democratic progressives and university professors who favored a classical curriculum with high academic standards. This traditional sort of high school, they argued, would prepare a small group of students for further academic work and leadership positions in society.

The *Report* emphasized the importance of an educational ladder and recommended eight years of primary education, four years of secondary education, and then university study. It rejected the "tracking" of students, noting that "every subject which is taught . . . should be taught in the same way . . . to every pupil . . . no matter [what] the probable destination of the pupil may be." In other words, the *Report* argued that vocational training for an occupation should not be the goal of education (*Committee of Ten on Secondary School Studies* 1892).

The backlash over the *Report* was swift and overwhelming. Authoritarian businessmen reformers such as William Bagley, Andrew Draper, Nicholas Murray Butler, and others attacked it and argued that a new direction in education was necessary. Their position was simple—the country desperately needed skilled workers that only a vocational high school curriculum could provide.

George Gerwig, secretary of Pittsburgh schools, summarized the basic argument of the authoritarian businessmen reformers. What America needed, he wrote, was a new sort of high school with lower academic standards that focused on vocational training. In his popular book, *Schools with a Perfect Score*, published in 1918, Gerwig wrote, "The trowel, or the compass, or the lathe is sometimes mightier than . . . either the pen or the sword." These schools would educate everyone—the college bound as well as those "industrially, commercially or otherwise inclined" (Gerwig 1918).

The debate over the direction of American high schools was joined by the African American community as well, pitting Booker T. Washington and W. E. B. DuBois against one another. Washington favored a vocational-oriented curriculum similar to the one he had established at his famous Tuskegee Institute in Alabama. He felt strongly that employment for African American men and women was the key to their success in America and, as such, he recommended an educational system that would create jobs and benefit people of color.

Washington's ideas were well received by the white authoritarian businessmen reformers of the day. And as a result, his Tuskegee Institute was supported by generous donations from the business community and a handful of wealthy philanthropists. This "accommodationist" position, as it was called by some, was not appreciated by everyone in the black community, however. W. E. B. DuBois (pronounced do-boys) was a harsh critic and offered a very different democratic-oriented approach to African American education.

For DuBois, vocational education was unacceptable. He argued that what Washington had proposed was for "black people to give up . . . three things—first, political power, second, insistence on civil rights and third, higher education for Negro youth." By advocating vocational training as the most acceptable form of black education, he noted, there had been "a steady withdrawal of aid from institutions for the higher training of the Negro" (DuBois 1903).

While DuBois was not necessarily against vocational training, he vehemently opposed it as the centerpiece of education for black children. Rather, he favored a more balanced approach—the same as that offered to white children. Tracking African American children into vocational training simply because of their race was unacceptable.

The debate over the direction of education raged during the first decades of the twentieth century. And although there was considerable opposition to this new vocational direction from both democratic, child-centered progressives and some African American leaders such as DuBois, the demand for change was unstoppable. It was in this charged environment that the important *Cardinal Principles of Secondary Education* was published in 1918 (*Cardinal Principles* 1918).

The *Cardinal Principles* represented an important shift in attitudes and policy toward secondary education. Nevertheless, the document was a creative compromise between vocational, industrial training as proposed by authoritarian, businessmen reformers and the democratic, educational approaches as outlined by the Committee of Ten, twenty-six years before.

The important document placed special emphasis on students' health, including physical education and diet. It also recommended the development of "Worthy Home Membership, Civic education," ethical character, and the worthy use of leisure. There was no mention of classical education such as the study of Greek and Latin or the development of the intellectual "faculties," though it did recommend that students gain a "command of fundamental processes" including "writing, reading, oral and written expression and math" (*Cardinal Principles* 1918).

On the other hand, the report did recommend vocational training, noting that a student should become acquainted with "a variety of careers so that . . . he . . . can choose the most suitable career." The report also proposed that these courses be taught by "those who are successful in a vocation" (*Cardinal Principles* 1918).

In short, the *Cardinal Principles* recommended that high school students become healthy, patriotic citizens who would be prepared to enter the job market. It helped to move high school education away from its classical orientation by embracing vocational training. But, in the spirit of child-centered progressives, it recommended new methods of teaching, including group projects and problem solving and explicitly rejected memorization and recitation as the primary method of instruction (*Cardinal Principles* 1918).

By the early 1920s, the American high school had successfully adapted to the growing student population of the nation. Educators recognized the need to educate all American students, rather than the select few who would go on to college or university study. They also moved slowly toward a vocational tracking system that would help direct students toward careers in the booming American economy. These institutions became the template for further consolidation of schools throughout the nation.

RURAL SCHOOL CONSOLIDATION

With this new model firmly in place, schools in America's hinterland also began to change. In fact, beginning in the first decades of the twentieth century, the rural school consolidation movement became the most important political and social issue for millions of Americans in small towns and rural communities. The debate raged in virtually every corner of the nation as school consolidators—often led by authoritarian businessmen reformers—clashed with leaders and everyday citizens in local communities (Parkerson and Parkerson 2015).

What was at stake in these communities was local control of their schools. These humble institutions—often one-room schoolhouses—were the cultural centers of their communities and were seen as essential in transmitting cherished values from generation to generation.

States such as Iowa had an incredible fourteen thousand local community schools at the turn of the twentieth century. As in other states across the nation, these schools provided important opportunities for community participation and leadership. Now that was being challenged by school consolidation reformers (Parkerson and Parkerson 2015).

School consolidation campaigns eventually were successful but not without bitter struggles that stormed through the countryside for nearly a half-century and involved local grassroots political action, legislative battles, and court challenges. School consolidators eventually crafted a plan that would convince the local citizenry that consolidated schools would provide their children with a better education while maintaining local cultural values. In addition, these schools would be more efficient and therefore would save taxpayers money.

The plan used by reformers had three central elements. First, they created state-level reform agencies that could coordinate consolidation efforts. In Iowa, for example, the superintendent of public instruction, with the help of local leaders, created the Better Iowa School Commission. Second, authoritarian reformers recognized that simply using their political clout to "bulldoze" opposition to achieve their goals was not the answer. Early political failures had demonstrated to them that these sorts of tactics simply strengthened the resolve of democratic local leaders (Parkerson and Parkerson 2015).

Finally, these reformers convinced the local citizenry that their children would benefit greatly from consolidation. In Iowa, and in other states throughout the country, this was the most difficult task.

First, universities throughout the states were encouraged to develop educational administration courses to meet the demand of these new rural consolidated schools. Second, reformers had to convince local community members that these new administrators would be sensitive to their needs. And finally, local communities often were promised new "cultural centers" as part of the consolidated school complex, thus assuring the maintenance and transmission of their values.

These strategies eventually were successful, and in state after state, the process of school consolidation proceeded through the middle of the twentieth century. Overall, this meant a reduction in the number of schools and school districts in these states. It also meant a parallel increase in the size of schools and school districts. And of course, it represented a dramatic decline in local control and democratic participation in the affairs of these schools.

URBAN SCHOOL CONSOLIDATION

While rural school consolidation spread rapidly across the countryside during these years, city schools also experienced dramatic changes. Led by a handful of authoritarian businessmen reformers such as Nicholas Murray Butler of New York, William Rainey Harper of Chicago, and Andrew Draper of Cleveland, urban schools throughout the nation were being consolidated and, school administrations were being centralized.

Nicholas Butler, founder of Teachers College and later the president of Columbia University, was the central figure in the reorganization and consolidation of New York public schools. His famous plan, aptly named the Butler Plan, was based on the corporate business model and aggressively restructured the administration of the New York public school system, essentially stripping administrative control from local neighborhood boards.

A central component of his plan was the creation of a new position of superintendent of New York Public Schools selected by a recently established board of superintendents. Unlike the local boards of education, these board members typically were businessmen, not educators, and they were elected "at large" from the city as a whole. This move effectively centralized the administrative control of public education.

Just below the newly elected members of the board of education in the administrative hierarchy were the school principals. These administrators typically were appointed from outside the local school districts, rather than from within. This essentially eliminated the traditional seniority system that allowed long-serving, exceptional teachers to move into the ranks of administration.

Teachers, of course, were relegated to the lower echelons of the administration and yet were responsible for the primary role of education—to teach young children. This change in the structure of schools placed teachers into positions of "workers" within the corporate business system rather than respected professionals within the educational community. This loss of status would have long-term consequences for the profession and for education in general.

The Butler Plan was presumed to be a great success by other likeminded businessmen reformers of this period. In one city after another, plans to consolidate the administrative structure of schools were implemented. In Chicago, for example, William Rainey Harper's school reorganization plan—fashioned after the Butler Plan—was put into place during these years. This scheme transformed the public schools by virtually eliminating local, neighborhood input and control. Similarly, Cleveland's schools were revamped by a similar design implemented by Andrew Draper, a close associate of Butler and Harper.

The reaction to these plans was dramatic. In Chicago, there was outrage from teacher organizations, local community leaders, parents, teachers, and even the students themselves. The fledgling Chicago Teachers Federation under the leadership of Margaret Haley, for example, was energized as a result of these actions and organized to challenge these policies. Students at the Clarke school in Chicago literally walked out of the school in protest over a new policy on testing, while mothers at one school reportedly "threw mud" at a "squad" of truant officers (Parkerson and Parkerson 2001, 180; Murphy 1990, 8–12).

Despite student walkouts, demonstrations, labor organization, and the mud throwing, however, the new authoritarian model of urban school consolidation was implemented throughout the nation during the first decades of the twentieth century. Just as thousands of new consolidated high schools were being built and as rural schools were consolidated in the countryside, urban schools also were being reconfigured into centralized institutions with a structure strikingly similar to the modern business corporation. The juggernaught of school consolidation was unstoppable.

DESEGREGATION CONSOLIDATION

The final phase of school consolidation during the twentieth century was what we have called "desegregation consolidation." This form of consolidation, of course, was not a planned effort to further consolidate American schools. But as an unintended consequence of the desegregation movement, it did just that (Parkerson and Parkerson 2015).

Desegregation consolidation often was initiated under the direction of the court as a result of pressure from civil rights activists and the Department of Justice. While the 1954 Supreme Court decision *Brown v. Board of Education* had declared an end to the policies of "separate but equal" school facilities, little had changed over the next decade of 1954 to 1964. States and communities often ignored the ruling, or when ordered, they engaged in stalling techniques (Parkerson and Parkerson 2015).

The Civil Rights Law of 1964—especially Title VI of the law, however, fundamentally changed this situation—especially in the South. Now the Department of Health, Education, and Welfare could penalize states and communities that did not comply with desegregation directives. As a result, communities throughout the nation—sometimes reluctantly—began to submit to federal orders (Parkerson and Parkerson 2015).

But compliance often meant that communities seeking to maintain their political and cultural control of the educational system simply transferred black students to larger white schools. These white schools typically maintained their names, professional staff, school mascots, and traditions. African American children, on the other hand, often lost their local schools and were bused to these larger white institutions. Desegregation was achieved, but white cultural hegemony was maintained. In addition, virtually every aspect of the black educational village was destroyed in the process.

In North Carolina, for example, the number of black principals declined dramatically in the wake of desegregation consolidation. From 1963–1970 the number of black principals in elementary schools fell from 620 to 170. In high schools, their numbers plunged from 209 to 10 and by the mid 1970s, there were only 3 black principals in North Carolina High Schools! African American teachers endured a similar fate. By 1972, over 3,000 black teachers had lost their positions because of these new policies (Cecelski 1994, 8–9).

In addition to the virtual elimination of black principals and teachers in North Carolina and other states throughout the nation, the African American educational village was damaged as a result of desegregation consolidation. Black students, who once walked to and from local schools and often stopped in black-owned stores and shops on their way home, were now being bused directly to and from consolidated schools.

The daily ritual of mingling with both members of the business community and neighbors, abruptly ended. The bonds between black students and the educational village began to disappear. The "eyes of the Street," as one scholar called it, now were closing, and the vital role they played in student behavior also ceased (Jacobs 1961).

Parents also became less engaged in the educational village. The new schools were remote—not just physically but socially as well. Parents did not know teachers, and teachers did not know parents. And more often than not, the new teachers were not African Americans from the local community. In short, the connection between the education village and the school was becoming much weaker.

Finally, many African American students found the new consolidated schools remote and alienating. They were often placed in remedial classes—"ghetto classes," as some called them—and they often felt as if they were strangers in their new schools. These schools may have been more comprehensive, but they were not *their* schools. More importantly, the accountability that was a central part of the neighborhood school was now gone—as students became more anonymous.

THE CONSOLIDATION CENTURY

The four phases of the consolidation century radically transformed American education. High schools provided the early template. They were larger, centrally located institutions and served students from a wide range of surrounding communities. They had a specialized teacher corps, often hired from outside the area, and they boasted a considerable depth of curricular offerings.

Using the high school model, rural and urban schools began the consolidation process in the early twentieth century. They centralized their school administration throughout the country and closed thousands of small local schools in favor of more "productive" consolidated institutions. Then, beginning in the middle of the twentieth century, as an unintended consequence of "desegregation," former black schools were closed and their students were bused to larger, predominately white schools.

The physical result of the consolidation century was dramatic as well. By the end of the nineteenth century, the number of American schools had grown considerably, peaking at about 270,000 on the eve of World War I in 1917. As the school consolidation movement took hold, however, the number of schools in the country declined for the next half-century to about 100,000 schools in the 1970s. Since then, that number of schools has remained relatively stable. One-room schoolhouses also were affected. In the early 1920s, there were about 150,000 of these local institutions, but today they have all but disappeared.

School districts, which had provided residents with opportunities for democratic participation, also declined during the consolidation century. Again, in the 1920s, the number of these districts peaked at about 130,000, but over the years they have declined to about 20,000 today.

Finally, while local schools and school districts were declining in number, they were becoming much larger in size. From the late nineteenth century to the early 1920s, for example, the average school size was a modest 50 to 75 students. As a result of the consolidation century, however, schools today now average about 450 students. School districts were also transformed. In 1920, school districts served about 250 students on average. Today districts represent ten times those numbers serving over 2,500 students on average (Parkerson and Parkerson 2015).

The dreams of authoritarian businessmen reformers at the turn of the twentieth century seemed to have been realized. Schools were firmly under the control of states and municipalities; teachers were specialized and more professional; schools often were enormous campus-like institutions that promised better education at a lower cost to taxpayers; and they were efficiently organized along the lines of giant American corporations.

THE CONSEQUENCES OF CONSOLIDATION

But as the self-congratulations began, something seemed to be wrong. The two central arguments of authoritarian school consolidation advocates were that these new larger schools would be less expensive to operate and that students would have greater educational opportunities with more specialized and better educated teachers as well as more expansive curricular offerings. Educational research, however, has demonstrated that both these assertions were either overstated or simply wrong (Parkerson and Parkerson 2015).

A number of educational researchers have shown that up to a point, school size and costs are inversely related. But once schools reached an "ideal size" of about four hundred students, expenditures began to increase. This "U-shaped" relationship demonstrates that large consolidated schools were not always cost effective (Fox 1981).

Similarly, promises concerning the quality of teachers and the diversity of curricular offerings in consolidated schools were overstated. Specialized teachers in large consolidated schools clearly had more education and training in their particular subject area. But these teachers were often drawn from a large geographic area and were not part of the educational village. This created a number of problems, including a greater transiency of teachers themselves and a growing distrust of them among parents and members of the community.

In addition, the specialized nature of consolidated schools often led to a decline in what educational researchers call "social integration." The greater the specialization and departmentalization within schools, the weaker the social connections between teachers and between teachers and students. This can create a climate of isolation and alienation that is not conducive to learning (Parkerson and Parkerson 2015).

With regard to the curricular-offerings argument, it is clear that while small schools offered fewer specialized courses, many scholars have demonstrated that there is an *inverted* "U-shaped" relationship between the breadth of the curriculum and the size of the school. Curricular offerings increased at first—up to the level of about four hundred students. After that point, however, they either leveled off or declined.

Moreover, it has been shown that even when there were specialized courses offered in schools, only a small proportion of the students—(about 10–20 percent) actually took advantage of them (Walberg and Walberg 1994; Barker and Gump 1964; Fowler and Walberg 1991; Howley 1994).

CONCLUSION

The school-consolidation century began with enthusiasm and promise. The stunning achievements of the American corporation beginning in the 1890s had provided authoritarian businessmen reformers with a model upon which they were determined to build the modern American school. These new schools would have a centralized administration that was hierarchically (top-down) organized. They would demand further professionalization of teachers with emphasis placed on specialization. And through "economies of scale" they would be cheaper to operate while their curricular offerings would be substantially greater.

As we have seen, however, many of these promises were either not met or were broken. Larger consolidated schools were not necessarily cheaper to operate. Teachers were more educated and specialized but were more transient and typically not part of the educational village. Curricular offerings did expand as school size increased but leveled off or declined once these schools reached an ideal size of about four hundred students. And perhaps more importantly, teachers, administrators, and students became more isolated and alienated from one another.

In short, educational researchers have shown rather conclusively that smaller, local schools—once seen as backward and inefficient—actually work best. These institutions allow a degree of community input into educational policy and strengthen the bonds of the educational village. Moreover, these schools typically adopt a more consistent and focused curriculum that encourages trust among parents, members of the community, students, teachers, and administrators (Parkerson and Parkerson 2015).

While these smaller local schools offered fewer courses, they promoted active learning and encouraged more democratic exchanges between teachers and students. This helped to develop trust and promoted an active learning environment.

Additionally, these schools often embraced cooperative learning, rather than competition. This benefits all students (high and low achievers) by stimulating collaborative interest and motivations. It also helps students develop a more caring attitude toward one another, rather than perceiving others as bitter rivals (Dewey 1916; Johnson and Johnson 1989; 1991; Slavin 1988).

In chapter 4, we turn to another central theme in American educational history—the ongoing struggle for diversity in American classrooms.

4

THE STRUGGLE FOR DIVERSITY

The Emergence of a Multicultural Consciousness

The struggle for diversity in American education is part of the monumental effort to achieve equality and "simple justice" for women, people

Figure 4.1. Following the *Brown v. the Board of Education* decision in 1954, schools gradually began the process of desegregation in the 1960s and 1970s. Courtesy of iStock by Getty Images, credit starfotograf.

of color, and immigrants throughout American history. It is a struggle that is far from over, though we have achieved a great deal over the years.

As we have seen, women typically were prohibited from attending school and, until the nineteenth century, they were not considered to be capable of teaching. Some women from wealthier families received an education from tutors or in the handful of private academies established in the late eighteenth and early nineteenth centuries. But they were the exception to the rule.

As the common schools took root and as the market revolution spread across the land beginning in the early 1800s, however, attitudes began to change, and women slowly were admitted to schools. Women also demonstrated their abilities to teach and eventually became an important part of the teaching profession.

Today, women dominate the teaching profession at the elementary level but are still underrepresented in secondary and higher education. Moreover, their salaries at all levels continue to lag behind those of men.

African Americans, on the other hand, came to this country in bondage and until the American Civil War (1861–1865) the vast majority was caught in the insidious web of slavery.

While a handful of slaves and free blacks were able to receive a basic education, most did not. In fact, those who sought an education as well as those who taught slaves to read and write were often punished severely.

For a brief, bright moment in the mid-1860s the Freedmen's Bureau schools offered African Americans—young and old—a chance at education, and countless thousands seized that opportunity. As Booker T. Washington remarked, the Freedmen's schools created a "veritable fever" for education in the black community (Parkerson and Parkerson 2001).

And yet, the dreams of education for African Americans faded as the nightmare of "Jim Crow" descended on the nation and blacks once again were subjected to overt discrimination and exclusion. The infamous *Plessy v. Ferguson* U.S. Supreme Court decision of 1896 then gave federal approval to a highly segregated society that set back African American educational dreams for generations. Only through the work of countless democratic activists and grassroots organizations did the legal forms of segregation begin to lessen, and the doors of schools began to open slightly for black students.

Today, African American students and teachers continue the struggle. Although education is now available to most people of color, the quality of that education varies dramatically from community to community. African American teachers also struggle to enter the classrooms of the nation, but latent forms of prejudice and discrimination continue to plague the nation.

Immigrants to this country have had similar experiences both in the society at large and in their efforts to receive an education. Unlike the African Americans who came to this country in bondage, however, immigrants from all over the world were drawn to this nation because of the promise of freedom, employment, and educational opportunities for their children. Most were recruited by businesses to help build the nation's infrastructure and work in factories and fields.

However the dreams of immigrants often were shattered once they arrived in this nation. Many were met with violence, discrimination, and distain. Others simply faced backbreaking work for low wages. Moreover, while some immigrant children entered the common schools of the nineteenth century, many faced ridicule and mockery because of their language, culture, or religion.

While democratic progressive educators have worked to accommodate immigrant children through dual-language education and other programs centered on inclusion, problems still exist. Latent prejudice often explodes as the number of immigrants coming to this country increases or during periods of economic slowdown when there is greater competition for jobs. And, of course, some students, teachers, and politicians across the nation promote prejudice through casual disrespect for the values, language, and religions that differ from their own.

In this chapter, we will examine the individual and collective struggles of women, African Americans, and immigrants as they have contended with prejudice and discrimination to enter the classrooms of the nation as both students and teachers. Their stories are very different and yet there is a common thread that runs through each. It is the story of great success and dramatic failure. But above all, it is the story of a constant idealistic movement to achieve freedom, dignity, and educational opportunities.

WOMEN

For much of early American history, education was controlled by white men. In this male dominated, patriarchal world, men were assumed to have superior intellects. In fact, this misdirected idea of male superiority had been woven into the fabric of many societies and cultures for millennia. And of course, this patriarchal worldview continues among some groups of Americans and in some regions of the world. Moreover, it is an important underpinning of many religions.

This male dominance certainly was reinforced by the fact that formal education was not seen as important for women, and they typically were prohibited from attending school. During the colonial era, for example, only a handful of young women were allowed in Puritan schools in the New England colonies. Some young women did go to religious primary schools in the colonies, and in the South a few girls from wealthy families occasionally received an education from a plantation tutor. Other than that, however, educational opportunities for young women were extremely limited.

In addition to their presumed superior intellect, men were seen as being better able to teach because of their physical strength. Until well into the nineteenth century, discipline in the classroom often meant being able to overpower young boys. The primary instruments of discipline were the ruler (sometimes called the ferule), the whipping post, the rattan, or the back of the hand. Young boys were routinely whipped, punched, slapped, and kicked for such "grave" offenses as whispering, talking, or simply not knowing their lessons. It's no surprise, then, that men monopolized the teaching profession from the colonial period into the nineteenth century.

While men would dominate teaching throughout the colonial era, it is important to note that there were four distinct types of teachers during this period—only one of which allowed women to teach. These included the New England schoolmasters, the church officials that taught religious education in the middle colonies and elsewhere, the private in-home tutors that educated wealthy plantation children in the South and the children of wealthy merchants in the North, and finally, a handful of women who taught in local or neighborhood schools—sometimes referred to as "dame schools."

New England Schoolmasters

Perhaps the best-known colonial teachers were the Puritan New England schoolmasters. One of the most celebrated of these stern masters was

Ezekiel Cheever, who taught for seventy years in his hometown of New Haven, Connecticut, then Ipswich, Massachusetts, then in Charlestown (Boston) and finally in Boston. Cheever published his *Short Introduction to the Latin Tongue* in 1645. This book, affectionately known as "Cheever's Accidence" was the mainstay of "grammar school" education throughout the colonial period and was still used well into the nineteenth century (Parkerson and Parkerson 2001).

While Cheever was well-known throughout the colonies, most schoolmasters taught in obscurity. Early on, most received their formal education in England while others had little formal training. By the mid-eighteenth century, however, many attended the new colleges of Yale and Harvard in preparation for the ministry and then taught a few years while they waited for a suitable pulpit. In fact, there was an old New England saying that went something like this: "scratch a teacher and find a preacher" (Parkerson and Parkerson 2001).

Church Schools

Elsewhere in the middle colonies and scattered through the North and South were church officials from a variety of denominations who taught school while attending to their spiritual responsibilities. These pastors, ministers, priests, and lay church leaders, taught in the Dutch Reformed, German Lutheran, Quaker, Roman Catholic, Moravian, and Mennonite churches, as well as hundreds of others.

Typically, these teachers provided children with a very rudimentary education in reading and spelling with special emphasis on their particular interpretation of the Scriptures. In many cases, these religious teachers instructed in their native language, such as German or Dutch, and were a central part of their immigrant community.

One such religious teacher was Christopher Dock from the Mennonite Church of Pennsylvania. Like many other religious teachers, Dock was profoundly influenced by the educational pioneer, John Amos Comenius, an early advocate of universal education.

In the early 1700s, Dock established a school that served both boys and girls; it didn't matter whether they were white or black. His instructional approach included singing hymns, reciting the Lord's Prayer and Ten Commandments followed by lessons in reading and writing. Dock's famous instructional work—*Schulordnung* (School Order)—became the standard text in a number of religious sects (Monroe 1901; Schubert 1986, 65, 85, 129).

Tutors

In addition to the New England schoolmasters and the religious teachers of the middle colonies were the tutors of colonial and early America. Early on, tutors typically were recruited from England or drawn from the ranks of educated indentured servants in the colonies. George Washington's tutor, Hobby, for example, was an indentured servant, and taught the future president of the United States to read and write. Hobby often boasted that "between his knees he had laid the foundation of Washington's greatness" (Heatwole 1916).

By the end of the colonial period and during the early Republic, tutors routinely received their education in this country from Harvard, Yale, Kings College, Queens College, or one of dozens of others. They often were recruited by affluent plantation owners or wealthy merchants to help prepare their children for college and university study. Sometimes they were given access to a small garden plot to grow their own vegetables; other times they were allowed to establish a small community school and charge their students a modest tuition. By the mid-nineteenth century, a handful of women, educated in female academies in the North were hired as tutors. Typically, however, most tutors were men.

Dame Schools

But while men dominated the profession during this period a small group of women did teach in what were called "dame schools." These early primary schools provided local neighborhood children with a rudimentary education to supplement the apprenticeship training they would receive later. And since most colonial Americans had little access to education, the need for educated and responsible women from the community to teach was increasing.

Changing Attitudes Toward Women

Dame schools gradually became more common by the early nineteenth century, and many communities employed female teachers to instruct their children. One New England town "paid Widow Walker ten shillings for schooling small children." Similarly, Hannah Beaman from Deerfield, Massachusetts, was hired to teach children in her village. Interestingly, Hannah's class was interrupted in the summer of 1694 by an Indian attack, and she and her children were forced to run for their lives. All, thankfully, were saved (Small 1969, 167).

During this same period, the American Revolution, the philosophy of the Enlightenment, and changing attitudes toward women promoted ideas of equality and democratic values that challenged the notion of female inferiority. Moreover, the concept of "Republican Motherhood" became widely accepted among the former colonists as women promoted ideas of equality, patriotism, and democracy among their children—especially boys (Reiner 1982).

The market revolution also challenged patriarchal ideas concerning the position of women in society. Central to the market economy was the idea of "meritocracy," the notion that your social standing was based on what you had achieved rather than what your traditional family position or gender may have been. While women were still not equal, change was in the air.

The Education of Women

Perhaps the most important factor that helped to change entrenched patriarchal attitudes toward women, however, was education. As we have seen, women had traditionally been barred from schools because of their assumed intellectual inferiority. And because of this, female illiteracy was very high, and patriarchal attitudes were reinforced. Women were caught in a cycle of oppression from which it was difficult to escape.

Nevertheless, in the years following the Revolution through the early 1800s, a number of "female academies" were established in young America. The earliest of these was the Young Ladies Academy of Philadelphia where women were introduced to a rigorous curriculum that centered on "Reading, Writing, Arithmetic, English Grammar, Composition, Rhetoric and Geography." The academy was a great success and drew women from all over the country. More importantly, it demonstrated that women were as capable as men—even in a challenging academic setting (Woody 1929).

By the early nineteenth century other important female academies were established. These included Emma Willard's Troy Female Seminary that opened in 1821. The Troy academy was a serious academic institution that focused on teacher training. Mary Lyon's Mount Holyoke Female Seminary was established a few years later and was designed to be comparable to men's colleges at the time. Lyon instituted a rigorous entrance examination and a curriculum that required seven courses in science and mathematics for graduation. Many of her graduates went on to have successful careers in education (Stowe 1887).

The important work of Emma Willard, Mary Lyon, and dozens of other women transformed the educational environment of young America. Hundreds of women entered the teaching profession during this period and created a kind of intellectual revolution in the nation. By the eve of the Civil War, between 60 and 70 percent of all young northern boys were attending school, and girls attended at about the same rate. While rates were lower in the South and West, there clearly had been progress with regard to female equality since the American colonial period (Parkerson and Parkerson 2008).

Women Teachers

The same factors that helped to change attitudes toward the education of women also helped to propel them into the teaching profession. As the common school movement of the early nineteenth century swept across young America, the demand for teachers grew steadily. School districts throughout the nation now had a pool of educated, ambitious, and clearly underemployed young women who were prepared to teach.

Gradually, women were preferred as teachers for three important reasons. The first was money, the second was a change in attitudes toward the discipline of children in the classroom, and the third was the urbanization of America in the second half of the nineteenth century.

For many district school leaders, the most important consideration for hiring a teacher was their willingness to work for less. Alonzo Potter, the great educational pedagogue of the nineteenth century, summed it up the best in his classic *The School and the School Master*. Potter bristled at pathetic wages paid to teachers during this period—especially women—noting that districts wanted the best teacher available "provided . . . they are the cheapest" (Potter 1842).

Given the fact that women had few employment opportunities, however, many reluctantly accepted lower wages in order to get their teaching position. In fact, women teachers typically earned 35 to 40 percent less than men in rural areas and actually were paid 40 percent less than common laborers in cities across America! Of course, teachers often received free room and board from a willing member of the community; nevertheless, their wages were still close to subsistence (Potter 1842, 198; Burton 1852).

As we have seen, men had been preferred as teachers because they were seen as more capable of disciplining unruly boys. But during this period, attitudes toward discipline were changing rapidly. In the early 1700s, John Locke published his revolutionary ideas concerning child rearing in *Some Thoughts Concerning Education*. In this important treatise, Locke recommended that physical punishment should be abandoned and replaced with more humane methods of praise for achievement and good behavior coupled with shame and humiliation for failure and poor deportment (Potter 1842; Locke 1705).

Gradually, these ideas were accepted by middle-class families throughout young America. Moreover, most democratic educational reformers, including Alonzo Potter, were convinced that these were the proper methods of discipline and, more importantly, that women were the most capable of implementing it. Potter argued that "in the government of schools, moral influence should be substituted as far as possible, in place of mere coercion [and] women are, in most respects, preeminently qualified to administer such discipline" (Potter 1842).

Finally, the growing urbanization of America in the second half of the nineteenth century helped to move women into the classrooms of the nation. By the end of the century, women teachers were common in the countryside—representing about a third of all rural classrooms. In the cities of America, however, 90 percent of all teachers were women! In the countryside, women had "higher economic utility" since "a daughter's domestic service was more highly valued." Moreover, in rural areas, women were more reluctant to enter the workforce because of entrenched conservative social values (Strober and Tyack 1980; Strober and Langford 1986).

In cities, however, things were different. First of all, women teachers were seen as more acceptable by democratic educators. And, because men had a greater range of employment opportunities in cities, many abandoned their low-paying teaching jobs for other higher paying occupations. This of course opened the door for greater opportunities in teaching for women. And women gladly took advantage of these opportunities.

AFRICAN AMERICANS

People of color faced a different set of problems from women, and yet they, too, were able to slowly enter the classrooms of America as well as the teaching profession. These achievements, however, did not come easily and have required decades of struggle against prejudice and misunderstanding.

Religious Schools for African Americans

As we have seen, African American slaves typically had little access to education from the colonial period through most of the nineteenth century. However, a few black children were able to take advantage of schools established by various religious institutions. In the late 1600s, for example, the Anglicans established the educational Society for the Propagation of the Gospel in Foreign Parts to help "Christianize" slaves in Maryland. Another school was established in Goose Creek, South Carolina, and yet another by Presbyterians in Virginia (Parkerson and Parkerson 2001).

In the North, a few African American schools were established in the eighteenth century. In 1704, for example, New York's Trinity Church founded a school that eventually enrolled two hundred slave children, while the Quakers chartered a number of slave schools in Rhode Island, Pennsylvania, and New Jersey. Following the Revolution, the African Free School was established in New York City, and by the end of the century, most northern states had established similar schools under the direction of the Quakers (Woody 1929).

And yet, racial prejudice, hatred, and violence often undermined these humanitarian efforts. Some schools were closed by law, others experienced mob violence, and in still others, both teachers and students were harassed by local residents. For example, Prudence Crandall's private school for girls in Canterbury, Connecticut, admitted a black girl in 1831, to the outrage of local residents. First, Crandall was threatened by local officials and then white parents removed their children from the school, forcing her to close her doors (Parkerson and Parkerson 2001).

Later, when Crandall established a school for girls of "color," the state passed a "black law" that effectively closed the school. She protested the law but was arrested and jailed. Later, the school was mysteriously destroyed by fire, and she was forced to leave town.

While not all teachers and black children in these schools were subjected to this kind of discrimination, violence, and legal maneuvering, it was not uncommon for them to experience some form of racial prejudice in the North. In the South, however, the level of prejudice and violence was much greater.

Prohibiting African American Education

Following South Carolina's Denmark Vesey slave uprising in 1822 and Virginia's Nat Turner slave rebellion in 1831, vague fears of slave uprisings became palpable among wealthy planters, and restrictive laws regarding the education of slaves and free blacks were rapidly instituted. The logic of these laws was simple—if a slave could read, he or she might become a threat to the existing order of the slave-owning society. Whippings were commonly inflicted on those who "dared" to get an education, and those providing that education—such as reading instruction—also were punished (Cohen 1974b).

As a result of these prohibitions, some black educators simply moved their schools "underground" in order to survive. Milla Granson, for example, was taught to read by her master's children. Later, when she was sold to a Mississippi plantation owner, she began teaching "midnight classes" in the back allies of Natchez, Mississippi. Her hard work paid off, and she eventually educated hundreds of slaves (Woodson 1968; Perkins 1989).

Freedmen's Bureau Schools

As we have seen, however, the turning point for African American education was the American Civil War and the creation of the Freedmen's Bureau schools in the early years of Reconstruction. Between 1866 and

1877, hundreds of these schools were established throughout the South. They created what Booker T. Washington later called "a veritable fever" for education. Thousands of young blacks and adults were educated by over nine thousand Freedmen's Bureau teachers—both black and white—recruited from all over the country (Parkerson and Parkerson 2001).

While this exciting moment in African American education faded with the end of Reconstruction in 1877, the struggle for access to education continued throughout the nineteenth and into the twentieth century. During the dark days of Jim Crow beginning in 1877, prejudice, violence, lynching, and legal restrictions against African American education grew. As we have seen, this was capped by the infamous *Plessey v. Ferguson* decision of 1896 that reinforced the misguided idea that "separate but equal" facilities were both legal and appropriate.

Educational Activism

And yet, through the work of activists and especially black teachers and their organizational work, the tide slowly began to turn with regard to African American education. The National Association of Teachers of Colored Schools (NATCS), for example, fought vigorously at the state and national levels to reform the curriculum of black schools, raise salaries of black teachers, increase the length of school terms, and secure better equipment and facilities. Their hard work eventually paid dividends.

The National Association for the Advancement of Colored People (NAACP) also played a major role in this area. Beginning in the 1930s, they initiated over thirty-five lawsuits demanding equal pay for black teachers. By the 1940s, over half of these suits had been settled in their favor. And of course, the work of the NAACP in desegregating schools reached a successful climax in 1954 with the *Brown v. Board of Education* U.S. Supreme Court decision.

As mentioned in chapter 3, the 1954 *Brown* decision of the Supreme Court was the first step toward desegregation of public schools in America. But for the next decade, states throughout the South engaged in "foot dragging" and noncompliance to the court's directives. Only through legislation—first the Civil Rights Act of 1964 and then the Voting Rights Act of 1965—did things begin to change. The court acted again in the early 1970s with the famous Mecklenburg Decision that essentially began forced desegregation through bussing.

The result of individual and collective activism, court decisions, and progressive legislation paid important dividends. By 1930, the proportion of African American children attending school had doubled to nearly 60 percent. And by the 1950s, it had grown to over 80 percent. Today, the percentage of black and white children attending school is roughly the same.

And yet, great barriers still exist for both the education of black children and the acceptance of black teachers and administrators in American public schools. For example, as discussed in the previous chapter, one of the great unintended consequences of the desegregation movement of the 1950s and 1960s was that by closing all-black, segregated schools, African American teachers and administrators also were purged from the teaching profession. Between 1963 and 1970 alone, for example, over three thousand black teachers in North Carolina lost their positions. Similarly, the number of black principals in the state's high schools plunged from 209 to three during roughly the same period (Cecelski 1994, 8–9).

Thus, while there has been considerable progress in the area of desegregation of schools, African Americans remain on the outside of the teaching profession. Moreover, in recent years, many states have abandoned their affirmative action policies that recruited black teachers. Also as our collective obsession with stricter licensure requirements, typically measured by standardized testing, has grown, the number of African American teachers entering the profession has declined significantly. Today, only 8 percent of teachers are African American, despite the growing percentage of black children in school.

IMMIGRANTS

The ongoing struggle of African Americans to both receive an education and enter the teaching profession has been monumental. Ethnically and culturally diverse immigrants to this nation, however, also have endured similar forms of prejudice, discrimination, and legal restrictions.

Immigrant Teachers in Religious Schools

A number of immigrant teachers did find success in private and religious schools over the years, but they struggled to enter the public school classrooms of the nation. During the colonial period, for example, the Dutch Reformed Church of New Amsterdam established nine schools in what is now New York City and hired dozens of Dutch-speaking teachers to teach school (Parkerson and Parkerson 2001).

In other colonies, such as Pennsylvania, Quakers took the lead and established dozens of schools. The Quakers also established a teacher apprenticeship system and were the first to "license" their teachers, including many who were born abroad. In addition, the Quakers were the first to embrace teacher diversity and educate young girls and African American, and immigrant children.

Numerous other religious groups, including the Moravians and Mennonites, also had a long tradition of promoting education and hiring foreign-born teachers. As we have seen, the Moravians taught new teachers the methods originally established by John Amos Comenius in the 1600s and also offered education to all children irrespective of race, gender, or national origin.

The Mennonites, for their part, established schools throughout the colonies but especially in Pennsylvania and North Carolina. And, as we have seen, teachers in the Mennonite tradition utilized an instructional method developed by Christopher Dock in the early eighteenth century, known as the *Schulordung* (Woody 1969).

Roman Catholics also were instrumental in this regard by offering Catholic immigrant children educational opportunities. In scattered northern settlements, especially in the mid-Atlantic colonies and in the Baltimore, Maryland, area, they established numerous schools during the colonial era and into the nineteenth century. The Jesuits, for example, established a school in St. Mary's City as early as 1640 and another in Newton in 1673. By the eighteenth century, Roman Catholic schools at the elementary and secondary level grew in both numbers and stature (McCluskey 1964).

The Exclusion of Foreign-Born Teachers

And yet, despite the efforts of these and other ethnic and religious schools, immigrant teachers and students often were the victims of prejudice, discrimination, and legal restrictions in public schools. As the common school developed in the nineteenth century, secular education became the standard. In this environment, there was little room for sectarian religious education. In fact, one of the early reforms of the common school was the elimination of religious education, creating a clear separation of church and school. Moreover, there was virtually no tolerance for either non-English-speaking immigrants or those whose culture differed from the norms of the day.

This is not to say that religious values were abandoned in the common school. They clearly were promoted. But those values were not specific to a particular religion or sect. As we have seen, they embraced a kind of secularized "pan Protestantism." D. Page, the important pedagogue of this period, clarified these values when he noted that Americans were dependent "on the life giving truths" of Protestant Christianity. However, "when I say religious training I do not mean sectarianism." Rather, these values were the "common ground we can occupy" (Page 1867).

As a result, there was strong opposition to religiously oriented schools during this period and the immigrant teachers that taught in these schools. Educators, politicians, and the general public typically embraced the unifying principle of the pan-Protestant common school as essential to unite the nation and provide young Americans with a common set of values. Linked to strong nationalism, the powerful idea of God and Country became one of the hallmarks of the common school movement.

The problem, of course, was that not all Americans accepted these values. Moreover, not everyone was a Protestant. As the nineteenth century progressed, more and more immigrants came to this country with different languages, religious views, and cultures. Over time, the Protestant-oriented curriculum became a growing source of division and discord.

Roman Catholic immigrants, for example, often were disrespected by Protestant America, and in the mid-1800s, there were a number of anti-Catholic riots across the country. The so-called Philadelphia Bible Riots, for example, left thirteen dead and dozens of Catholic churches in ruins. The cause of these riots was the demand by Catholics to use the "Roman

Catholic" Bible for instruction in predominantly Catholic public schools in that city. Similar anti-Catholic riots occurred in New York City in 1842 (Higham 1970; McCluskey 1964).

Immigrants to young America also were troubled by the values that were being promoted in the common schools. For example, most primary readers of this era, including the influential McGuffey series, routinely underscored the "evils of drink" in their readings. While this idea resonated with white, middle-class Protestants, it conflicted with the culture of Roman Catholics and Jewish Americans who used alcohol in their services and sometimes drank wine with the evening meal.

Finally, the issue of "English only" instruction in primary and secondary schools created dramatic tension within communities across the nation—as it sometimes does today. It caused resentment among German, Polish, Russian, Italian, and other non-English-speaking immigrants, and it became a rallying cry for "native White Americans" who objected to immigrants' requests for dual-language instruction.

The result of these tensions created a growing animosity toward immigrants to this country, and immigrant teachers often found themselves in the middle. These tensions isolated newcomers from the mainstream culture of America, it alienated young immigrants who were often ridiculed by their classmates and their teachers because of their "different ways" and it systematically helped to purge immigrant teachers from the classrooms of the nation.

By the end of the nineteenth century, the pattern of discrimination and exclusion was in place. The number of immigrants would rise and fall, the race and ethnicity of these groups would change, and the political climate would shift. But latent prejudice would linger and then reappear on a regular basis. However, the fact remains that we have always had difficulty accepting those who are different.

Today, because of the hard work of such groups as the National Coalition of Advocates for Students (NCAS), the doors of classrooms across the nations are opening slightly to both immigrant students and teachers. And yet, progress remains slow. Like women and African American teachers before them, they will contend with cultural stereotypes, prejudice, and blatant discrimination. Like other groups that preceded them, they will have to struggle individually and collectively to achieve change. And that change is absolutely necessary!

Our greatest strength as a nation as well as the basis of our social turmoil is our diversity. This irony should come as no surprise since the struggle for acceptance and inclusion for women, African Americans, and immigrants from around the world has been a central theme in American history as well as the history of education.

As we move forward into the twenty-first century, the job of teachers will be to help break down the barriers that discriminate against women, blacks, and those with cultures that are not part of the mainstream. Providing quality education for all children and creating an environment that both engages student learning and promotes a culture of acceptance is our primary responsibility. Teachers must change the world—one student, one class, one school at a time. If not us, then who?

In the next chapter, we turn to the curriculum of American schools. As with other aspects of our educational history, the curriculum has been the mirror to the nation. It has reflected the prevailing vision of the country and continues to demonstrate the constant tension between the democratic and authoritarian schools of teaching.

5

THE CURRICULUM

From Religious to Secular and Comprehensive

The curriculum of the American school has undergone a fundamental transformation over the years. As with other aspects of American educational history, the curriculum has been the mirror to the history of the nation itself. It has reflected the prevailing vision of the country and continues to demonstrate the constant tension between the authoritarian and democratic perspectives on teaching.

As we have seen, the early curriculum of the colonies focused on religion. In New England, for example, Puritan leaders felt that the primary purpose of education was religious instruction. In fact, as noted in previous chapters, the first compulsory educational law in the colonies was The Old Deluder Law. This law stated that the purpose of education was to teach children to read the Bible in order to "thwart the delusions of Satan."

To achieve that goal, the classic "hornbook" was used to teach reading, writing, and spelling. The hornbook was a paddle-shaped piece of thin wood inscribed with the letters of the alphabet and the Lord's Prayer. It was covered with a transparent sheet of a cow's horn to protect it—thus the name hornbook.

Teachers often punched a hole in the handle and attached it to a leather strap so that it could hang from the child's waist or neck. These simple learning devices typically displayed both printed and cursive letters of the alphabet that were copied by generations of Puritan children. The Lord's

Figure 5.1. In the early public schools, children often did not have textbooks, but used books that were available from the teacher or from home. Today, students have access to a wide range of curricular materials, both online and in print. Courtesy of iStock by Getty Images, credit AndrzejSowa.

Prayer was memorized, and the words of the prayer were used for spelling lessons (Blackwell Museum of History of Education).

As the number of Puritan children in school increased during the next generation, *The New England Primer* was introduced. This book was based loosely on *The Royal Primer* from England and served as both a catechism and a reader. *The New England Primer* provided children with religious instruction in the form of questions and answers, for example, "Who made you?" and then gave answers such as "God made me." In addition, the primer listed the letters of the alphabet—"easie" syllables for children to memorize, words of increasing difficulty, and finally, a picture alphabet with rhymes (Ford [1897] 1962).

Notably missing in these primers was arithmetic. However, they did include roman numerals to help children find chapters, psalms, and verses of the Bible. Teachers soon realized, however, that their students needed to learn to "cipher," and many created their own handwritten "sum books" for that purpose (Ford [1897] 1962).

Students would copy the numbers in the sum book to create their own book for studying. Ciphering consisted of addition, subtraction, multiplication, and some division. Teachers recognized that as the country slowly moved from a bartering to a cash economy, the ability to add and subtract had become crucial (Ford [1897] 1962).

During the 1780s, Nicholas Pike published an arithmetic book fondly referred to as "Old Pike." The book may seem rather bewildering to us today, and perhaps it did as well to the children who used it in school. It contained many biblical references, and arithmetic problems typically had a religious focus. For example, one lesson required students to consider the "proportions and tonnage of Noah's Arc." The complexity of this text made it appropriate for upper-level students (Ford [1897] 1962).

In the middle colonies of New York, New Jersey, and Pennsylvania, a religious curriculum also was the norm. Numerous sects from the Quakers to the Mennonites established schools to promote their particular vision of the world, taught on the hard benches of local schools.

During this period, for example, the Quakers found a home in Pennsylvania and quickly established hundreds of religious schools in their local communities. Typically, these schools offered a religiously oriented curriculum to all children including young women and a handful of African Americans.

Similarly, Mennonite settlements scattered throughout this region also promoted religious education. And as we have seen, they typically followed the curriculum established by Christopher Dock in his famous *Schulordung*. Like many other religious schools of the time, their curriculum centered on the memorization and recitation of the Ten Commandments and the Lord's Prayer. In addition, singing religious hymns was an important part of the school day (Monroe 1901; Schubert 1986).

THE COMMON SCHOOL

While a basic religious education was accepted by many colonists, the American Revolution and the market revolution of the early nineteenth century changed attitudes toward education as well as the basic curriculum.

As we have seen, a diverse group of intellectuals, political leaders, workingmen, small-business owners, and commercial farmers called for a new kind of secularly oriented school that emphasized God and country, as well as the values of the marketplace. This was the common school.

These democratic reformers felt strongly that our new nation required a solid, nationalistic foundation. Young students, moreover, not only needed a "God-fearing" discipline and moral direction but also the lessons of competition, persistence, and punctuality. It was these values that defined the curriculum of the common school.

With the publication of the McGuffey *Readers* in 1830s, these values became more standardized. Religious content was minimized with only one in four selections in the *Readers* making reference to God or the Bible (Parkerson and Parkerson 1998).

Rather, the central content of the *Readers* promoted the secular values of nationalism and patriotism. Selections about George Washington's famous cherry tree incident and Paul Revere's midnight ride were typical. Some of these stories were parables, but in more advanced *Readers* they included actual speeches by the founding fathers that students memorized and then recited to the teacher (Parkerson and Parkerson 1998).

Other selections of the McGuffey *Readers* reinforced the market values of competition, punctuality, perseverance, and hard work. Common school teachers often conducted bees to reinforce the spirit of competition. Warren Burton reflected that the "thrill of competition" seemed to bring out the best of every student. The spelling competitions were something of a sport, and as we have seen, parents and members of the community often traveled miles to see the entertainment (Burton 1852).

Teachers encouraged the value of punctuality by punishing (and sometimes humiliating) students who were tardy. Punishment would include staying after school, forfeiting recess, sitting in the corner with a dunce cap, and so on. It was widely held that children needed to learn the value of being punctual because it was essential in the workplace.

The value of perseverance—also important in the new market economy—often was reinforced by common school teachers through the pacing of lessons. Students had to successfully memorize their lesson before proceeding to the next. For example, in their spelling lessons, students were required to correctly spell each word before advancing.

The McGuffey *Readers* and the *Blue Backed Speller* also helped to reinforce this value. A selection in the *Second Eclectic Reader*, titled "Puss and Her Kittens," for example, told the story of a cat who lived in the cellar with her three kittens. One day, Puss decided to move her kittens to the attic and carried them up one by one.

The servant in the house thought that this was not the proper place for the kittens and moved them back to the cellar. The mother cat then moved her kittens back to the attic again, and the servant removed them once more. Puss persevered and once again moved her kittens back to the attic. This time the servant gave up, and all the cats remained in the attic.

The moral of the lesson was perseverance. Puss felt that her kittens would be safer in the attic and was determined to achieve this goal. Teachers would explain to their students that just like Puss, perseverance was an important trait for success in life (McGuffey 1836b).

Hard work also was emphasized in the McGuffey *Readers*. This value was woven through many selections. In the *Fifth Eclectic Reader*, for example, there was a selection titled "No Excellence Without Labor" that stated, "The education . . . of every individual must be chiefly his own work." Later in the reading, the author, William Wirt, wrote (in all caps) "THERE IS NO EXCELLENCE WITHOUT GREAT LABOR" (McGuffey 1879, 242–43).

THE NEW AMERICAN CURRICULUM

By the end of the nineteenth century, young America had matured into a modern, powerful nation experiencing tremendous population growth as well as greater ethnic and religious diversity. American schools, once again, responded to these changes with yet another transformation of their curriculum.

The common school curriculum of an earlier era had been successful in many ways. It taught young Americans how to spell, helped to develop their basic arithmetic skills, promoted a God-fearing morality, fostered a patriotic vision of our developing nation, and helped to prepare students for the emerging market economy.

But now, the common school appeared "old-fashioned" and ill equipped to deal with the problems and possibilities of the new modern nation. As we have seen in chapter 2, the structure and organization of American schools was changing dramatically during this period as a result of state control and school consolidation. And now educational reformers sought a transformation of the curriculum as well.

At the same time, democratic educational researchers had demonstrated that as children aged, they progressed through distinct developmental stages, with certain subjects appropriate at each stage. The graded school—rather than the one-room schoolhouse of the past—clearly was needed. Eventually, the graded school was matched with high schools to create a sort of educational ladder with teachers trained in specific academic specialties.

The New High School Curriculum

But as the graded elementary school curriculum slowly took shape during this period, a great debate raged over the direction of secondary education. As we have seen, by the end of the nineteenth century, the population of the United States had become more diverse, and the market economy had matured. Now businesses needed more trained and educated workers. The question was whether high schools should continue to exclusively focus on small groups of upper middle-class students and offer a classically based education, or should they begin to accommodate the growing multicultural, middle-class population?

Businessmen reformers and authoritarian educators of this era typically saw education as a preparation for jobs. As such, they favored a curriculum that "tracked" students into specific occupations. They wanted a curriculum that focused more on vocational and manual-skills training rather than academic subjects. In this way, they argued, the high school could accommodate the needs of a rapidly growing body of students and help the economy grow. They also claimed that since high schools were publicly funded, their mission should not be simply to educate an elite group of students (Parkerson and Parkerson 2015, 28–29).

Progressive democratic educators, on the other hand, understood well the needs of a growing population and economy but nevertheless argued that the nation would be best served through a classically oriented high school curriculum. They typically embraced innovations in teaching such as collaborative learning and group work but rejected the idea that the primary function of education was to train individuals for a job.

As we have seen, this great debate was framed by two important educational reports. The first was the *Committee of Ten Report* of 1892 and the second was the *Cardinal Principles of Secondary Education* published in 1917. The *Committee of Ten Report*, generally promoted by the democratic reformers, passionately advocated the traditional classical curriculum of the high school that was designed to prepare a small group of students for college and university study (*Committee of Ten on Secondary School Studies* 1892; *Cardinal Principles* 1918).

The Cardinal Principles of Secondary Education, on the other hand, was a creative synthesis of the authoritarian and democratic positions and called for a shift in the curricular focus of high schools. It accommodated businessmen reformers by recommending a tracking system that would include vocational and industrial training. In fact, the report detailed seven recommendations—only one of which was academically based: the "Command of Fundamental Processes" that included "writing, reading, oral and written expression and math" (*Cardinal Principles* 1918).

But the report also subscribed to some progressive democratic ideas by recommending that academic subjects be taught with newer material and newer methods. It also placed a great deal of emphasis on the development of health, physical activity, civic education, and "worthy" leisure activities (*Cardinal Principles* 1918).

As we have seen, the debate surrounding the curriculum of the high school also raged among African Americans. Booker T. Washington, for example, favored a vocationally based curriculum. He felt that this approach would help African Americans get jobs. His goal was to lift blacks out of poverty through an educational system that provided them the skills to get jobs. His Tuskegee Institute, founded in 1881, was designed for this purpose (Washington 1974).

Actually, Lewis Adams was responsible for the creation of Tuskegee. Adams, a former slave, had become a successful tradesman. In the late 1870s, he struck a deal with several state politicians to "deliver the African-American vote" if the Alabama legislature passed a bill to "establish a Normal School for colored teachers." The deal was agreed upon, and Tuskegee was established.

Adams and George Campbell (a former slave owner) then recruited Booker T. Washington as the principal of the school. Adams initially contributed a "good horse," a wagon, harness, and plow to help students plant vegetables to eat.

For his part, Booker T. Washington devoted his life to the Tuskegee Institute. He recruited remarkable African Americans to join the faculty, including notables such as George Washington Carver. Moreover, he also successfully solicited substantial monetary support from businessmen and politicians (Washington 1974).

As already noted, however, W. E. B. DuBois took a very different position on the education of African Americans. DuBois had earned his doctorate in history from Harvard University in 1895. Perhaps as a result he felt strongly that equality could only be achieved when blacks had access to the same classical curriculum as whites. Thus, he strongly opposed the practice of tracking African American students into vocational and technical training.

DuBois called Washington's approach "accommodationist" and argued that only through an academic curriculum could blacks rise to positions of leadership in politics and business. Although his ideas were considered radical in the early 1900s, they eventually gained acceptance in the black community during the 1950s and 1960s as racial integration became more of a reality (DuBois 1903).

Despite this conflict, an uneasy compromise over the direction of the high school curriculum was achieved. The high school curriculum developed during the next few decades included health education, physical education, civics, government, art, and music.

In addition, new scientific and technological discoveries demanded that high schools expand their curriculum and offer courses in biology, physics, and chemistry. Similarly, America's new position as an international power required that high school students learn modern foreign languages such as German, Spanish, and Russian, rather than Greek or Latin. And, in order to help students understand this new complex world, they were instructed in courses such as history, geography, civics, and government.

Also, in accordance with the recommendations presented in the *Cardinal Principles*, the school day gradually included extracurricular activities such as football, basketball, baseball, and club sports such as golf, tennis, volleyball, and archery. Other leisure activities also were introduced during the school day or after school, such as student council, drama club, debate team, chorus, chess club, and bridge. Finally, a variety of extracurricular academic and social clubs also were launched during this period such as Hi-Y (High School YMCA), French clubs, speech clubs, math clubs, and history clubs.

Authoritarian businessmen reformers were happy that the high standards of the classical high school were being relaxed and that vocational training was now considered important. Democratic progressive educators, on the other hand, were encouraged by the expansion of the curriculum in order to develop the "whole child." They also were satisfied that new methods of instruction were now being promoted throughout the nation.

Vocational and technical training, of course, would remain an important part of the curriculum. At the high school level, tracking became more commonplace, with entire programs such as precollege and business education eventually emerging. Nevertheless it has been shown that for students in the vocational track, only about 17 percent of their coursework involved vocational courses. The remainder of their coursework was spent on more traditional academic courses such as math, English, and science (Labaree 1986).

The Ongoing Influence of Progressive Education

Over the next few decades, however, progressive education gradually would play a greater and greater role in the curriculum. The central curricular innovation of the progressives was group instruction with the integration of subjects around real-life problems or issues. These progressive approaches continued to develop in tandem with the more innovative and diverse curriculum of math, science, the arts, and humanities.

A single topic would be used to focus the curriculum in order to demonstrate to students how learning relates to the real world. For example, with a theme such as growing a garden, students would learn about science, math, reading, and writing. In science, they would be introduced to plants and nutrients. In math, the layout of the garden and the potential harvest might be discussed.

In reading, students would discuss the occupation of farming and the important role of agriculture in our society. And by keeping a journal on the development of the garden, students would gain important experiences in writing. These ideas were an application of John Dewey's theories of learning as well as Kilpatrick's project method (Parkerson and Parkerson 2008).

Progressive education continued to develop during the 1960s with programs such as Head Start. This program helped to prepare "underprivileged" children for school. Children learned readiness skills such as learning the alphabet, counting, and listening to stories read aloud by the teacher. This helped students get ready for reading and math in the primary grades.

Innovative curriculum ideas also were implemented. The open classroom, for example, was employed in some schools. Here, several teachers would group their students into a large open area and pool their teaching strengths around a central learning theme. For example, using the theme "A Trip to the Moon," students would build a "rocket" to take them to the moon.

Students would read science articles about space travel and the environment of the moon. A science teacher would guide these activities. Math would be used to construct the rocket ship in the correct proportions, and students would be led by the math teacher in this task. Language arts also would be incorporated through journaling the progress that was made each day. Social studies would involve learning about space travel and experiments in the past, and art would focus on the actual design and construction of the spaceship.

In elementary schools, whole language became an important curricular theme. Once again, a general topic was used to organize various subjects. In language arts, for example, reading, speech, writing, and listening were integrated. Students would share experiences, such as baking bread. Their speech might be recorded and later would be available for listening and reading. In this approach, interacting with language skills was the goal. Learning to spell correctly was not considered important because that skill would be developed later.

Another progressive change in the curriculum was in response to the integration of our public schools in the 1960s and 1970s. As we have seen, throughout much of American educational history, the curriculum had focused on the cultural, scientific, and literary contributions of white men. The contributions of African Americans, ethnic groups, and women typically were ignored. This had sent a message to children that racial minorities, immigrants, and women were not important.

This "hidden curriculum" was well-known to democratic progressive reformers who vigorously advocated an open curriculum that was more inclusive and multicultural. As a result of this pressure, basal readers, such as the Scott Foresman Dick and Jane series gradually began to include stories of black families and of women working outside the household. Moreover, at the secondary level, the curriculum began to include selections written by black authors, such as James Baldwin's *Go*

Tell It on the Mountain and by women authors, such as Jane Austen's *Pride and Prejudice*.

Social studies and history textbooks published during this period also began to include the notable contributions of blacks such as Booker T. Washington, as well as pioneering women such as Clara Barton, founder of the American Red Cross.

Science textbooks also began to reflect this multicultural perspective and slowly included the mention of important women scientists such as Marie Curie, who conducted groundbreaking research on radioactivity. The contributions of people of color such as George Washington Carver, the scientist and innovator who developed new uses for peanuts and sweet potatoes, also made their way into textbooks. This inclusion of notable contributions made by minorities and women sent an important message to children—all people are important.

The Move Toward Authoritarian Education

By the early 1980s, however, the American school curriculum entered a new phase. A wave of conservatism swept into the classrooms of the nation and transformed the curriculum once again. As we have seen, in 1983 the presidential report on the status of education in America titled *A Nation at Risk* was released.

This report focused on America's low standardized-test scores noting that "the educational foundations of our society are presently being eroded by a rising tide of mediocrity that threatens our very future as a nation and people." Authoritarian critics argued that the "warm and fuzzy" curriculum of progressive education was to blame for this "dire" situation (National Commission on Excellence in Education 1983).

Many authoritarian educators, administrators, and politicians also advocated a more scientific education curriculum and eventually promoted a new curricular direction with the creation of STEM programs (science, technology, engineering, and math). This curriculum acquired special funding from the federal government to advance these subjects. The goal was to encourage more students to enter these fields to address a perceived shortage of specialists in these areas.

Slowly, under the direction of Presidents Ronald Reagan and George H. W. Bush with Secretaries of Education Terrell Bell, William Bennett, and Lauro Cavazos, our entire school curriculum was revamped to help focus on math and science along with other "crucial" courses to improve test scores.

In the elementary schools, this new curricular movement was referred to as "Back to Basics." Courses deemed as nonessential, such as art, music, and physical education (as well as recess) were cut or simply minimized to make room for test preparation. At the secondary level, courses in the humanities often were eliminated as were courses such as health, band, chorus, physical education, and art. The emphasis on testing gradually began to dominate the curriculum.

This conservative authoritarian movement in education lasted over two decades. In 2001, it reached a kind of crescendo with the passage of the No Child Left Behind Act (NCLB). Ironically, this draconian piece of legislation actually was a reauthorization of the democratic progressive–inspired Elementary and Secondary Education Act (ESEA) of 1965.

The idea supporting this new law was that if students were required to pass a standardized achievement exam, they would work harder to meet these expectations. Under provisions of the law, states were required to develop an accountability plan for all public K–12 schools. These plans typically mandated that teachers and administrators be held accountable for student achievement and that "failing" schools could be closed with students being allowed to transfer to other schools in the district (Dee and Jacob 2010).

Once again, the curriculum narrowed to allow teachers to focus on the subjects that were being tested. As a result, there were dramatic funding cuts at the state level to courses in foreign languages, art, social studies, music, and physical education.

NCLB required annual testing in reading and math in grades three to eight and at least once in grades ten through twelve. As a result, math and reading gradually became the primary focus of the curriculum. Test-taking skills were emphasized, and students spent much of their day (especially at the end of the school term) studying material that would be on the test and practicing test taking.

Many students and teachers found this new curricular emphasis to be boring, monotonous, and terrifying. The curriculum was dominated by the test and yet there was little educational "progress" made. Over the next few years, there was some improvement in fourth-grade-math test scores and slight improvements in eighth-grade-math scores. However, there was virtually no improvement in reading scores (Dee and Jacob 2010).

Approximately forty states used the NAEP (National Assessment of Educational Progress) to meet the NCLB requirement for reading and math for grades three and eight and in high school. The remaining states used another standardized exam of their choosing to meet the NCLB requirement. In grades four, five, six, and seven, schools were required to have their students take a standardized exam in science and math.

An indirect result of all this was the development of the Common Core curriculum. The goal here was to standardize the curriculum so that students in each grade level would be exposed to the same competencies across the country for direct comparisons. These competencies were broad based and each state or local district was required to develop strategies to integrate them into their curriculum.

Of course, the NCLB testing and Common Core regulations were federally mandated. This annoyed administrators, teachers, and some political leaders, who felt that the federal government had overstepped its authority and should not dictate policy to the state and local school districts. State and local districts should set their own policies and innovations.

Eventually, both the authoritarian conservative and democratic progressive leaders in Congress began to turn against the NCLB. Conservatives perceived the federal government as overreaching its authority and wanted to give that power back to the states. Progressives, on the other hand, had opposed the NCLB for years because it forced teachers to teach to the test.

As a result, an unexpected consensus was reached in December 2015 when Congress passed the Every Student Succeeds Act. This law reauthorized the ESEA once again and scrapped the NCLB. This law returned control of the curriculum to the individual states, where administrators and teachers (at least theoretically) could once again set standards and adopt innovative methods (http://www.ed.gov/essa).

Clearly, the curriculum of American public schools has changed over time. It has been impacted by our society, the economy, and the perceived needs of the country as well as the political climate. In the next chapter, we will discuss classroom instruction and how it also changed in relation to these external societal forces.

6

INSTRUCTION

From Memorization to Comprehension

Classroom instruction, like curriculum, was transformed as a result of economic, societal, and political change as well as the powerful influence of both authoritarian and democratic educational reformers. As we have seen, the authoritarian approach favored a subject-centered approach to learning and stressed the products of learning. The democratic approach, on the other hand, emphasized the process of learning and generally was student centered.

The authoritarian approach to education dominated early colonial education. During this period, instruction was based on *The New England Primer* with its catechism and religious readings. It involved a three-stage process of memorization, beginning with mastery of the alphabet and letter combinations such as vowels and consonants. These were referred to as the "abs" (*ab, ac, ad, af, ag,* etc.) (Ford 1961).

Once these were mastered, students would proceed to phonetic sounds called the "easie" syllables (*ba, be, bo, bu, ca, ce,* etc.). Finally, students would learn one-syllable words, two-syllable words and then three-, four-, and five-syllable words that were contained in the *Primer* (Burton 1852; Ford 1862).

At this point, students would progress to rhymed verses accompanied by simple pictures. These verses would be memorized and recited to the teacher. For example, for the letter *A* was the selection, "In Adam's fall, We sinned all." For the letter *B* was the phrase, "Heaven to find: The

Figure 6.1. During the nineteenth century, children sat on hard benches in the common schools. Sometimes young children's feet could not touch the floor. Courtesy of iStock by Getty Images, credit esokolovskaya.

Bible mind." Students would memorize each lesson before continuing to the next lesson in the book (Burton 1852; Ford [1897] 1962).

Spelling also was mastered by memorizing words from the *Primer* and then reciting those words back to the teacher. Spelling was considered a valuable skill and, later, spelling bees provided great competition and, as we have seen, an important source of entertainment for the community.

The emphasis on memorization was noted by Warren Burton in his recollections of *The District School as It Was*. He vividly recalled a classmate "Memorus Wordwell," a young boy who could spell every word in their book. However, he did not know the meaning of any of the words that he spelled so easily.

One day, Jonas Patch, a big boy of about fourteen years of age was sent outside by the teacher to cut and split wood for the classroom stove. After a while, the teacher asked Memorus to "go out and spell Jonas." Memorus knew only one meaning of the word "spell" and that was to say the letters that make up a word.

He went outside with his spelling book and went through all the words in the spelling lesson with Jonas. He proudly stood on top of the pile of wood and asked Jonas to spell, word by word, while Jonas chopped. Memorus was actually hit in the nose by a flying wood chip!

When the schoolmaster went out to check on the boys, he was surprised that Memorus was actually hearing Jonas spell. Both boys returned to the classroom, but a few minutes later Memorus announced, "I have heard him spell clean through the whole lesson, and he didn't spell hardly none of 'em right." The schoolmaster burst out in laughter (Burton 1852).

Besides reading, the skill of handwriting or penmanship was another important component of classroom instruction because it was the main form of written communication. If available, children copied letters from a "copybook" with a quill pen and ink. Typically, quills were made and repaired by the teacher.

Copybooks also were handmade by teachers. Students would write the example on the page over and over until they had mastered it. In short, the use of rote memory in instruction and the teacher's ability to produce these learning aids were the measure of a good teacher and a successful school (Johnson 1963).

By the 1830s, slates and pencils also had become important instructional aids. They were easier to use than quill pens and were less expensive. Typically, slates were used to teach children to write, and once mastered, they would "graduate" to pencil and paper as well as quill pen. The teacher often would use a larger slate for instruction in the front of the room. These slates later evolved into blackboards and became very popular in classrooms for decades (Johnson 1963).

As the common school emerged in the early to mid-nineteenth century, instruction began to change. As we have seen, during this period the McGuffey *Readers* first appeared. These *Readers* had a less sectarian religious focus with a greater emphasis on pride in country and the values of the marketplace.

Memorization was still important, but now speaking eloquently also was stressed. Presentations often included the use of classical gestures complete with appropriate bows before and after a performance. As one common school student of the period noted, the purpose of reciting memorized materials was to "read fast, mind the stops and marks and speak up loud" (Burton 1852).

The problem with memorization, however, was that there often was little understanding of the meaning of the reading selection, or the words spelled. The McGuffey *Reader* took an important step forward in this regard by including a number of discussion questions and vocabulary words at the end of some selections. By addressing these questions, teachers helped students begin to understand what they had read.

Memorization and recitation, however, continued to be the important instructional method for several reasons. Although the McGuffey *Readers* were commonly used during this period, many rural school children did not have access to them because the school district could not afford to purchase them.

Children in these remote rural schools used a hodgepodge of reading materials. The teacher might contribute a few books of her own and some children would bring a book from home, usually the Bible. Moreover, they would often have to share a book. Students would recite lessons aloud or in chorus—in what was often referred to as a "blab" school. This form of recitation, moreover, continued to be used by teachers for many years as a means of "testing" what the student had learned.

As we have seen, the bee also emerged during this period as a form of instruction and assessment. As an added benefit, parents, administrators, and other members of the community enjoyed the spelling bees, recitations, and math contests.

School trustees and members of the school board often would come to the schoolhouse to listen and evaluate how well the students recited their lessons. And sometimes these visits were unannounced! The quality of these presentations, as well as how quiet other children were, became an important form of assessment and would determine whether the teacher would be rehired for the next term.

COMPREHENSION

By the end of the nineteenth century, newer editions of the McGuffey *Readers* and other similar readers had become more widely available. These texts typically stressed the importance of understanding, as opposed to simple memorization. The movement away from memorization to understanding also was promoted by early progressive democratic educators such as Johann Pestalozzi and Jean-Jacques Rousseau.

This new emphasis on reading comprehension was gradually incorporated into methods of instruction throughout the nation. Once again, McGuffey was important in that transition. "Old Guff," as he was called, included a section in his books titled "Suggestions to Teachers," where he noted that "nothing can be more fatiguing to the teacher than a recitation conducted on . . . verbatim answers." This method "would be a little more than an exercise of memory to the neglect of other faculties" (McGuffey 1873).

McGuffey then referred teachers to his expanded "Discussion Questions" to guide them through a conversation about the reading in order "to engage" them with the selection. Discussion questions were included initially in the *Second Eclectic Reader* but were more common in each succeeding *Reader*. This was an important step in the evolution of instructional methods—from memorization to reading comprehension—though many students did not progress beyond the second *Reader* (McGuffey 1873).

CIPHERING

During this period, there also was a growing emphasis on ciphering (arithmetic) as our economy became more market based. Teachers understood that students needed to be able to count money and make change to be successful in this new economy.

Math typically was taught by having students copy problems from the teacher's math notebook. Word problems with contemporary themes also were very common. Moreover, as we have seen, a number of "arithmetic books" such as the standard "Old Pike" published during this period helped to improve the ciphering skills of common school students.

CHANGES IN HIGH SCHOOL INSTRUCTION

As discussed in chapter 5, ("The Curriculum"), by the end of the nineteenth century, more young people were attending high schools throughout the nation. Consequently, both the curriculum and classroom instruction changed. The high school curriculum abandoned its classical format and gradually became more vocationally based. At the same time, instruction shifted from memorization to hands-on experiences and group learning.

Students in vocational programs took courses to prepare them for a career such as carpentry, tailoring, and bookkeeping. Teachers would demonstrate techniques and guide students through their activities. In more traditional courses, teachers often used hands-on experiences and group learning as a basis of instruction.

The turning point for these dramatic changes was the publication of the *Cardinal Principles of Secondary Education* in 1918. The report specifically recommended some vocational preparation as well as citizenship, unification, and "worthy use of leisure time."

In order to encourage student participation, extracurricular activities such as school government associations were promoted. For example, teachers might guide students into activities in civics to become involved in "mock governments." To promote unity, school sports were developed, and students who were not athletically inclined often participated as cheerleaders or joined the marching band or the pep club. Similarly, pep rallies frequently were held during school hours to promote school spirit.

The leisure activities principle also was included among the extracurricular activities, and some were taught as content courses, such as band, chorus, art, physical education, and journalism. In the latter case, students might actually contribute to the school newspaper, publish it, and distribute it to the student body.

Other extracurricular activities included intramural sports, debate clubs, and drama clubs, as well as social clubs that focused on community service. These might include Hi-Y or Red Cross organizations. In the case of career interests, DECA (Distributive Education Clubs of America) and FFA (Future Farmers of America) also were established.

These clubs and organizations were composed of students with the approval of the school administration, with teachers serving as advisors. Students, however, typically ran the clubs themselves. They elected their officers and selected their own projects and activities. Many of these organizations were part of state or national organizations, and school groups joined as a chapter.

The important instructional principle here was to encourage student participation in groups to make decisions and carry out activities. In this way, these organizations also provided important training for student leaders. Through these activities, students learned critical ideas articulated in the *Cardinal Principles*, such as leadership, taking part in a democracy and unification (*Cardinal Principles* 1918).

The new focus on student participation in clubs and organizations was an extension of the democratic progressive reform principle of group learning by actively, engaging students with hands-on experiences and activities.

John Dewey had championed these ideas and promoted progressive ideas throughout his long career. Dewey built on the earlier work of Rousseau and Pestalozzi and used objects to aid in the learning process. He reinforced the notion that learning does not take place in the abstract and that students needed to connect ideas with objects. In short, he promoted the concept of "learning by doing."

In his Chicago Lab School, developed under the supervision of his wife and colleague, Alice Chipman Dewey, these ideas were put into practice. For example, in the context of a grocery store, students would learn to count, make change, keep an inventory, and purchase goods. Students would learn these lessons in the context of actually using objects in the store. Finally, students typically worked together in groups, learning important ideas of cooperation rather than more traditional competition (Dewey 1899).

Based in part on these democratic progressive ideas, William H. Kilpatrick developed his Project Method. This learning approach helped students understand how our society had become fragmented as a result of industrialization. His goal was to help them reestablish societal connections in the classroom through group work and cooperation (Kilpatrick 1918).

The Project Method was an important element of progressive education. Rather than receiving direct instruction, students used problem-solving techniques, with the teacher as a facilitator rather than a director. Students learned through exploration and experience and pursued topics of their own interest or those of the class in general. Memorization was abandoned; rather a form of experiential learning was emphasized (Kilpatrick 1918).

While democratic progressive instructional methods remained an important part of public schools during this period, other authoritarian methods also were adopted. Perhaps the most important of these was Johann Herbart's lesson plan.

This plan was based on sequencing and included five steps: preparation (establishing the learners interest and creating a mindset for learning); presentation (the actual instruction, demonstrations, questions); association (comparison with other ideas or knowledge); generalizing (encourage students to make conclusions); and application (where students demonstrated what they had learned through worksheet assignments and tests (Herbart 1904).

Over time, other versions of the lesson plan were developed. Their primary focus, however, was on the teacher presenting knowledge with students acting as passive recipients. The teacher was the center of instruction, and the textbook was the basis of the curriculum. Students typically worked alone, and teachers assessed their individual written work (Binder 1970; Parkerson and Parkerson 2008, 124).

BASAL READERS

By the 1930s, the movement toward reading comprehension (rather than memorization and recitation) had reached an important milestone with the emergence of the basal reader. This democratic development expanded the ideas of a number of important educational researchers such as Herbart and Kilpatrick as well as of the earlier work by Pestalozzi.

The basal readers that emerged during this period gradually replaced the McGuffey *Readers*. These new readers embraced the idea of students' developmental levels along with the use of "controlled vocabulary." For example, in the famous "Dick and Jane" series published by Scott Foresman, books were arranged by graded difficulty levels.

These readers also used a controlled vocabulary—with groups of words taught directly using the "look-say" method (also referred to as "sight words"). In each story, this initial block of words was repeated, and then a new group of words was introduced. This approach led to repetition of words in the stories, and eventually to the mastery of those words (Parkerson and Parkerson 2001, 112–15).

The basal readers drew on Kilpatrick's idea of building on children's interests and experiences. In the "Dick and Jane" series, stories were based on Dick and his sister Jane and their mother and father. Educational researchers understood that the family was a theme to which all school-age children could relate.

The readers also drew on Herbart's lesson plan in terms of presentation and review of materials. Finally, they used Pestalozzi's idea of using objects, by including vivid illustrations that accompanied each page with several lines of text below (Parkerson and Parkerson 2001, 112–15).

Since the readers were graded according to difficulty, students could actually understand what they read. Comprehension had become increasingly important. The stories were based on a white middle-class family that lived in a white house in a small community. Most of their experiences were in their house and yard as they interacted with other members of their family including Baby Sally, Spot the dog, and Puff the cat.

The family was modeled on what was seen as "traditional" values of the time. Mother was a housewife; she cooked, cleaned, and took care of the children. She always wore a dress. Father always wore a suit and went to work every day. The children had gender-specific roles: Dick rode his bike and played ball, while Jane played with dolls, jumped rope, and helped her mother (Parkerson and Parkerson 2001, 112–15).

The readers used a variety of instructional materials that contributed to their popularity. It was the first series that included teacher manuals that detailed how lessons should be taught. This was a critically important aid for the classroom teacher. Based on Herbart's lesson plan, the teacher's editions provided detailed lessons that included four basic steps: preparing for reading, interpreting the story, extending skills and abilities, and extending interest. These manuals were very popular, especially with beginning teachers (Parkerson and Parkerson 2001, 112–15).

There were numerous other instructional aids that accompanied the readers, including workbooks, worksheets (with a teacher's answer guide), and tests. These packages made up the core of reading instruction. There also were a number of other materials available for purchase, including word cards, word charts, and tape-recorded stories, though many school districts could not purchase them because of the expense.

Some teachers improvised and made their own word cards using index cards. Alternatively teachers might have family and friends save "shirt cardboards" that could be cut up and used for this purpose.

In keeping with the growing emphasis placed on standardized testing during this period, many of the basal readers also provided tests to measure reading achievement. This also added to the popularity of the series.

While these basal readers embraced some elements of the democratic progressive approach, they were firmly rooted in the authoritarian, subject-centered approach to curriculum and instruction. By the 1960s, however, the democratic learner-centered approach slowly reemerged as an important instructional focus. As we have seen, these instructional approaches encouraged student interaction with the instructor and other students through cooperative learning.

In addition, other progressive instructional ideas also were introduced during this period. These included inquiry-based instruction, cooperative learning (based on the project method), flexible scheduling, team teaching, and the open classroom.

Inquiry-based instruction encouraged student learning through experimentation, with the teacher as a facilitator. Memorization was not the goal; rather, understanding and meaning, once again, were emphasized.

Students frequently worked in groups, and through their interaction with one another, they learned the importance of cooperation rather than competition. Frequently, students grappled with social issues such as the degradation of the environment, war, or intolerance. This resurgent interest in a form of the project method persisted well into the 1970s and it is still used in some classrooms today (Parkerson and Parkerson 2008, 166).

Later, flexible scheduling also was introduced in many schools in the form of the "block curriculum." Here, the typical forty-five- or fifty-minute class period was expanded to ninety minutes to allow more in-depth study, experimental learning, simulated activities, and group work.

Another progressive democratic instructional innovation of the 1960s was the open classroom, using team teaching. In this method, two or three classes would be grouped in a large room, and teachers would pool their instructional specialties.

For example, one teacher might instruct students in language arts, while another would teach social studies, and yet another would lead science lessons. Learning would be centered on an important topic, such as the destruction of the rainforest. Finally, teachers also would plan and work together to share ideas and help create a more positive learning environment for their students.

The desegregation of schools during the 1960s and 1970s also energized democratic forms of instruction. As we have seen, traditional authoritarian instructional methods typically emphasized the contributions of white, male Protestants in subjects such as literature, history, social studies, and science.

This "hidden curriculum" and accompanying instructional approaches promoted the idea that only white, male Protestants had made significant contributions to our society. As we have seen, democratic progressives had long understood this problem because students were being sent a clear message that African Americans, immigrants, and women were not important. Certainly this made some students feel isolated and devalued.

Democratic progressive teachers also recognized that they were role models for their students and through their instructional techniques must demonstrate tolerance and acceptance of all people regardless of race, ethnicity, or gender. Teachers were encouraged to celebrate cultural differences and select books and instructional topics that reflected different cultures and the acceptance of all groups in our society.

A number of basal reading series also were transformed as a result of the resurgence of progressive ideas in the 1960s and 1970s. Influenced by such new ideas as inclusion, they began to develop a more diverse approach to their reading materials.

First the "color" of people in their illustrations began to change to portray people of different races and ethnicities. Then the physical settings of the reading selections were revised to portray families in larger communities as well as those living in apartment buildings and in extended households. In these new series, children often would take the bus or ride the Metro to go to school.

Readers also began to include stories about children of other racial or ethnic groups as well as selections about important individuals in history, such as Harriet Tubman and George Washington Carver. Democratic teachers built on these stories and encouraged students to create bulletin boards that emphasized diversity in society.

Others had their students grapple with the important social problems of racism, ethnic hatred, or misogyny by having them work in groups to create murals or work individually and write in their journals. These activities helped to send an important message to students concerning the inherent value of all people.

Gradually, the Scott Foresman readers as well as other similar readers began to include women in expanded roles outside the home—such as working mothers. Mothers occasionally were portrayed as teachers, nurses, or secretaries. They were no longer "just housewives," but had other occupations available.

In these new, more progressive readers, both boys and girls helped with household chores and cared for younger children. These efforts helped move us away from gender stereotyping. Democratic teachers reinforced these values through discussions of notable women. Students also were encouraged to read biographies of women and do further research. In cooperative groups, students might reenact their important contributions.

Other textbooks in history, social studies, and science that appeared during this period also embraced a more multicultural perspective. Democratic teachers often used these textbooks as a starting point for supplementary follow-up activities such as group work on skits, dioramas, posters, and exhibits. Again, through their instructional techniques, teachers were telegraphing an important message to students—people of all races, ethnicities, and genders were important.

As we have seen, however, with the publication of *A Nation at Risk* in 1983, the pendulum of change once again swung toward the more authoritarian model of instruction. The report stated that the U.S. standardized-test scores had declined in both science and math and seemed to suggest that the "rising tide of mediocrity" in schools was the result of democratic progressive education programs of the 1960s and 1970s (National Commission on Excellence in Education 1983).

Once again, the curriculum and classroom instruction shifted. Authoritarian whole-class instruction that focused on reading, science, and math became the norm, while "progressive frills" were minimized or dropped. During this period, the integration of subject matter and group projects that centered on cooperation typically was abandoned in favor of the more traditional focus on competition to improve test scores.

As a result, students, once again, became passive recipients of knowledge imparted through textbooks, teacher lectures, and lessons. Instruction in fine arts and physical education was reduced and sometimes eliminated, while the role of the teacher dramatically shifted away from facilitator to lecturer and assessor.

Multicultural education became less important in this new environment, and complex material often was ignored because it did not conform to the dictates of the standardized exam.

The testing movement gained momentum during this period, and as we have seen, it reached a crescendo with the passage of the No Child Left Behind Act of 2001. By then, the curriculum had become more focused on the tests, and instruction often centered on test preparation. The effect on instruction was to fundamentally limit the creativity of the teacher, to the neglect of student participation and enthusiasm.

The recent passage of the All Students Succeed Act in 2015 effectively rescinded the NCLB Act, and suggests that the twenty-five-year ascendency of the authoritarian vision of education has quietly passed (Every Student Succeeds Act, www.congress.gov , 2015).

Perhaps as we once again reconsider more democratic progressive options of curriculum development and instruction, American public schools will return to an earlier time when teachers tested students on the material that was presented in the classroom, when a multicultural focus was center stage in the curriculum, when instruction did not "teach to the test," where cooperative learning was favored over competition, where comprehension was more important than memorizing for an abstract standardized examination, and where many teachers employed multiple methods of assessment such as portfolios, skits, journals, and exhibits.

We remain cautiously optimistic.

7

DISCIPLINE IN THE CLASSROOM
From Corporal Punishment to Preventative Techniques

Classroom discipline in public schools has been one of the most contentious and controversial aspects of American education. Nevertheless, as with other aspects of education, it directly reflects the norms of society. As we shall see, changes in disciplinary techniques over the course of American educational history involved a shift from corporal, or physical, punishment of children to a variety of psychological forms of behavior modification and preventative discipline.

TRADITIONAL DISCIPLINARY METHODS

Traditional authoritarian attitudes toward the discipline of children may seem draconian by today's standards but were rooted in the Judeo-Christian idea of "original sin" built around the assumption that children were "stained" at birth, and only through severe discipline could they be wrested from the influence of the devil.

Biblical imperatives such as "Spare the rod and spoil the child" appear in a slightly different form in Proverbs 13:24 and had a profound impact on attitudes toward children. In fact, the book of Proverbs mentions discipline in six different passages. Proverbs 23:14, for example, notes, "Thou shalt beat him with the rod, and shalt deliver his soul from hell." Similarly, Proverbs 22:15 states, "Foolishness is bound in the heart of a child;

Figure 7.1. In the common school, discipline was often harsh. In this image, a schoolmaster is ready to cane the young boy. Such punishment was administered for relatively minor offenses, such as talking in class, tardiness, or not completing schoolwork. Today, more humane forms of discipline are typically used in public schools. Courtesy of iStock by Getty Images, credit TonyBaggett.

but the rod of correction shall drive it far from him (*Holy Bible, King James Version* 1978).

By the early 1500s, these ideas had become commonplace in the secular literature. Richard Mulcaster, famed pedagogue and tutor to Princess Elizabeth, for example, addressed this issue in his important work *Training up of Children*. While he wrote that whipping a child because he had failed to learn his lessons was "worse than madness," he did say that the "rod may no more be spared in schools, than the sworde may in the Prince's hand" (Oliphant 1903).

Corporal Punishment in the American Colonies

By the early 1600s, these attitudes made their way to the American colonies from New England to the Carolinas and persisted well into the 1700s. Educators saw physical punishment as both a lesson to errant students as well as a warning to other students in the classroom. As a result, the use of the ferule, as it was called, was applied vigorously to young boys in school.

In the Massachusetts Bay colonies, corporal punishment was common. John Robinson from the Plymouth colony, for example, routinely used physical punishment on his students noting that "there is in all children . . . a stubbornness and stoutness of mind . . . which must in the first place be broken down and beaten down." Similarly, John Bernard, a Boston student of the legendary Ezekiel Cheever noted that he "was often beaten for my play and my little roguish tricks" (Axtell 1974).

CHANGING ATTITUDES TOWARD DISCIPLINE—FOUR DEVELOPMENTS

And yet, change was in the air. By the middle of the 1700s, four important developments gradually began to alter our attitudes toward discipline. The first was the philosophical revolution initiated by such visionaries as John Locke, Jean-Jacques Rousseau, and other Enlightenment figures. The second was the First Great Awakening, the third was the American Revolution, and the fourth was the market revolution that swept across the nation beginning in the early 1800s.

A Philosophical Revolution

During the early eighteenth century, traditional values and beliefs were challenged by a handful of iconic visionaries such as John Locke and Jean-Jacques Rousseau. Along with other Enlightenment philosophers of this era, they promoted a fundamental transformation of secular attitudes toward discipline.

John Locke, for example, challenged the prevailing biblical ideas regarding human nature in his influential work *Some Thoughts Concerning Education*, published in 1705. He argued that man was not evil at birth but rather was "white paper void of all character." Locke wrote that rather than attempting to drive out evil from a young boy, praise for good behavior and excellent work matched with humiliation for failure and misbehavior were two ends of the same disciplinary technique (Locke [1705] 1968).

Jean-Jacques Rousseau, on the other hand, outlined his ideas regarding the nature of humankind and effective methods of discipline in his novel *Emile*. Like Locke, Rousseau argued that children were not inherently evil at birth and that physical punishment was not appropriate. But he differed from the great philosopher and argued that children were not blank slates, either. Rather, Rousseau noted that young people came into the world with an innate goodness that was corrupted by society. The best form of learning and discipline was to allow children to do as they wished as long as they understood and then experienced the consequences of their actions (Rousseau 1974).

Partly as a result of these new ideas, by the end of the 1700s and into the early 1800s, there were important changes in disciplinary attitudes toward soldiers, sailors, prisoners, and of course children in school. Flogging of members of the military—the primary means of punishment for centuries—gradually declined. Corporal punishment of criminals such as pillorying and whipping was replaced over time by imprisonment and rehabilitation. And of course, the beating of children at home and in school gradually lost favor during this period (Dinwiddy 1982).

The First Great Awakening

In addition to these important changes in our secular philosophy, the spiritual world was transformed during these years by what historians refer to as the First Great Awakening. For nearly a half-century, before the American Revolution, traditional religious beliefs were challenged by a new kind of evangelical approach to preaching. At camp meetings and city church services, charismatic preachers—often Methodists and Baptists—delivered a new and exciting message that salvation did not depend on adherence to the formal teachings of the church but, rather, was a personal matter (Kidd 2009).

These preachers reached out to ordinary people throughout the established colonies and on the frontier promoting a more tolerant vision of religious diversity. They also helped to challenge the vision of the basic depravity of humankind as well as the notion that most people were predestined to go to hell (Kidd 2009).

Two Revolutions

While there was a fundamental challenge to both traditional secular and religious beliefs during the eighteenth century, it was the American Revolution and the market revolution that thrust this nation toward a new vision of individualism, liberty, democracy, and freedom. The American colonies, long held in check by the most powerful colonial power in the world, now began to embrace a new perspective of human dignity and individual freedom. It was this exciting concept that helped to promote modern attitudes toward discipline and punishment.

The American Revolution was the opening act that would help transform those attitudes. The market revolution that followed completed this fundamental transition. At the heart of these two revolutions was the notion of the "merit-based society," what we now call a "meritocracy." It was this new worldview that demanded a different rationale for discipline.

In traditional society, "deference" was the basis of social order. Individuals were expected to respect and obey their "betters" because of their noble birth. The nobility, of course, had controlled the economy, politics, and society for well over a thousand years and was seen as the cornerstone of the "natural order."

With the emergence of the new revolutionary ideas of freedom, individualism, and democracy, however, that natural order was challenged, and the power of deference declined rapidly. As the meritocratic society took hold of Americans following the Revolution, social position evolved from being based on the class into which you were born to your achievements in life. No longer would individuals simply defer to the authority of someone simply because of his or her ascribed status (Parkerson and Parkerson 2001).

Students in this postrevolutionary age also were less likely to follow the arbitrary directions of a cruel schoolmaster. They now expected mutual respect between teachers and students. Like others, students were becoming more forcefully democratic in this new market-oriented society of young America (Parkerson and Parkerson 2001).

Rather than simply demanding obedience with threats of a beating, progressive teachers gradually developed a new kind of "disciplinary power" to achieve classroom control. This new approach was based on constant supervision, establishing clear norms of achievement, and eventually, the written examination. By continual monitoring of student behavior and by controlling the content and administration of the exam, these new teachers were able to establish their authority in the modern classroom (Parkerson and Parkerson 1998).

Standardized Readers

By the mid-nineteenth century, the accepted method of discipline in the classroom had quietly begun to shift from violent corporal punishment to these more modern methods. These approaches, moreover, were reinforced by a new generation of standardized readers typified by the McGuffey *Readers*, first published in the late 1830s. These new readers developed the important idea of subordinating one's individual interests to a higher, secular authority.

McGuffey's first *Reader*, for example, contained five selections that emphasized the importance of obedience to parents. These lessons, moreover, did not simply command the student to obey but provided logical reasons why they should curb their individual interests to appease parental authority. Lessons in more advanced *Readers* expanded these ideas by demonstrating to students the importance of subjugating one's self-interest to the greater good of the community and nation (Parkerson and Parkerson 1998, 87–89).

COMMUNITIES REACT TO DISCIPLINARY CHANGES

And yet, sometimes there was a price to pay as democratically oriented teachers slowly abandoned whipping as the primary form of discipline. Community members often responded to these changes with anger and frustration. One upstate New York teacher, Benjamin Gue, for example, wrote that his benefactor, Mr. Hawley, often told him that he "did not whip enough." When Ben responded that "no scholar had refused to mind . . . [and] he had no occasion for whipping," an angry Mr. Hawley responded that he "thought it was a good plan to whip sometimes" (Gue 1962).

Lester Ward was fired from his teaching position after only one month in the classroom because of his restraint in using the whip. He was tempted one day when two young boys—Emerson Bull and William Drake—disrupted his class. He noted in his diary that he "got a whip this morning but I hope I shall have no occasion to use it." Lester never used that whip, but within a week that restraint cost him his job. He wrote in his diary on January 5, 1861, that Mr. Smith, the local trustee, called him out of the classroom and fired him on the spot. Mr. Smith "was sick of hearing so many rumors and complaints against the order in the school." (Ward 1935).

Mary Augusta Roper of Templeton, Massachusetts, also lost her job because of her progressive policies toward discipline. Following her graduation from the Hartford Institute, she took her first teaching position at Mill Point, Michigan. Mary used patience and restraint with her students and "never used the rod unless a scholar refused to obey." But her new techniques were simply too much for this conservative community, and she was "removed" because she "don't *lick* them at all" (Kaufman 1984, 163).

In order to keep their jobs, teachers often were forced to adapt to the mores of the community and occasionally use older, more authoritarian forms of corporal punishment. They adopted policies that required them to "whip enough" to satisfy the more primitive instincts of parents and school board members, but they also used reason, kindness, and praise to maintain classroom discipline. The shift to more humane democratic disciplinary techniques was a slow but important transition in American education.

By the end of the nineteenth century, the routine practice of using corporal punishment in the classroom had begun to fade, especially in urban communities. The dunce cap had symbolically replaced the whip as the primary symbol of discipline. And yet, as immigration from Europe increased and hundreds of thousands of young children flooded into America, schools were faced with a new set of problems.

INDUSTRIAL DISCIPLINE AND THE REGIMENTATION OF STUDENTS

As a result, schools often adopted an authoritarian approach to discipline by creating new administrative positions of disciplinarians, new forms of standardized architecture, and embracing new ideas of student regimentation. In large urban schools, for example, principals or assistant principals often assumed the role of "disciplinarian." Being sent to the principal's office often struck terror in the hearts of an unruly boy or girl who might receive a vicious tongue lashing, suspension, or in some cases, a paddling.

New forms of school architecture also were developed during this period to deal with the growing numbers of students in schools. C. B. J. Snyder, for example, created what would become the new standard of classroom design. His plan involved symmetrical rows of identical desks bolted to the floor with attached chairs. All desks would face the teacher and the blackboard. In the lower grades, there were forty-eight desks; in middle grades, forty-five; and in grades seven and eight, there were forty (Cuban 1984).

While the new administrative position of school disciplinarian and the standardized design of classroom architecture helped to provide order for enormous classes during this era, new forms of student regimentation also were introduced into schools during this period. In response to this perceived need, William Bagley developed a new system of student control outlined in his popular book *Classroom Management* (Bagley [1907] 1925).

Bagley, an authoritarian reformer, argued that the primary purpose of schools was to develop habits that would allow students to successfully enter the new modern industrial society. In short, the teacher's central role in education was to enforce strict rules of conduct and to promote regimentation. Bagley noted that he could judge the quality and efficiency of a teacher simply by observing "the manner in which lines pass to and from the room" (Bagley [1907] 1925).

Under Bagley's plan, students were expected to quietly enter the classroom, go to their desks, place their "feet flat on the floor," and remain silent until the teacher called "attention." In this way discipline was "maintained" and the classroom would remain conducive for learning. In short, discipline under the new Bagley model was not just a supplement to learning but central to the educational experience (Bagley [1907] 1925).

By the first decades of the twentieth century, these new forms of discipline had become common in the schools across America. Administrators were now placed in charge of disciplining unruly students, a new standardized form of school architecture provided constant surveillance, and more effective discipline of students and new ideas regarding regimentation became extremely popular in both large and small schools throughout the country.

THE BEHAVIORISTS

While many educators of this period embraced student regimentation and standard classroom architecture as a solution to disciplinary problems in the schools, psychologists such as John Watson, B. F. Skinner, and other authoritarian educators were demonstrating the importance of behavior modification in both learning and discipline of students.

Watson was an early pioneer in this area and argued that all human behavior was a response to external conditioning. He demonstrated in his experiments that through "stimulus-response," behavior could be molded. As we have seen, his classic work with children that demonstrated how a baby first reaches for the flame of a candle, gets burned, and then "learns" that she should never touch the candle again was a powerful example of stimulus-response (Watson 1924).

B. F. Skinner built on the work of Watson and eventually developed the idea of "reinforcement." Skinner noted that "by carefully constructing certain 'contingencies of reinforcement' it is possible to change behavior quickly and to maintain it in strength for long periods of time." In his classic work *Beyond Freedom and Dignity*, Skinner recommended that teachers aggressively and consciously discipline students because they were vulnerable to both the media and their peers. In addition, he advocated subtle manipulation of the classroom environment to maintain discipline in the classroom (Skinner 1971).

While many behaviorists advocated reinforcement as an important method of behavior modification, they typically rejected all forms of shame and humiliation. Skinner, for example, recommended that teachers ignore a student's bad behavior as much as possible but quickly reward their good behavior. These ideas have been embraced by so-called neo-Skinnerians such as Fredric Jones and Lee and Marlene Canter.

In his *Positive Classroom Discipline*, published in 1987, Fredric Jones placed special emphasis on nonverbal methods of communication including body language, facial expressions, and eye contact. He argued that these forms of stimulus can have a dramatic impact on classroom discipline. The Canters, on the other hand, developed an entire system of discipline in their works *Assertive Discipline* (1976) and *Succeeding with Difficult Students* (1993).

These "competency-based" packaged programs called for teachers to take a very assertive approach to discipline. They recommended that teachers establish clear limits of behavior in the classroom that rewarded good behavior but strictly prohibited activities that interfered with learning. While they broke slightly with Skinner by recommending punishment under certain conditions, they did favor incentives for good behavior, such as expanded recess periods or story reading at the end of the day.

Today, the legacy of the industrial-discipline approach can be seen in classrooms throughout the country. School uniforms are common (though losing favor) as are programs such as Louisiana's "Yes Sir/Yes Ma'am" laws that require all students in the state to "address public school system employees . . . with the respectful terms 'yes sir/yes ma'am'. . ." (Justia 2006).

Similarly, the influence of the behaviorists is everywhere. The use of praise for student achievement can be seen on virtually every elementary and middle school bulletin board in the country. Even a cursory glance at these bulletin boards shows that they are typically adorned with lists of students who have excelled and arrays of silver and gold stars, smiley faces, and certificates of student achievement and good behavior. Behaviorism is alive and well in American public (and private) schools.

THE PROGRESSIVE, HUMANISTIC APPROACH TO DISCIPLINE

The authoritarian-industrial approach to discipline linked with some form of stimulus-response behaviorism appealed to many educators in the late nineteenth and early twentieth centuries. Classrooms were quiet, students were well behaved, and there was an air of formality in the schools.

Parents were impressed with this environment, and business leaders were delighted that students seemed to be prepared for the workplace once they graduated.

And yet, not everyone was happy with these approaches. Democratic progressives, for example, were appalled by the regimentation and manipulation of students. They argued that these systems had begun to suppress students' natural curiosity. A quiet classroom was not a place for learning, and immovable desks and chairs in symmetrical patterns would not allow group learning and student interaction. Moreover, they saw stimulus-response behaviorist techniques as a kind of brutal authoritarianism that was unacceptable in the classroom.

The Roots of Progressive Education

Many of the democratic progressive approaches to discipline and learning were derived from the work of Jean-Jacques Rousseau and Johann Pestalozzi. Rousseau had demonstrated that constant activity with familiar objects that interested the student was the best form of preventative discipline. Pestalozzi, on the other hand, recommended a child-centered approach to learning and discipline that focused the curriculum on individual student needs, rather than imposing a rigid structure of external rules, regulations, and expectations.

In his famous educational novel *Leonard and Gertrude*, Pestalozzi also promoted what may be the most important element of teaching—especially at the primary level—love. As Pestalozzi wrote, Gertrude's love for each of her students was clear, and her discipline was a natural product of that love (Pestalozzi [1791] 1901).

Pestalozzi argued that mental order (learning) and moral order (discipline) were two sides of the same coin. Mental order was achieved through practical work—such as spinning and weaving cloth, led by Gertrude. Moral order, on the other hand, was the product of Gertrude's love for each of her students. This sort of love in the classroom, he argued, created a sort of inner peace among her students that in turn led to contentment and beneficial interaction with others (Pestalozzi [1791] 1901).

Pestalozzi's ideas of learning and discipline quietly made their way to young America in the nineteenth century. John Griscom, an early educational reformer from America, had traveled to Switzerland to observe Pestalozzi in 1805 and then published a book, *A Year in Europe*, three years later. This work praised Pestalozzi's techniques and referred to their "moral charm" in producing an intelligent and moral citizenry (Knight 1930).

Within just a few years, Charles Mayo applied some of Pestalozzi's ideas in his "infant schools" and later Friedrich Froebel used them as the basis of his kindergarten instruction. By the mid-nineteenth century Edward Sheldon, founder of Oswego State Normal School in New York, promoted Pestalozzi's ideas at the school and later helped to popularize them in a series of public lectures known as the "Oswego movement" (Knight 1930).

By the end of the nineteenth century, these ideas were becoming well-known among educators in America. Francis Parker, for example, clearly was influenced by both Rousseau and Pestalozzi. Parker's methods were adopted by the public schools in Quincy, Massachusetts, and soon they had become famous as the "Quincy Methods" (Parker 1883).

One observer of these schools (Lelia E. Partridge) wrote that in these schools, the "child was the objective point and not the courses of study, examinations or promotions." While she noted that innovative methods were an important part of the Quincy curriculum, the schools were "joyous" and were built on the "comradeship of teacher and pupils." Discipline was not a problem, she noted, since there was an environment of mutual "courtesy and respect." Clearly, the model of the democratic classroom was emerging by the late nineteenth century (Partridge 1885).

John Dewey and the Progressives

By the turn of the twentieth century, the democratic progressive education movement was taking shape. Building on the work of Rousseau, Pestalozzi, Parker, and others, John Dewey and Alice Chipman Dewey established the famous Lab School at the University of Chicago. This school would become the cornerstone of their progressive educational ideas (Dewey 1899).

As we have seen, democratic progressives like the Deweys were troubled by the industrial approach to education and discipline. They were especially concerned by the effect of industrialization on the social cohesion of Americans. In a number of important works, John Dewey argued that as a result of the industrial revolution, we had embraced individualism and personal success to such a degree that we had lost our sense of community—*Me* had essentially eclipsed *We* (Dewey 1899).

The concern over these important issues led the Deweys to experiment with a number of instructional strategies at their Lab School at the University of Chicago. Their overall focus, however, was to help students develop a stronger connection to society, which in turn would give them a greater stake in their communities. This would reduce alienation (a major cause of discipline problems in the classroom) and help develop moral habits of social cooperation.

For John Dewey and Alice Chipman Dewey, discipline was inseparable from instruction. Through group work and constant activity that emphasized social cooperation, students would not only learn, but they would also develop important social habits. This cooperation was the foundation of effective classroom discipline.

Other important democratic progressive educators followed the lead of the Deweys. Marietta Johnson's School of Organic Education, for example, developed a child-centered curriculum that was reinforced by the love and nurturing of the teacher. Discipline was achieved not by regimenting or punishing students but through peer pressure and the persuasive power of the instructor (Dewey and Dewey 1915).

J. L. Meriam's lab school at the University of Missouri was similar. Meriam developed flexible class schedules and a curriculum that was centered on the interests of the students. His disciplinary approach, moreover, emphasized democratic responsibilities of both students and teachers to act respectfully to one another (Dewey and Dewey 1915).

Students in these and other progressive schools were highly motivated and typically had little need of intensive discipline. Nevertheless, the policies developed by these democratic progressive educational pioneers provided an important alternative to the regimentation of the industrial discipline model and the manipulative techniques of the behaviorists.

Progressives understood that by regimenting, denigrating, and manipulating students, they also stripped them of their self-esteem and diminished their natural curiosity. Here was the basis of the emerging democratic progressive classroom.

MODERN DISCIPLINARY TECHNIQUES

Progressive approaches to discipline effectively challenged both the use of corporal punishment in the classroom and the use of regimentation and manipulation popular at the turn of the twentieth century. These ideas have persisted to the present day and offer an alternative for today's teachers.

Building on the work of these visionaries were a number of educators and psychologists who helped develop modern, preventative disciplinary approaches. They include Rudolph Dreikers, Jacob Kounin, and Haim Ginott. Dreikers focused on democratic teaching, Kounin developed a program of preventative discipline, and Ginott centered his work on developing self-esteem among students.

Democratic Teaching

For nearly a century, the accepted method of dealing with mental disturbances—most notably neurosis—was Freudian psychology. While this was complex, Sigmund Freud argued that the key to understanding mental problems was to reveal past experiences of psychic trauma or unresolved conflicts. By identifying these repressed memories and then discussing them with a trained psychotherapist, problems could be resolved.

By the 1960s, however, a number of psychologists began to challenge this form of psychotherapy as inadequate. William Glasser, for example, rejected the Freudian approach and argued that since individuals could not change past events, searching for answers among repressed memories was counterproductive (Glasser 1965).

But individuals do have the ability to change their behavior in order to make more productive choices about their futures. This idea, what he referred to as "reality therapy," was developed in a number of books including *Reality Therapy: A New Approach to Psychiatry* (1965) and *Schools without Failure* (1969).

Glasser argued that before teachers turn their attention to individuals with antisocial tendencies or aggressive, disruptive behaviors, however, a democratic classroom must be created where teachers and students show respect for one another and where the school is a "good place to be." Only then can the teacher begin to address the needs of individuals with disciplinary problems (Glasser 1965; 1969).

The first step is to have the "problem child" recognize his or her own misbehavior. It's much easier, of course, to simply tell the student what he is doing wrong, but this will not allow him to take responsibility for his actions. In addition, it was not the job of the teacher to try to uncover the presumed basis of the misbehavior. Glasser argued that this is simply making excuses.

Once the student has identified his misbehavior, he must be encouraged to articulate exactly why that behavior is a problem. Again, the teacher should not simply *tell* the student why it is a problem because this tends to shift responsibility away from the student. Then comes a plan of action. Here the student makes a commitment to correct that behavior and if at all possible, designs a written "contract" where he specifies both the problem and the solution to that problem (Glasser 1977).

The teacher, for her part, must strictly enforce the "contract" but never use punishment if it is violated. Rather, trust must be developed throughout the entire process. Finally, Glasser recommended persistence and patience. His advice to teachers was simple: "never give up." Teachers must "hang in there longer than the student thinks you will" (Glasser 1977).

A Comprehensive Approach to Discipline

Over the years, educators have learned a great deal about discipline in the classroom. And yet, as frustration mounts, some teachers resort to public humiliation as a form of discipline. Calling out, insulting, or simply disrespecting a student may appear to have results, but it often backfires. It disrupts the entire class and sends a message that disrespect for one another is an acceptable behavior. And of course, the use of physical punishment—sometimes sanctioned by state law—can perpetuate the culture of violence in our society.

Today we understand that the causes of severe discipline problems are complex and require comprehensive solutions. Some children come from homes where violence is common. Others lack the necessary self-esteem to achieve success in the classroom or to act appropriately with others. Still others misbehave because their basic needs of security are not being met.

Active intervention through counseling and special programs can be useful. For example, conflict resolution strategies are very helpful, and the development of remedial skills is sometimes valuable as well. As a last resort, the temporary placement of students in special schools may also be appropriate. Clearly, we have come a long way from assuming that discipline in the classroom can be achieved by beating an unruly or headstrong boy or girl.

CONCLUSION

Discipline in the classroom has changed dramatically over the past centuries. During the colonial era, children were seen as inherently corrupt because of the stain of original sin. As a result, the use of corporal punishment was seen as the only method to establish discipline. By using the whip or the ferule on a low-achieving student or one who disrupted the class, teachers managed to maintain "control" of their classroom.

However, new philosophical ideas from scholars such as John Locke and Jean-Jacques Rousseau and dramatic changes in religion initiated by the First Great Awakening began to alter our ideas toward discipline. A new, more humane perspective regarding punishment was emerging in both Europe and in young America. The brutal beatings of soldiers, sailors, and prisoners declined during the late eighteenth and early nineteenth centuries. And of course, attitudes toward the discipline of children gradually changed as well.

Slowly, the whipping post and ferule gave way to other forms of democratic discipline. Praise and incentives along with various forms of humiliation became common. Similarly, new standardized readers such as the McGuffey *Readers* helped students understand the importance of respecting others and subordinating their own self-interests to their parents, classroom, community, and nation.

However, as millions of new immigrants poured into the nation during the first years of the twentieth century, authoritarian educators became alarmed and recommended regimentation, vocational training, and standardized classroom architecture to deal with potential disciplinary problems. These new approaches had the desired effect of subduing active children in the classroom, but there were unintended consequences that progressive educators clearly recognized.

Regimented classrooms were quiet, students moved through the halls in lockstep, and both parents and administrators were pleased with the results. However, individual creativity, group interaction, and learning suffered. The reaction to this "industrial discipline" approach helped to launch a new perspective on discipline. These programs developed by progressive educators were democratic in focus, demanded mutual respect, and recognized the need to develop self-esteem in all students.

Building on the work of the progressives, educators today have embraced the democratic classroom and have also moved toward a disciplinary system that balances learning with a number of preventative techniques. Classrooms may not be as quiet as they once were, but group work encouraging cooperation rather than competition and projects that develop a sense of community among students have transformed our understanding of discipline and learning in general.

As we write these words, we are all saddened by another horrific mass killing, in Orlando, Florida. This massacre is not the first and certainly will not be the last. School shootings at Columbine and Sandy Hook have tormented the nation as a whole. Moreover the heartrending fact that a child is shot to death every other day in the United States seems incomprehensible (Child Trends 2015).

Nevertheless, things continue to improve in the schools themselves. This is due primarily to progressive teachers employing democratic and preventative disciplinary techniques. Students today have higher rates of enrollment than at any time in American history. They volunteer for service work more than other generations; they are generally less violent in the classroom and are less likely to take their own lives (Report on Violence in the Public Schools 2000).

Clearly, we live in a world where we often turn to violence to solve our problems. Thankfully, American teachers are helping to break that cycle of violence, one student at a time.

8

MORAL EDUCATION

From Virtue Centered to Cognitive Moral Development

In addition to the dramatic changes in classroom discipline over the years, there has been a similar transition in moral education. As we have seen, severe corporal discipline was common throughout the American colonies and was centered on a set of beliefs regarding child rearing derived from the Bible. Paralleling the imperative of "Spare the rod and spoil the child" were moral prerogatives drawn from the Ten Commandments and other biblical scriptures.

From the Calvinists of Massachusetts Bay Colony, the Quakers and Mennonites in Pennsylvania, and the Roman Catholics in Maryland to the Anglicans and Baptists in the Carolinas and Georgia, religious-based education thrived during the colonial period. These schools promoted a vision of moral behavior that matched their religious teachings. In fact, the central role of these schools was to promote a specific set of religious beliefs and moral values to their young children.

The basis of instruction in these schools was the catechism. The early religious primers provided children with an unambiguous set of moral behaviors usually presented in a question-and-answer format. The original *New England Primer*, for example, had its "Shorter Catechism" that consisted of a number of questions and answers regarding the Puritan vision of religion. For example, Q: Where is the moral law summarily

Figure 8.1. As we slowly moved away from corporal punishment, women teachers used love and nurture to help students understand their moral and social duties. Courtesy of iStock by Getty Images, credit JonnyJim.

comprehended? A: The moral law is summarily comprehended in the Ten Commandments (Ford [1897] 1962).

In addition to including the "Shorter Catechism," the *Primer* also centered on religious teachings. For example, the famous twenty-four pictures with alphabetical rhymes in the *Primer* incorporated moral lessons for young Puritan boys and girls. The letter "A" for example, included the sentence that reinforced religious beliefs surrounding original sin "In Adams Fall We Sinned all." For the letter "F" the accompanying sentence reinforced industriousness and correct behavior "The Idle Fool is whipt at School" (Ford [1897] 1962).

Once students had mastered both the alphabet and each moral precept, they went on to memorize a variety of religious tracts including "The Dutiful Child's Promise," "The Lord's Prayer, "The Creed," and the books of the Bible. It was not unusual to hear a young Puritan child struggling to recite this material before a stern schoolmaster. Mastery of these verses and religious tracts was seen as essential for moral development (Ford [1897] 1962).

Young boys who were unable to attend school also were expected to receive moral training. Typically, this training was derived from the family and later as they learned their trade. During his apprenticeship period, a young boy would master the skills of a craftsman and also would be instructed in the values of obedience, hard work, persistence, and perhaps most importantly, fear of God.

Young girls also received moral lessons in the family kitchen or garden. Mothers, grandmothers, aunts, and sisters often provided moral lessons while they prepared the family meal, washed clothes, or tended the kitchen garden. And during quiet moments, young girls recited prayers and scriptures with their sisters and cousins. In this way, moral teachings were woven into the fabric of everyday life.

Providing moral lessons for young children of the faith, however, was not just the province of the family or artisan guild. Members of the community also were expected to take part in this important function. Not only were villagers expected to act responsibility and morally in their relations with children, and to provide them with role models, it also was assumed that they would speak out when appropriate to warn children of the dangers of misbehavior and to promote moral life lessons as well. Clearly, it did take a village to raise a moral child.

MORAL EDUCATION AND THE COMMON SCHOOL

While the family, church, guild, and community would continue their important role in the moral development of children, the nature of moral education began to change following the American Revolution and the market revolution of the early nineteenth century.

As we have seen, Americans began to rethink the nature of education during this period and recognized that the religious education that had been so widespread during the colonial period was no longer viable. These schools were simply not capable of providing students with the social and political cohesion necessary for the new republic.

Gradually, the idea of the "common school" promoted by democratic reformers was seen as necessary not only to help unite the thirteen states into a union but to provide young Americans with a sense of patriotism and individual achievement. In addition, however, non-sectarian, pan-Protestant religious references were often part of the common school curriculum.

The common school developed rapidly during the early nineteenth century and provided students with a basic education that included reading, spelling, and arithmetic. As we have seen, students first learned the letters of the alphabet, vowels, and consonants. They then proceeded to various syllable combinations—sometimes referred to as the "syllabarium." Once these were mastered they began their reading instruction from any book that was available—often the Bible—and then recited memorized passages or verses to the teacher.

Similarly, spelling was important in the common school, and words were often derived from the Bible or early religious primer. Competition between individuals or groups in the school—and sometimes between schools—took the form of spelling bees. Once again, these bees became an important form of entertainment for the community and also a primary method of assessment of both students and teachers.

Finally, basic arithmetic was taught by counting money, making change, and performing simple arithmetic functions such as addition, subtraction, division, and multiplication, often on slates. Early math textbooks often had a moral purpose, such as Franklin's *Arithmetic* published in 1832. This book included word problems such as: "Judas, one of the twelve apostles, hung himself; how many were there left?" (Johnson 1963, 156).

THE VIRTOUS BALANCED CURRICULUM

As we have seen, however, the American Revolution and the market revolution that followed had transformed young America. The American

Revolution had shattered the political and social basis of traditional authority that gave deference to the nobility. In this new aggressively democratic world, however, everyday Americans no longer would simply accept the authority of an individual simply because of his or her noble birth. Now that respect had to be earned.

In addition, the market revolution further weakened traditional authority. In this new economy, an individual's status was no longer based on the class into which he or she was born but was a function of what he or she had accomplished in life. Individual achievement associated with the market economy was quickly becoming the central value in American society.

The emerging values of both egalitarianism and individualism were the cherished symbols of the new Republic but they had unintended consequences for educators. As young Americans were "cut loose" from their strict social moorings of deference, they seemed to have little respect for authority or moral direction. In fact, American children were often perceived by outsiders as rebellious and disrespectful. Recognizing this problem, teachers in the common school embraced what was called the "virtuous balanced curriculum" to deal with it.

The idea of the "virtuous balanced curriculum" was first expressed in America by Noah Webster in his essay "On the Education of Youth in America." In this work, he argued that students in common schools should be instructed in basic subjects but should also have a good understanding of his or her "moral and social duties" (Webster [1790] 1972).

Later, Charles Northend, in his important work on teaching entitled *The Teacher and the Parent*, made a similar argument. Northend wrote that the primary aim of common schools should be to demonstrate to students their "true relation to God and his fellow beings and . . . obligations laid on him by these" (Northend 1853, 96).

In this new world of egalitarianism and individualism, religion would continue to play a role in the moral development of students, but now common schools were emphasizing the importance of becoming useful citizens and balancing individual desire and achievement with a sense of community and nation. In the words of the great pedagogue Alanzo Potter, education should help students develop "a power of self control and a habit of postponing present indulgences to a greater . . . good" (Potter 1842, 103).

THE MCGUFFEY *READERS*

Many of these ideas were integrated into the standardized readers of the day, most notably, the McGuffey *Readers*. While these *Readers* did make reference to God and also included some biblical passages, their primary focus was to help students to develop into useful citizens who could balance their individualism with a sense of community. Early readers focused on the idea that simply because something pleased you did not make it right. In more advanced *Readers*, students were introduced to the concept of patriotism (Parkerson and Parkerson 1998).

In McGuffey's *Second Reader*, for example, young students read a story called "Robbing Birds' Nests" where a little boy celebrated "his good fortune" when he took a bird's nest from a tree. When his sister explained that he had done something wrong the boy "yielded to the sweet impulse of humanity" and returned the nest to the tree (McGuffey 1836/1982b).

In McGuffey's *Fifth Reader*, moral lessons had shifted to promoting values of patriotism and love of country. One selection focused on the heroism of John Adams during the American Revolution and quoted him as saying, "Sink or Swim, live or die, survive or perish, I give my hand and my heart to this vote. It is true that in the beginning we aimed not at Independence. But *there's a divinity that shapes our ends*. (McGuffey 1879/1962).

The move from traditional biblical imperatives that demanded that children obey absolute moral principles to a more secular approach embedded in the virtuous balanced curriculum was an important transition in common school classrooms of the mid- to late nineteenth century. These new ideas were promoted by important pedagogues such as Webster, Northend, and Potter and were supported in the vast majority of teachers institutes during this period. With the help of readers such as the McGuffey series, teachers—many of whom were now women—transmitted these values to hundreds of thousands of students on the hard benches of the old schoolhouse.

THE PROGRESSIVE CHALLENGE TO THE VIRTUOUS BALANCED CURRICULUM

The virtuous balanced curriculum was a successful approach to promoting morality among common school students in young America. The simple moral lessons of the McGuffey *Readers* seemed appropriate for a nation that was relatively homogenous, rural, and agricultural. By the end of the nineteenth century, however, young America had developed into a powerful nation that was more heterogeneous, urban, and industrial.

Rapid immigration, a dramatic population shift to American cities, and a furious industrial revolution had transformed the nation and classrooms across the country. Schools typically were larger and more complex. The social and political issues facing young Americans, moreover, seemed more confusing than ever. No longer did the simple moral stories of the McGuffey *Readers* seem appropriate in this new, complex world.

John Dewey recognized these changes and recommended a different approach to moral education in America. In his influential book *Moral Principles in Education*, he noted that "moral principles are not arbitrary . . . they are not 'transcendental.'" What was needed was a more flexible approach to moral education (Dewey 1909).

Dewey made an important distinction between an individual's personal behavior and one's civic responsibility. The virtue-oriented moral curriculum of the nineteenth century had centered its attention on personal behavior—what he called moral habits—such as attending church, abstaining from alcohol and refraining from sex before marriage.

This "goody-goody" approach, as he called it, was misdirected. Instead, Dewey recommended a civic approach to moral education that would allow students to respond to a wide range of ambiguous moral dilemmas that they would face throughout their lives. Dewey and other progressive educators of this period argued that students must develop a "social intelligence" in the "service of social interests and aims" (Dewey 1909).

Rather than simply forcing children to memorize a set of rigid moral codes, speeches, and passages, students should be confronted with social problems that might be solved through scientific reasoning and democratic engagement. Problem solving in a group context rather than memorizing rules of behavior was the key to developing a social intelligence.

Many of these democratic progressive moral education proposals were promoted through the Social Education Association (SEC), founded in 1906. Under the leadership of Colin Scott, a colleague and friend of John Dewey, the SEC published its influential journal *Social Education* as well as a number of books and activity plans for teachers. This body of work promoted a progressive vision of moral education to help prepare students for a socially purposeful life (Scott 1908).

William Heard Kilpatrick's "project method" was another important component of this new progressive approach to moral education. Like other democratic progressives of this era, Kilpatrick saw instruction, discipline, and moral teaching as inseparable. In his important work *The Project Method,* published in 1918, he argued that the student who "regulates his life with reference to worthy social aims meets at once the demands for practical efficiency and of moral responsibility" (Kilpatrick 1918).

THE AUTHORITARIAN BACKLASH

Progressive approaches to moral education reflected both the problems and possibilities of any democracy. Students who were part of these new programs tended to be more flexible when facing moral dilemmas and were less likely to submit to arbitrary authority. They also were more apt to abandon traditions, if necessary. Students were also more inclined to try new approaches to problem solving and to experiment. Above all, they were keenly aware of the relative nature of morality and understood that in this new multicultural world, not everyone had the same moral compass.

But it was this very question of "relativity" that troubled more conservative authoritarian educators. They argued that in the absence of a strict moral code, parental influence would be weakened. Moreover, students might be influenced more directly by their peers or passing fads. Immature students might have difficulty choosing the right path of behavior, while others might perceive moral relativism as a signal that "anything goes."

In short, the legacy of progressive moral education was mixed. Some students benefited from this approach that allowed them to deal with difficult moral dilemmas and comprehend the complexities of the modern, multicultural world. Others were confused by the moral ambiguity that was part of the "relativity" of progressive moral education.

As a result, moral education became a hot-button political issue during these years. Democratically-oriented, progressive educators embraced the ideas of Dewey, Scott, Kilpatrick, and others. Other more authoritarian-oriented educators and communities rejected these approaches as dangerous and renewed their commitment to virtue-centered morality. The fact that over fifteen million copies of the McGuffey *Readers* were sold during this period testifies to this more conservative approach.

Some communities were caught in the crossfire of politically charged rhetoric and often adopted some selective elements of a progressive moral approach as well as more conservative moral codes. This method, however, sent mixed signals that were both democratic and authoritarian at the same time, puzzling both educators and students. Confusion reigned.

CHARACTER EDUCATION

While democratic progressive and authoritarian virtue-centered approaches to moral education waged a political battle over the direction of moral education during these years, another alternative emerged. This alternative was character education. Character educators, like the progressives, understood the changing nature of American society and economy and argued that new approaches to education were necessary—especially in the area of moral education.

Like the progressives, character educators rejected the traditional virtue-centered approach to moral education and argued that a more "civic approach" was necessary. They also supported group activities and a problem-solving curriculum because it would prepare individuals for work in the emerging corporate world. To help achieve these goals and promote their ideas, they established the Character Education Association (McClellan 1992).

But character educators parted ways with their progressive colleagues over the question of relativity. Like the virtue-centered authoritarian moral educators and their lineal decedents today, such as William Bennett and others, they sought to promote an absolute moral code to guide students. The code they envisioned would be reinforced through peer influence and student clubs.

Character educators were profoundly influenced by the great success of clubs such as the Boy Scouts of America and the 4-H clubs established in the first years of the twentieth century. One element of these clubs that appealed to character educators was the pledge that they used to promote their values. The Boy Scout Oath, for example, required that scouts pledge to be trustworthy, loyal, helpful, friendly, courteous, kind, obedient, cheerful, thrifty, brave, clean, and (later) reverent.

In 1917, the Character Education Association adopted its own pledge written by William Hutchins. This "Children's Morality Code," as it was called, specified "ten laws of right living" and focused on mental and physical hygiene as well as moral development. Its simplicity made it very popular, and it was adopted by thousands of schools as part of their moral education curriculum. Students were required to memorize the pledge and promise to obey these ten principles (Parkerson and Parkerson 2015).

Within a few years, a number of competing "codes" were developed, such as the one introduced by *Collier's* magazine in the early 1920s. This and other codes were adopted by numerous student clubs like the national Uncle Sam's Boys and Girls Clubs, and local organizations such as Boston's Courtesy Club (McClellan 1992).

The idea of character education captured the imagination of the American people and educators alike. In its important report *Cardinal Principles of Secondary Education*, published in 1918, the NEA (National Education Association) acknowledged the importance of moral education with two of its principles. The first was the development of an ethical character and the second focused on the importance of "unification," what they referred to as the "democratic ideal that brought people together to provide them with a common set of ideas" (*Cardinal Principles* 1918).

The *Cardinal Principles* also encouraged schools to establish activities and clubs that would promote "unification." These included student newspapers and academic clubs, as well as intramural sport teams. The report suggested that these activities would advance democratic principles and foster social cooperation and teamwork. In addition, "school spirit" would be enhanced among those who did not directly participate in these activities (*Cardinal Principles* 1918).

Perhaps more importantly was the *Cardinal Principles*' suggestion that schools promote "model governments" that would both help students understand the workings of our political system and promote a sense of unity and patriotism. In short, the NEA, through the publication of its *Cardinal Principles*, provided direct support to the emerging idea of character education.

Through the establishment of school clubs and activities, centered on a set of moral codes and oaths, students would learn lessons of unity, cooperation, and teamwork accompanied by a set of absolute rules of moral behavior (*Cardinal Principles* 1918).

Over the next several decades, educators and the public at large would struggle with these two competing visions of moral education. Democratic progressives, for their part, promoted an educational system that would prepare students to rationally deal with the ambiguous moral dilemmas facing society. Problem solving through group interaction was at the heart of these democratic programs. Moreover, they argued that students must understand that in the modern multicultural world of the twentieth century, morals and values were relative.

Character educators, on the other hand, supported a civic approach to moral education and encouraged the use of student clubs and activities to help promote ideas of democracy and good government. Unlike the democratic progressives, however, authoritarian character educators rejected relativism and argued that students must adhere to an absolute moral code on which to base their lives. This could be achieved through the memorization of oaths and pledges.

As this bitter debate continued, however, America would face dramatic challenges over the next decades that would test the moral education principles of both democratic progressives and authoritarian moral educators. World War I, the Great Depression, and World War II fundamentally altered the debate. Educators understood that a strong nation matched with a consensus over the direction of moral education was essential if the nation was to endure.

To meet this challenge, the NEA in conjunction with the American Association of School Supervisors issued the important report titled *Moral and Spiritual Values in the Public Schools* in 1951. The goal of the report was to forge a compromise between competing ideas regarding moral education in America (National Education Association 1951).

Elements of character education were included in the report and recommended that a "generally accepted body of values" be promoted among public school students. On the other hand, the report also embraced ideas of the democratic progressives by recommending that students should clearly understand that these values were not absolute. In order to satisfy parents and the educational village, moreover, they recommended that members of the local community work with teachers and administrators to develop a moral agenda that was in accordance with their way of life (National Education Association 1951).

As with all compromises, not everyone was happy with these recommendations. But during this turbulent period, an uneasy consensus was achieved. Soon, however, that compromise would collapse in the face of even greater changes that were sweeping across the nation and its public schools.

Three challenges in particular were transforming the debate over moral education. The first was a growing demand for more rigorous academic subjects, the second was the intensification of anticommunism during the Cold War, and the third was emerging "culture wars" in America.

A MORE RIGOROUS ACADEMIC CURRICULUM

Following World War II, America emerged as the undisputed leader of the world. And with this new position of responsibility, politicians, educators, and communities throughout the nation realized that there was a need for an expansion of the scientific and technological curriculum of colleges, universities, and secondary schools. The addition of these courses, however, had the unintended consequence of essentially "squeezing out" moral education as an educational priority. Thus, while our STEM curriculum—as we call it today—grew, our moral compass seemed to be missing.

FEAR OF COMMUNISM

Additionally, during these years, our growing fear of communism began to affect our politics and our educational system. The turmoil associated with World War II, the Chinese Revolution and creation of the Peoples

Republic of China in 1949, the Soviet Union detonating a nuclear device in 1950, as well as the Korean War that ended with thirty-six thousand Americans and millions of Koreans killed, enhanced this growing anxiety.

Politicians such as Republican Senator Joseph McCarthy and others capitalized on this anxiety and contributed to the growing hysteria over the spread of communism and the threat of nuclear war. For their part, educators responded to this growing fear by Americans and repackaged what was left of the moral education curriculum into new anticommunism courses. There seemed to be no room in the curriculum for other moral issues as Americans felt they were in a death struggle with communism!

As the fear-mongering of Joseph McCarthy waned and the senator was formally censured by his colleagues in the U.S. Senate, the hysteria over communism slowly subsided. Educators in turn gradually abandoned their anticommunism focus but with it, the fabric of the moral education curriculum began to unravel.

AMERICA'S CULTURE WARS

But it was the "culture wars" that began in the 1960s that was the final "nail in the coffin" of moral education. It was during this decade that a series of progressive Supreme Court decisions as well as the passage of an astounding number of progressive laws helped to trigger our long ideological struggle between authoritarian, conservative, religious reformers and democratic, progressive liberal "secular humanists."

Supreme Court rulings such as *Engle v. Vitale* that declared mandatory prayer in schools unconstitutional and *Roe v. Wade* that upheld women's reproductive rights regarding abortion outraged religious conservatives and mobilized them into a powerful conservative political force. Similarly, legislation establishing programs such as Medicare and Medicaid as well as the War on Poverty programs, the Civil Rights Act, and the Voting Rights Act was a "call to arms" for small-government conservatives. As these groups coalesced into a powerful political force, the culture wars took shape over the next two decades.

Because of the polarized political climate that resulted from these culture wars, moral education in public schools was virtually abandoned during this period. New conservative groups, for example, demanded that schools return to a traditional, religiously based form of moral education and pressured local school boards to allow Bible reading in the classroom and posting the Ten Commandments on classroom walls (Shimron 2000).

School administrators found themselves in a difficult political situation, torn between two powerful political ideological forces. Their response typically was to distance themselves from any policy of moral education by drawing a firm line between the public and private spheres of education. They hoped that these actions would eliminate the hostile political climate that was part of these culture wars. The result, however, was the "sanitation" of the moral issue in schools and the virtual elimination of most moral education programs in schools by the late 1970s.

As moral education was abandoned in the midst of political turmoil, however, educators turned their attention to other problems in society. Just as they had addressed communism in the 1950s and early 1960s, in the 1970s, schools turned to the issue of illegal drug use. In almost messianic fashion, programs were designed to inform students of the dangers of drug and alcohol use.

One of the most successful of these programs was DARE (Drug Assistance Resistance Education). Typically these programs begin in the fifth grade and are often led by a police officer. Students are encouraged to resist peer pressure and "just say no" to drug use. Workbooks and role-play activities are often used in later grades to help students make the right choices. Eventually, students are encouraged to sign a pledge never to use drugs (or alcohol), and then they are awarded buttons, bumper stickers, and other antidrug paraphernalia when they graduate from the program (DARE 1995).

And yet, most educators understood that simply focusing on drug and alcohol use—though important—was simply not enough to encourage moral development among their students. In our complex world, there were many problems, and schools needed to address them in a comprehensive manner.

CONTEMPORARY APPROACHES TO MORAL EDUCATION

Two distinct approaches to moral education gradually emerged during this period—each reminiscent of programs rooted in the previous century.

Democratic, neo-progressives typically embraced either the "values clarification" approach or what has been called "cognitive-based values development." Authoritarian conservatives, on the other hand, turned to traditional virtue-centered moral education, popular during the 1800s.

Values Clarification

The values-clarification movement was launched with the publication of *Values and Teaching* by Louis Raths and his colleagues in 1966. This book not only provided educators with an important theory of why moral education was essential in the schools but also suggested classroom activities that would help implement these ideas. Values clarification embraced the democratic progressive idea that societal values were relative and argued that moral education should help students make life choices that were "positive, purposeful, enthusiastic, and proud" (Raths, Harmin, and Simon 1966).

Values clarification advocates also rejected the idea of memorizing moral rules, codes, or pledges. Rather, they supported group discussions organized around films or media events, intensive "dialogues" with the teacher and the use of "value sheets" where students would grapple with ambiguous moral dilemmas such as our involvement in wars or military incursions. Using a form of the Socratic Method, moreover, teachers would not provide answers to students but would guide their discussion in order to help them make their own ethical decisions (Raths, Harmin, and Simon 1966).

Although values clarification has become quite popular among teachers in recent years, it has also received its share of criticism. Some conservative politicians, for example, argue that it fosters a kind of ethical relativism that is dangerous for society. Others suggest that this form of moral education is a kind of indoctrination. William Casement, for example, has written that some values sheets used in the classroom ask students to list things they could do for the environment. Casement argues that this is indoctrination because it assumes that protecting the environment is a positive good (Casement 1984). Apparently, he does not!

Cognitive Moral Development

In addition to values clarification, other democratic, neo-progressives have also embraced "cognitive moral development" as an important approach to moral education in the classroom. Cognitive moral development was first developed by Lawrence Kohlberg during the 1960s. In a series of scholarly articles, he argued that students developed through six distinct stages of moral reasoning as they evolve cognitively from self-orientation to a moral perspective that is principle based (Kohlberg 1975).

Using this method, teachers engage students in discussions to help them advance from one cognitive level to another. Kohlberg argued that his approach was principle based rather than centered on rules or codes. Rules and codes—however commendable—specify certain behaviors, while principles are guides to help students make moral choices (Kohlberg 1975).

As expected, Kohlberg's approach also has been criticized by authoritarian conservatives. But women's rights activists have challenged this approach, as well. Conservatives have argued that Kohlberg has a strong liberal bias in defining his cognitive levels, while feminists have noted that his approach does not account for gender differences. Nevertheless, cognitive moral reasoning has helped educators understand that moral reasoning is not simply abstract theory but is rooted in scientific research. This has opened an important new direction in our understanding of moral education.

Character Education

While democratic neo-progressive approaches to moral education have become very popular in the last few decades, traditional character education also has its advocates. The "new" character education movement emerged in the 1970s as a response to the growing culture wars in America. Two groups dominated this movement. The first was formed by traditional character educators who organized the American Institute of Character Education (AICE). The AICE developed a comprehensive package of instructional materials and focused on memorizing of codes and pledges.

The second group of character educators emerged from the conservative political revolution of the 1980s (sometimes called the "Reagan revolution") and embraced a more political agenda. This group was led by then Secretary of Education William Bennett and promoted the more traditional virtue-centered approach to moral education popular during the nineteenth century. Bennett's approach—similar to that used in the McGuffey *Readers*—was to fully integrate moral teachings into instruction itself.

Bennett's popular *The Book of Virtues* was the sort of material that appealed to these virtue-centered moral education advocates. Like the McGuffey *Readers* that preceded it, *The Book of Virtues* included patriotic and religious selections as well as moral tales that would encourage what Bennett called "moral literacy" (Bennett 1993).

One other constituent of the conservative, virtue-centered moral education is Christian education and home schooling. Since the beginning of the culture wars, the number of students enrolled in conservative Christian schools has grown exponentially. These schools often use the Accelerated Christian Education (ACE) program, an integrated system of learning and Christian teachings (McClellan 1992).

Strikingly similar to traditional Christian instruction of the colonial era and beyond, the ACE program has a rigidly focused conservative agenda that condemns socialism, liberalism, humanism, and occasionally, Catholicism and Judaism. These individualized lessons are coordinated through a series of workbooks, which avoids direct classroom instruction. Typically "teachers" are not certified and simply monitor the progress of students as they quietly complete their assigned workbook pages (McClellan 1992).

CONCLUSION

The future of moral education is unclear. Competing with increased emphasis on academic subjects and competitive standardized testing, there seems to be little room for any form of character or moral education. Politically charged issues such as antismoking, antialcohol, and antidrug have emerged periodically as have occasional forays into sex education.

But comprehensive moral education is often caught in the web of partisan politics in the wake of the ongoing culture wars. Teachers and students, of course, are once again caught in that web. There is not enough time in the day it seems, to demonstrate complex ideas of civic virtue when these ideas certainly will not be included in end-of-year, high-stakes exams.

And yet there is hope. We have learned from our educational history that moral education is not a separate component of learning but part of learning itself. Moreover, we now understand that to sanitize the curriculum of all elements of moral education to avoid criticism from authoritarian conservatives and democratic progressives alike is also unproductive. We have managed this fine balancing act in the past, and we must do so in the future as well.

9

TESTING AND ASSESSMENT

From Recitation to Standardized Assessment

Some form of testing and assessment has been an important part of the American educational experience since the colonial period. The form of that assessment, however, has changed dramatically over the years.

Throughout the American colonies, schools were religiously based. In New England, for example, the primary goal of education was to "thwart the delusions of Satan." Testing was oral and based on memorization and recitation. As other children sat on hard school benches, reading and working independently, one child after another would appear before the schoolmaster—sometimes with a lash in hand—to recite their biblical passages and other lessons.

Testing often was traumatic for a young student, and assessment was based exclusively on his or her performance rather than an understanding of the passage. As Warren Burton recalled from his days in school, what was read meant little, it was simply how well it was read. Lost in the process were "the ideas hidden in the great long words and spacious sentences" (Hewett 1884; Northend 1853).

A young man who did not have the opportunity or desire to attend school often was sent to a skilled craftsman to work as an apprentice. After a period of five to seven years of training, he would be tested in the traditional manner by journeymen and masters in the guild in order to receive his journeyman's status. Building a cabinet, sewing a pair of

Figure 9.1. By the end of the twentieth century, standardized testing in schools had become common. Courtesy of iStock by Getty Images, credit deimage.

shoes, or creating a piece of stained glass before the guild examiners was the culmination of his apprenticeship training.

Young women in colonial America did not have the same educational opportunities as men but learned the life lessons of sewing, cooking, baking, cleaning, washing clothes, gardening, and raising children under the watchful eyes of mothers, aunts, and sisters. For these young women, testing was constant but not formalized. Learning the skills of the kitchen, garden, and field was a lifelong task, and their progress was closely monitored by members of the household. Reciting or singing the lessons of domestic work, often infused with spiritual songs, was common.

By the nineteenth century, little had changed in the way young men and women were assessed. The same hard benches so familiar to schoolchildren throughout the colonial era continued to be places of study, reading, and preparation for the coming recitation. As before, students memorized material from their readers—now often secular stories and rousing tales of patriots—and then recited them to the teacher. In addition to delivering the passage, some teachers required that students use classical gestures, borrowed directly from the Greek and Roman educational systems.

THE BEE

In addition to these age-old methods of evaluation, however, a new sort of assessment emerged during this period—the bee! As we have seen, bees were communal gatherings common on the frontier and in rural agricultural areas of young America. Settlers would come to hear the recitations, presentations, or spelling contests of local school children.

These regular contests were a source of entertainment, amusement, and assessment. They also were important social occasions for the community, complete with picnic lunches and speeches from town officials, school commissioners, and teachers. The highlight of the day's events, however, were the all-important matches themselves.

Students who distinguished themselves became local celebrities, and teachers who guided their work often were rehired and respected. If the class did not perform well, on the other hand, teaching contracts were canceled, and students were shamed in town as dullards. This was assessment in its rawest form.

WRITTEN EXAMINATIONS

By the mid-nineteenth century, educators began to recognize the importance of some form of written examination and grading (marking) of students. Edwin Hewitt, for example, in his *A Treatise on Pedagogy for Young Teachers,* noted that examination marks were an important "written record of the teacher's estimate concerning the relative success of the pupil's efforts." Earlier, Charles Northend echoed these thoughts in his classic *The Teacher and the Parent*, explaining that the written examination was an important "auxiliary in the great work of education" (Hewett 1884; Northend 1853).

The turning point for the acceptance of the written examination, however, came in 1845. For years, Horace Mann—secretary of the Massachusetts State Board of Education—had been critical of the "uneven" quality of education in his state. This criticism led to a virtual war with local schoolmasters who demanded complete autonomy of instructional methods and curriculum—without the interference of the new state administration led by Mann (Hanson 1994).

The struggle came to a head when Mann challenged the powerful local schoolmasters in and around Boston to test their students in arithmetic, grammar, history, and geography and then compare their scores. The schoolmasters reluctantly agreed, and Mann tested five hundred grade-school students (average age thirteen) in these subjects. His predictions regarding the unevenness of education were confirmed and were published in the October issue of *The Common School Journal*. Dramatic changes were ahead for Massachusetts's schools—the age of the written, quantitative exam had arrived (Hanson 1994).

In the coming decades, written exams in the common schools became more widespread. Eventually, the weekly tests as well as the dreaded report card—complete with grades for academic performance and deportment—became a central part of the school experience.

NEW ATTITUDES TOWARD TESTING

By the end of the nineteenth century and the beginning of the twentieth, there was a distinct shift in Americans' attitudes toward testing and assessment. During this period, two important factors prompted these changes. The first was the development of statistical analysis by Francis Galton, Karl Pearson, Ronald Fisher, and others. The second was the emergence of "achievement" and "intelligence" tests and their implementation, during World War I, with the famous Army Alpha Tests. These two factors propelled standardized testing into the classrooms of America during the early 1920s (Parkerson and Parkerson 2015, 72–74).

FRANCIS GALTON AND HIS DISCIPLES

The publication of Charles Darwin's *On the Origin of Species* in 1859 stunned both intellectuals and communities at large and had a profound impact on Darwin's half cousin—the famous explorer Francis Galton. In early July of 1860, following a conference in Oxford to discuss Darwin's work, Galton set out to scientifically study variations in human intelligence. Eventually, he would argue that intelligence was inherited. This research turned out to be his life's work, and along the way he developed basic statistical concepts such as normal distribution, correlation, and techniques of regression analysis (Parkerson and Parkerson 2015).

Colleagues and students of Galton successfully built on this work. Karl Pearson refined Galton's concept of correlation and developed the Pearson Product Moment Correlation, chi-square, and p value. Moreover, he extended the work of his mentor and laid the mathematical foundation of multiple regression analysis. Ronald Fisher also was influenced by Galton and developed statistical techniques of analysis of variance (ANOVA) as well as the F test associated with probability (Parkerson and Parkerson 2015).

In 1890, Galton's colleague, James Cattell, introduced a series of mental tests and administered them at Columbia University. Cattell noted that the world of testing was growing rapidly, and he identified at least ten tests that were available at that time that measured strength of grip, reactions to sounds, and rote memory (Freeman 1939).

The following year, Thaddeus L. Bolton developed an exam for children to determine their "memory span for digits" and published his results in the prestigious *American Journal of Psychology* in April of 1892. A year later at the Colombian Exposition in Chicago, Joseph Jastrow created a sensation with his test of "mental abilities." Volunteers flocked to his booth on the Midway to take the test. Clearly, Americans were becoming captivated with "scientific" testing (Freeman 1939, 40).

Soon thereafter, Alfred Binet entered the field of mental testing. Binet was fascinated with the work of Francis Galton as well as John Stuart Mill's ideas on intelligence—what he called "associationism." Soon, Binet was commissioned by the French Ministry of Public Instruction to help identify empirically what we now refer to as "learning disabled children" (Fancher 1985).

This research led to his publication of *Experimental Studies of Intelligence*, where he developed a methodology to distinguish between "normal and . . . abnormal" children. This was an important step in the development of a true "mental testing" instrument. Then in 1905, he collaborated with his student, Theodore Simon, to create a simple test known as the Binet-Simon Scale—the first real intelligence test (Fancher 1985).

TESTING COMES TO AMERICA

The link between the work of Binet and Simon in France and the American testing movement was Henry H. Goddard, sometimes referred to as the "father of intelligence testing." Goddard translated the Binet-Simon Scale into English and employed it as part of his research at the Vinland Training School for Feebleminded Girls and Boys, where he served as director of research. Eventually he would distribute over twenty-two thousand copies of the test to schools throughout the country (Fancher 1985; Zenderland 1998).

Goddard's reputation grew rapidly during this period, with the publication of *The Kallikak Family: A Study of the Heredity of Feeblemindedness* in 1912. It was in this work that he introduced a new classification of individuals with low IQs—namely, "morons," "imbeciles," and "idiots." He further expanded this research with a new testing program at Ellis Island and later boasted that because of his tests "the numbers of aliens deported because of feeblemindedness . . . increased approximately 350 percent in 1913 and 570 percent in 1914 over what it had been in each of the five preceding years" (Zenderland 1998; Goddard 1917, 271).

While Goddard's work had a major impact on the testing movement in this country, it was Lewis Terman who revised the Binet-Simon test and reissued it as the *Stanford Revision of the Binet-Simon Scale*. The test came to be known as the Stanford-Binet exam, which is now in its fifth revision. And although it originally was designed to identify children who were developmentally disabled, it has become the standard, general intelligence test today.

TESTING AND EUGENICS

The work of Goddard and Terman, however, reveals the darker side of the mental-testing movement. While the original purpose of mental testing by such pioneers as Binet and Simon was primarily the diagnosis of learning problems among students, Goddard, Terman, and many others used testing for another purpose: namely, to classify and sort individuals.

Whether testing was used to identify immigrants to be deported because of their "mental inadequacies," to track students who scored low on

IQ tests into vocational programs, to identify "mentally deficient" women to be sterilized, or simply to place "deficient individuals" into institutions, the purpose of testing had shifted dramatically during these years from diagnosis to sorting. This function would become the legacy of the mental testing movement moving forward (Parkerson and Parkerson 2015).

THE ALPHA TEST

While work on mental testing developed slowly during the first decades of the twentieth century, the breakthrough came during World War I. The suddenness of American involvement into the conflict and the need to mobilize over two million troops created an environment of pragmatism among military and political leaders.

Into this setting, Robert Yerkes, then president of the young American Psychological Association (APA), lobbied politicians and military leaders alike to adopt mental testing. His message was clear and simple: mental testing would "increase the efficiency of the Army and the Navy" (Parkerson and Parkerson 2015).

Yerkes understood that while the idea of mental testing was becoming more accepted among the American people, there was still a great deal of skepticism among educators and especially the military. In order to change these attitudes, Yerkes became the chair of the APA's Psychological Examination of Recruits Committee to promote the use of testing in the military.

The committee developed a comprehensive proposal for the military command to demonstrate the importance of testing and the identification of men of ability for "responsible types of service commissions." Despite continued skepticism, the military reluctantly agreed and gave Yerkes a commission as a major in what was called the Sanitary Corps (Kevles 1968, 73).

Yerkes recruited over forty young psychologists from universities and private practices to work on this project, and within a matter of months his team had developed a battery of exams and tested over eighty thousand men. This success caught the attention of the adjunct of the War College, and by the end of 1917, extensive testing was approved for the military (Gould 1991, 73).

What came to be known as the Alpha test eventually was administered to hundreds of thousands of enlistees and draftees into the U.S. Army. At its peak in early 1918, over two hundred thousand men were being tested each month! Soon thereafter, the Beta test was developed to test "illiterates." And yet, given the vast numbers of conscripts, it was impossible to keep up with demand for these tests.

It was at this point that General "Black Jack" Pershing, commanding general of the army, essentially called for further testing. His call to improve the "quality" of recruits into the army eventually led to General Order no. 74, which gave the testing movement its full support (Kevles 1968).

By the end of the war, nearly two million recruits had been tested by a large group of young, ambitious psychologists. These young men became the "shock troops" of the mental testing juggernaught that soon would be embraced by educators and the general public. Armed with both statistical theory and glowing reports of the successful implementation of the Alpha Test, they promoted the "gospel of standardized testing" for the rest of the twentieth century (Parkerson and Parkerson 2015).

THE LEGACY OF THE ALPHA TESTS

The army examinations were a clear sign of the abysmal state of education in America. Most recruits had not attended high school, and the overall median educational level was a mere 6.9 years of education. Immigrants' median education was 4.6 years, while among southern blacks, it was a pathetic 2.6 years. In addition, nearly a third of all recruits were classified as "illiterate!" Educators clearly had their work cut out for them (Kennedy 1980).

Moreover, the army's Alpha and Beta tests also represented an important crossroads in testing. The success of these testing programs helped to fundamentally transform the attitudes of the American people regarding the validity and importance of standardized testing. And although some skepticism would remain, a new era had begun.

Authoritarian educators were especially fascinated with standardized testing and scrambled to use these new instruments of assessment in the classrooms of the nation. It appeared to them that they finally had a scientifically proven instrument to measure a student's mental ability for both diagnostic and sorting purposes.

STANDARDIZED TESTING COMES TO AMERICAN CLASSROOMS

Then, following the war, in 1919, the Education Board of the Rockefeller Foundation granted the National Research Council $25,000 to develop tests similar to the Alpha and Beta exams used by the army. A committee of five influential psychologists and educators was created to direct this project and develop tests that could be used in the schools (Clarke et al. 2000).

The result of this work was astonishing. The National Achievement Test was developed and implemented in twenty-one schools across the nation. The results of these exams were tabulated and then reconfigured at Columbia University. National distribution followed and by 1922, over eight hundred thousand copies of the exam were administered. In 1923 alone, it was estimated that "one firm which deals particularly in mental tests had sold over 2,500, 000 intelligence tests" (Whipple 1921; Freeman 39, 3).

THE SAT

While primary and secondary schools scrambled to adopt the National Achievement Test and other tests in the coming years, universities slowly began to recognize the use of standardized exams for college admissions. As a result of this growing interest, the College Entrance Examination Board introduced its new Scholastic Aptitude Test (SAT) in 1926 and then tested and revised it over the next few years. The result of this work led to the creation of the modern SAT exam in 1930 with two distinctive sections: verbal and math (Lawrence et al. 2002).

Within just a few years, the SAT was adopted by Harvard University. Then-President James Bryant Conant and his staff felt strongly that the use of such an exam would help to democratize the process of admissions and open the doors of Harvard to deserving students. Conant also saw the exam, more broadly, as a leveler of society and perhaps a tool to slow the process of the economic stratification of American society. For the idealistic, democratically-oriented Conant, the standardized exam held out the promise of a classless social order (Conant 1940; 1943).

By the end of the 1930s, there was a growing consensus that standardized exams were valuable. Both democratic and authoritarian educators now generally accepted these exams as useful. Authoritarian educators, of course, embraced these exams early on because their vision of education focused on the memorization of primary facts that now could be tested with regular multiple-choice exams. Democratic educators, although remaining skeptical, now saw a limited use of these exams as a leveler of society as well as a diagnostic tool. The standardized multiple-choice test was no longer a novelty—it had become an article of faith in education!

POLITICS AND TESTING

Gradually, education succumbed to the power of the exam, and the curriculum itself became "exam driven." Material that was not easily "testable" was often overlooked in multiple-choice standardized exams, and measuring a student's ability to express complex ideas in written essays were slowly replaced or eliminated.

In addition, international comparisons of educational achievement slowly began to drive the direction of education itself. During the 1950s, in the midst of the Cold War with the Soviet Union, for example, crude test-score comparisons between Soviet and American students in science and math led some politicians and educators to believe that America was "falling behind" the Soviets.

Admiral Hyman Rickover, a leader in this movement, testified before the U.S. House of Representatives and sounded a grave alarm about the growing education gap with the Soviet Union as evidenced by test-score comparisons. He noted that "only the massive upgrading of the scholastic standards of schools would guarantee the future prosperity and freedom of the Republic" (Rickover 1959; 1963).

THE PROGRESSIVE RENAISSANCE—1960S

And yet, not all educators agreed with this assessment. Some discounted the crude test-score comparisons between the Soviet Union and the United States. They argued that only an elite group of Soviet students actually was being tested, while in the United States, most students' scores were reported. Others challenged the exam-driven nature of the curriculum that was literally "squeezing out" other important subjects such as history, art, music, and physical education.

As fears of the Soviet Union began to fade—at least temporarily—progressive educators were reinvigorated and moved to expand the humanities and arts curriculum and to minimize the intrusive use of standardized, multiple-choice exams. As we have seen, educational innovations such as the new basal reader, the look-say method of reading, the open classroom, and whole language—just to name a few—gradually returned to classrooms throughout the nation.

THE MODERN TESTING MOVEMENT

But by the 1970s, many of these innovations were, once again, being criticized by more conservative politicians and authoritarian educators. Many were alarmed that student SAT scores had declined steadily since the early 1960s. Once again, there were calls for more rigor in education centered on the standardized assessment of students.

Some educators called for greater accountability of students through "competency-based" instructional programs. Others suggested a form of computer-assisted instruction (CAI) as the solution to our educational "woes." Still others resurrected the vocational, business approach to education linked with competency-based exams. Sidney Marland, commissioner of education under President Richard Nixon, for example, promoted a "back to basics" and vocational education curriculum and rejected most of the innovations of the progressives during the 1960s (Marland 1971).

By the early 1980s, the persistent criticism of American education reached a crescendo with the publication of *A Nation at Risk: The Imperative for Educational Reform.* This powerful report was the final document presented by President Ronald Reagan's National Commission on

Excellence in Education. As we have seen, the report used dramatic language to urge educators, politicians, and the American people to act (National Commission on Excellence in Education 1983).

A Nation at Risk clearly alarmed the American people with its incendiary language. It stated that (based on test scores of American students) "for the first time in the history of our country the educational skill of one generation will not surpass, will not equal and will not even approach those of their parents." It concluded by warning the American people that "the educational foundations of our society are presently being eroded by a rising tide of mediocrity that threatens our very future as a nation and a people (National Commission on Excellence in Education 1983).

The publication of *A Nation at Risk* launched the modern-day testing movement in America. The document recommended that "standardized tests of achievement should be administered at major transition points from one level of schooling to another and particularly from high school to college or work." The purpose of these tests would be to "certify the students' credentials" (National Commission on Excellence in Education 1983).

In one sweeping statement, this document had elevated standardized exams to a position of national importance and by implication suggested that teachers' judgments were simply not adequate. Standardized tests were needed to "certify" the accuracy of teacher assessments.

A Nation at Risk had a profound effect on educators, politicians, and the American people in general. While there was some criticism from democratic educators regarding the objectivity, language, and findings of the report, there was a curious, uncritical acceptance of its conclusions. Americans seemed to agree that higher test scores among students would help to create a more productive workforce and allow us to compete more effectively in the new global economy. Testing, it appeared, was as American as apple pie!

AMERICA 2000

Within just a few years, ambitious education projects were launched throughout the nation that centered on new forms of testing, accountability, and comparison of schools. One of the most important of these was the America 2000 project, initiated by President George H. W. Bush in the late 1980s.

President Bush called a "national education summit" to be held in Charlottesville, Virginia. The group developed a plan of action that embraced six educational goals that were eventually published in 1991 as *America 2000: An Education Strategy*. This plan was a comprehensive accountability package that encompassed a number of standardized tests that would allow comparisons of students' performance at the national, state, and district levels (New American Schools Development Corporation 1991).

Business leaders were brought into the project to form the New American Schools Development Corporation (NASDC), whose stated goal was to "unleash America's creative genius . . . invent . . . the best schools in the world . . . [and] achieve a quantum leap in learning" (New American Schools Development Corporation 1991).

As part of this effort, Christopher Whittle, then president of NASDC, established the "Edison Project," so named because the private schools created under the program would be superior to public schools as the light bulb was to the candle. Enthusiasm ran high for this project, but when test scores from Edison schools failed to compare favorably to public institutions, the plan was quietly abandoned (Kozol 1992).

In addition to the Edison Project and other plans for privatization of schools, America 2000 proposed a voluntary national exam called the American Achievement Test. This test was seen as a potential admissions test for college and President Bush suggested that it might also be used by employers when hiring workers. While the test never was developed because of strong opposition to it, many politicians and some authoritarian educators saw it as a high-stakes career track examination that was necessary for all American students (Kozol 1992).

Clearly, by the early 1990s, the testing pendulum had once again swung away from diagnostic uses and toward the sorting of individuals. Once again, the enthusiasm for standardized testing had reached a crescendo in America. Politicians, news commentators, and some administrators and teachers saw these high-stakes tests as a simple (and relatively cheap) method to retain poor students and close poor schools. This uncritical—often punitive—use of standardized tests was becoming a dark national reality.

During the 1990s, President Bill Clinton continued support of the national standardized testing movement. As governor of Arkansas, President Clinton had endorsed President Bush's America 2000 plan, and during his presidency he called for regular testing of fourth and eighth graders to achieve "national standards" (Parkerson and Parkerson 2001).

Then in his State of the Union Address on January 23, 1996, Clinton proposed that "every school and every state . . . adopt national standards of excellence; to measure whether schools are meeting those standards . . . and to hold them accountable for those results. That's what our Goals 2000 initiative is all about" (Clinton 1996).

ASSESSMENT OF TEACHERS

In addition to the testing of students, teachers were being subjected to new forms of assessment. Throughout the 1980s, there had been a growing demand among conservative politicians and authoritarian educators to "raise the standards" of teachers. No longer would a passing score on the venerable National Teachers Exam and earning a degree from an accredited institution of teacher education be sufficient. Now, their credentials had to be be assessed by the state as well.

By the early 1990s, the Educational Testing Service (ETS) capitalized on this opportunity and launched the PRAXIS series of exams that they billed as a "new generation of teacher assessments." The PRAXIS series soon became the accepted assessment instrument for teachers, and today hundreds of thousands of these exams are administered to teachers at a total cost of tens of millions of dollars. And of course, *teachers* typically bear these costs (Educational Testing Service 1999a; 1999b; 1999c).

NO CHILD LEFT BEHIND

By the turn of the twenty-first century, terms such as *privatization, accountability, high-stakes testing, assessment,* and *standards* had become part of the American lexicon. And yet, with all the bluster and confidence of supporters of national standardized testing, there was little progress in raising test scores. The year 2000 had come and gone, and the monumental promises of an educational transformation never materialized. Yes, students continued to learn, and teachers continued to teach. But standardized testing had not revolutionized education as promised.

And yet, the most far-reaching testing program ever imagined by Americans was about to be launched by the U.S. Congress. Just days after the contested election of 2000 had been decided by the U.S. Supreme Court, Congress reauthorized the 1965 Elementary and Secondary Education Act as the No Child Left Behind Act (No Child Left Behind 2001).

This extensive piece of legislation called for "stronger accountability for results," in schools and initiated punitive measures against those schools that did not make "progress" (i.e., improvement in overall test scores) within two years. Schools were essentially placed on probation for two years and if "progress" was not forthcoming, parents had the right to transfer their children to a different public school or a charter school in their district (No Child Left Behind 2001).

Authoritarian supporters of No Child Left Behind argued that this program would help to improve the quality of schools through sanctions and the threat of closing altogether. Moreover, they argued that poor test scores among students were a threat to our national security and our global competitiveness and as such should be a legislative priority.

Opposition to No Child Left Behind was muted during the early years of the twenty-first century but grew to become a major opposition force. Some democratic reformers saw the law as unredeemable and called for its immediate repeal. One opponent argued that "its main effect has been to sentence poor children to an endless regimen of test preparation drills." Others such as a coalition of 135 civil rights and religious organizations called for an elimination of "sanctions" with a greater emphasis on funding education and "holding states and localities accountable for making the systemic changes that improve student achievement" (Kohn 2007).

Today we find ourselves in a difficult position as educators. On the one hand, we understand the importance of assessing our students to assure that they are heading in the right direction academically. On the other hand, we are often overwhelmed by the powerful testing establishment that has successfully promoted an ever-growing set of standardized exams for our students that often do not measure the content of the curriculum.

It may be time to reconsider the role of assessment in public schools. Certainly a balance can be achieved—one that measures academic progress but also places testing back in the hands of teachers. With the recent repeal of No Child Left Behind, we are cautiously optimistic.

10

RIGHTS AND RESPONSIBILITIES OF TEACHERS AND STUDENTS

From *in loco parentis* to Individual Rights

The U.S. Constitution neither mentioned education nor assigned a federal role in its development. By default, then, the responsibility for education fell to the states and local communities. As a result, local control of public education often has been seen as the cornerstone of American democracy: a privilege derived from the principles of divided government as outlined by the founding fathers.

And yet, this patriotic nostalgia obscures the darker side of local control. As we look back on the development of public education, we clearly can see that local communities and states often have acted irresponsibly with regard to the hiring and firing of teachers and administrators; they imposed their personal religious beliefs on students and teachers; they segregated their schools on the basis of gender and race; and they deprived both teachers and students of their basic civil and academic rights.

This is not to suggest that all communities acted irresponsibly—but many did. And as a result, the fight for civil, academic, and individual rights in the schools over the years has been a struggle with local communities, what educational historian Ellwood Cubberly called, "the dog in the manger."

Like other aspects of education, the crusade to achieve equal rights for women and minorities, as well as individual and academic freedom in the public schools, has been a reflection of society at large. Discrimination

Figure 10.1. In the last half of the twentieth century, the courts played an important role in protecting the rights of students and teachers. Courtesy of iStock by Getty Images, credit utah78.

against female students and teachers, African Americans, immigrants, the poor, the handicapped, the sick, and more recently the LGBTQ community has been a constant refrain both inside and outside of America's classrooms.

Progress against these various forms of discrimination has been slow, and only in the last decades of the twentieth century and the beginning of the twenty-first century have we seen real improvement. This has resulted from consistent grassroots struggle by a mix of individuals and organizations coupled with favorable court rulings and democratic progressive legislation.

GENDER EQUALITY

From the beginning of the colonial era, women and young girls suffered discrimination both in the schools and in society as a whole. Women could not vote, they had no legal rights, and their economic mobility was constrained by a very conservative, male hierarchical society.

Young girls typically were not allowed in New England's public schools, and when they finally were admitted, they were required to attend segregated classes that offered an inferior education. In Boston, for example, girls were excluded from public schools until 1789, and then they were rotated with boys. This policy continued for nearly a half-century until 1828 when girls finally were allowed to attend school with boys.

But even when girls were admitted to private or common schools, discrimination continued. Male teachers often refused to offer them a thorough and rigorous education. Susan B. Anthony recalled her school days with some bitterness, noting that her schoolmaster in upstate New York refused to teach her and her sisters long division. The schoolmaster had decided that certain subjects were simply unnecessary for women, who should be focusing on how to sew, cook, and clean the house (Parkerson and Parkerson 2001).

Secondary education, much less college, was out of the question for most women until the late 1700s and early 1800s when a number of "female academies" were established. One of the earliest and most important of these female institutions was the Young Ladies Academy of Philadelphia, established in 1787. Unlike earlier female "finishing schools" where flower arranging, serving tea, and gentile "manners" were taught, this academy provided instruction in reading, writing, arithmetic, rhetoric, and geography. Its purpose was to demonstrate that women were intellectually equal to men and could compete academically (Fairbanks 1898).

The Young Ladies Academy soon became recognized as a first-rate educational institution, and women from all over the country sought admission. The academic achievement of the "young ladies" was monitored by a board of "gentlemen visitors" who awarded prizes for outstanding performance (Lerner 1977; Woody 1929).

The success of the Young Ladies Academy led to the establishment of a number of other schools for women during the early nineteenth century. In 1821, for example, Emma Willard established the Troy Female Seminary. Like its counterpart in Philadelphia, the Troy Seminary had a strong academic curriculum. Moreover, it was the first school in the country to prepare women teachers for the common schools. By 1869, hundreds of women had been trained as teachers.

In 1837, Mary Lyons established the prestigious Mount Holyoke College in South Hadley, Massachusetts. Lyons introduced written composition into the curriculum and courses in math, English, science, and foreign languages. She encouraged her female graduates to become scientists and college teachers and to "go where no one else will go and do what no one else will do" (Stowe 1887).

The graduates of these institutions and thousands of other educated women helped to launch the mid-nineteenth-century women's movement. Capped by a number of national conventions beginning in 1848 at Seneca Falls, New York, the struggle for equal rights began in earnest.

Though progress was slow, things did change. The Nineteenth Amendment to the Constitution granted American women the right to vote, and although the Equal Rights Amendment (first introduced by Alice Paul in 1923) eventually "died" in the 1980s, other laws have helped to eliminate some discrimination against women.

Title IX of the Higher Education Act of 1972, for example, put an end to arbitrary firing of women when they married or became pregnant. It also made sex discrimination and sexual harassment illegal—enforced by the Department of Education's Office of Civil Rights. The impact of this law has been dramatic. Prior to 1972, young women students who married or became pregnant could be prohibited from attending school by law. Today these students are protected under Title IX.

Sexual discrimination and sexual harassment of teachers and students (male or female) has also been made illegal under the provisions of Title IX. The Department of Education's Office of Civil Rights, moreover, has the power to enforce this provision. This provision was affirmed under the 1992 Supreme Court ruling *Franklin v. Gwinnet County Schools* (*Franklin v. Gwinnet* 1992—www.law.cornell.edu).

One other example is worth noting. Prior to the passage of Title IX legislation in 1972, women were consistently discriminated against with regard to their participation in school sports. Programs were not offered, scholarships were not provided, and there was little encouragement for women to participate. Since 1972, however, things have changed dramatically. On the eve of its passage, for example, only 295,000 women participated in organized sports in schools. Today that number is over 2.7

million! More active and healthy women are emerging from schools today (White 1999).

And yet, while progress clearly has been made, the Supreme Court in its 2007 *Ledbetter v. Goodyear* decision ruled that claims of discrimination must be made within 180 days of the initial act of discrimination. For its part, Congress passed the Lilly Ledbetter Fair Pay Act in January 2009 that essentially reversed this decision. The recent Women's March on Washington on January 21, 2017, moreover, suggests that the struggle continues.

While subtle and pernicious forms of female-teacher and student harassment persists, it appears that a new more respectful attitude toward women is slowly emerging—very gradually changing the culture of the nation. Only when that culture changes, however, will gender equality be achieved. Despite some recent setbacks, we remain optimistic.

AFRICAN AMERICANS

While gender discrimination has been a consistent problem in American educational history, segregation and discrimination based on race have been a perpetual problem in this country since the colonial era. As we have seen, slaves were forbidden by state laws and local custom from attending school, and even freed slaves and freedmen in the North faced discrimination and violence when seeking an education.

During the early decades of the nineteenth century, in the wake of a number of slave rebellions, states throughout the South passed punitive laws to forbid slave education. As we have seen, North Carolina, as just one example, prohibited the teaching of slaves with a fine of $100 (approximately $1,000 today)—or imprisonment for a white person who broke the law. A slave who attempted to learn to read could receive "39 lashes on his or her bare back" (Cohen 1974).

The Freedmen's Bureau, established in the years following the American Civil War, briefly brought education to both younger and older blacks in the South, but the experiment ended as white rule returned to the South during the 1870s.

Some African Americans attended their own schools, often held in churches and taught by the pastor or another member of the congregation. Others went to philanthropic schools such as the Jeanes Schools. But the segregation policies of states and local communities were essentially given the stamp of approval with the infamous *Plessy v. Ferguson* decision of 1896. This Supreme Court decision allowed segregation as long as the segregated facilities were "equal" to white schools. This "separate but equal" doctrine stained the civil rights landscape for the first half of the twentieth century.

The turning point, of course, was the *Brown v. Board of Education* Supreme Court ruling in 1954 that struck down *Plessy* and essentially launched a half-century of civil rights protest, legislation, and court decisions. These included the struggle of African Americans during the 1950s and 1960s, the Civil Rights Act of 1964, the Voting Rights Act of 1965, the *Swan v. Charlotte-Mecklenburg* Supreme Court busing decision of 1971, and the Black Lives Matter movement of today.

Problems still exist, however. Some people have pointed to a subtle "resegregation" of schools in the last twenty years. Others note that academic tracking has created a two-tiered educational system with blacks, some ethnic minorities, and poor children directed into vocational or remedial programs, while white students are tracked into "upper ability tracks" or college preparatory courses (Parkerson and Parkerson 2015).

Still others have noted that the enormous consolidated mega-schools of today create an atmosphere of isolation and anomie especially for African American, immigrant, and poor children. As a result, these children often do poorly or drop out of school (Parkerson and Parkerson 2015).

IMMIGRANTS

While immigrant children were not subjected to the brutality of slavery and vicious segregation, they did endure (and continue to endure) discrimination both in and out of school. Informal bans on immigrants attending schools were common throughout the nineteenth century and well into the twentieth.

Even more common were school policies of English-only instruction that limited the progress of young immigrant children. Today, new programs of bilingual instruction have become more available, and immigrant children have greater educational opportunities. On the other hand, during the nineteenth century, Irish Catholics eventually were forced to establish private schools to educate their children. This tradition continues to the present day.

Nativism, as well as religious and ethnic discrimination, also persists in America as we struggle to embrace our emerging multicultural society. But as with gender equality, a new sense of optimism is gradually emerging despite recent political setbacks.

OTHER OPPRESSED GROUPS

In recent years, democratic progressive reformers have begun to recognize that other groups in American society have been silent victims of discrimination. In 1975, Congress enacted P.L. 94-142 to protect the rights of handicapped people, including handicapped students. This law was strengthened with the passage of the Individuals with Disabilities Education Act (IDEA) in 1990. Today, access to and inclusion in classrooms throughout the nation is assured by this law.

In addition, with the creation of the Office of Special Education Programs at the federal level (established under IDEA), these special children are guaranteed their basic rights. Finally, the court also has ruled that students infected with HIV cannot be denied education, under provisions of P.L. 94-142.

Discrimination against LGBTQ students has had a long, though mostly silent history in America. Gay students have been harassed informally by both teachers and students over the years and have typically been forced "into the closet," fearful of reprisal because of their sexual orientation. The movement for gay rights began in earnest in the late 1960s and made great progress during the 1970s.

The AIDS crisis that emerged in the early 1980s and continues to plague both gay and straight Americans today, however, was a major setback for the LGBTQ community. Many Americans incorrectly blamed homosexuals for spreading the disease, and gays were often condemned by religious groups and the society at large. In recent years, as a new generation of Americans has begun to express itself, some progress has been made. The recent ruling by the Supreme Court regarding gay marriage (*Obergefell v. Hodges*) has empowered the LGBTQ community, and more progress is expected.

Nevertheless, recent regressive legislation at the state level, such as North Carolina's HB2 (bathroom law) has been another setback for the LGBTQ community (and for North Carolina and the nation as a whole). And while schools have quietly challenged this law with "gender neutral" facilities, it is clear that this struggle is far from over.

And yet, the silent discrimination and bullying in classrooms, playgrounds, and in the workplace continues. Once again, only when there is a change in the collective cultural attitudes of Americans will real progress be made.

INDIVIDUAL RIGHTS OF STUDENTS

Finally, there is the question of student rights in general. Although they are citizens of this country, students have traditionally been the victims of discrimination. As we have seen, corporal punishment, beginning in the colonial period and continuing in some communities—even today—is a stain on American justice.

Moreover, until recently, students did not have the right to sue, they had had no access to their personal school records, they had no due process when accused of a crime, they had no protection from unlawful search and seizure, and they certainly had little freedom of speech. Only in the last generation have we begun to see students as having fundamental constitutional rights rather than as children under the protection of schools *in loco parentis* (in place of parents).

Corporal Punishment

As we have seen, corporal punishment is still legal in twenty-eight states and the District of Columbia. The Supreme Court ruled in its landmark decision *Ingraham v. Wright* (1977) that schools had the right to choose whether to use corporal punishment or not. Perhaps as a result of this decision, the Department of Education, Office of Civil Rights, has reported that in 2002–2003 over three hundred thousand school children in the United States were subjected to physical punishment by teachers and administrators (U.S. Department of Education, Office of Civil Rights 2002).

The Right to Sue

The right of students and their parents to sue a teacher, administrator, or member of the school has, until relatively recently, been denied. However, because of the landmark Supreme Court decision *Wood v. Strickland* (1975), that right has been secured (*Wood v. Strickland* 1975—www.law.cornell.edu).

This important case, sometimes referred to as the "spiked punch" decision involved two tenth-grade girls (Peggy and Virginia) from Mena Public High School in Arkansas. As a prank, Peggy and Virginia "spiked the punch" with two bottles of malt liquor at a home economics meeting. The school took quick action and suspended the girls for the balance of the school year—about three months. The girls and their family sued the school claiming that they had been punished unfairly and had been denied due process since they were not allowed to attend the suspension hearing and defend themselves.

The case was heard by a lower court that ruled the punishment was excessive. The school board, for their part, claimed it had "qualified immunity" because they were unaware that they had violated the student's constitutional rights. However, the Supreme Court agreed with the lower court and noted that ignorance of the law was no defense. A federal judge in Arkansas then ruled that students had the right to sue individual school board members but not the school district or the board of education itself (*Wood v. Strickland* 1975—www.law.cornell.edu).

Due Process—Access to Personal Records

The two girls in the "spiked punch" case, Peggy and Virginia, had secured for all students and their parents, the right to sue members of the school board for their actions. Student access to their personal records, however, also was a critical issue. In fact, during the early 1970s there were numerous challenges to the age-old tradition of holding *"incognito"* all personal records from students and parents. These records included test scores, grades, health and attendance records, and teachers' comments on students' work, as well as disciplinary actions.

This tradition had made it difficult for students and parents to dispute decisions by the school in matters of promotion, retention, or discipline. As a result, there were a number of cases brought before the court in the

1970s that challenged this age-old authoritarian "tradition." Eventually, Congress passed landmark legislation and then amended that legislation as P.L. 93-568—known as the Buckley Amendment. This law made it possible for students and parents to examine their personal records. Moreover, it changed the relationship between teachers and students from *in loco parentis* to guaranteeing students' rights (Parkerson and Parkerson 2001).

While many teachers and administrators (as well as most students and parents) are unaware of the Buckley Amendment (P.L. 93-568), it quietly has become the cornerstone of student rights today. Parents and guardians now have access to all personal records of their children, and students over the age of sixteen can access those records as well. In this case, the democratic progressive struggle for individual rights has been successful.

Due Process—The Right to Tell Their Side of the Story

When the Fourteenth Amendment to the U.S. Constitution was ratified in 1868, it not only provided civil rights to former slaves, but it also guaranteed that states could not "deny to any person within its jurisdiction the equal protection of the laws." And yet, while this amendment clearly included *all* citizens, students have traditionally been denied "due process" in the classrooms of the nation.

Once again, in the early 1970s, this tradition was challenged by numerous students and their parents. One such case involved several students, including Dwight Lopez, who was suspended from Central High School for "causing a disturbance in the lunchroom." However, Dwight and his fellow students were not allowed to attend their suspension hearings. As a result, he and his parents sued the school alleging that he had been denied his constitutional rights under the Fourteenth Amendment.

The case went all the way to the Supreme Court, and in its famous *Goss v. Lopez* decision (1975), the court ruled in favor of Dwight and his parents. The Justices argued simply that "students have property and liberty interests that give them due process rights when they are suspended from schools." Students now have the right to tell their side of the story (*Goss v. Lopez* 1975—www.law.cornell.edu).

Freedom of Speech

While the issue of having the right to represent yourself in a disciplinary hearing is what legal analysts call "procedural due process," the right of free speech is referred to as "substantive due process." Throughout much of American educational history, students have had few rights in this area. As with other legal matters, free speech typically has been denied under the broad tradition of *in loco parentis*.

This tradition, however, was challenged over and over again—especially during the turbulent 1960s and 1970s. The breakthrough came in 1965 when three young students (John and Mary Beth Tinker and Christopher Eckhart) from Des Moines, Iowa, protested America's involvement in the war in Vietnam by wearing black armbands to school. The principal was outraged by their behavior and suspended them from school.

The students and their families sued the school board for their actions, arguing that they had been denied their First Amendment right of free speech. The district court heard their case and ruled in favor of the school board. But in an unprecedented decision by the Supreme Court of the United States (*Tinker v. Des Moines* 1969) this ruling was overturned, essentially guaranteeing the right of free speech for students and teachers. In his legendary majority decision, Justice Fortas wrote that "teachers and students do not shed constitutional rights at the schoolhouse gate" (*Tinker v. Des Moines* 1969—www.law.cornell.edu).

And yet, the concept of "free speech" is somewhat ambiguous and can be interpreted in a number of ways. While *Tinker v. Des Moines* appeared to have settled the issue, fifteen years later, in 1983, Matthew Frasier was suspended from Bethel High School because of alleged vulgarity during a speech to the student body. The school argued that Matthew used an "elaborate graphic and explicit sexual metaphor" to promote his friend who was running for student office. In addition to the three-day suspension, Matthew was not allowed to give his valedictorian speech at commencement (Parkerson and Parkerson 2008, 259).

While there was no "obscenity" in Matthew's speech, his sexual analogies were considered "vulgar." Matthew and his family sued the school board, arguing that it had violated his First Amendment rights. The case made its way to the U.S. Supreme Court, and in their 1986 decision *Bethel School District v. Frasier*, they sided with the school. The court ruled that since the speech was not a political issue, and was vulgar, the school had the right to suspend him (*Bethel School District v. Frazier* 1986—www.law.cornell.edu).

Search and Seizure

The issue of free speech continues to be debated by teachers, students, administrators, and the courts. Like other legal issues, it is somewhat indeterminate. Such is the case of "search and seizure." The court has ruled over the years that certain kinds of searches—such as "strip searches"—are illegal, while other searches are seen as legal and can be conducted by school administrators.

Once again, during the tumultuous 1970s, the issue of illegal search and seizure was challenged by students and their parents. Two young students from Graham Elementary School, Cassandra and Onieka, were accused of stealing $4.50. They were taken to the school bathroom and, according to the girls, they were ordered to pull down their underpants to "check their clothes for the money" (Parkerson and Parkerson 2008).

The girls and their parents sued the school district, arguing that they had been subjected to an illegal "strip search." The lower court agreed and ruled in *Bellnier v. Lund* (1977) that since strip searches "are inherently among the most intrusive of all searches," they are unconstitutional under the provisions of the Fourth Amendment to the U.S. Constitution. The Supreme Court affirmed that ruling in its *New Jersey v. T.L.O.* (1985).

And yet, the court has allowed other kinds of student searches. Searching a student's locker or car is considered legal if an administrator suspects that illegal firearms or drugs are present. However, administrators and teachers are held to a higher standard with regard to personal searches and must have "reasonable suspicion" that the student is carrying a weapon of some sort.

Drug Testing

Drug testing, however, is another category of the "search and seizure" issue and is very controversial. Since the onset of America's War on Drugs in the 1980s, drug testing has become common in virtually all areas of life—including schools. As we have seen, routine searches of student lockers and automobiles are legal under the law, but drug testing is another matter.

Beginning in the 1980s, in a wave of controversial authoritarian reforms, numerous communities throughout the country initiated antidrug campaigns. Some, as in Vernonia, Oregon, began an aggressive policy to test all their student athletes. In 1989, the Vernonia school board began its Student Athletes Drug Policy. Student athletes were required to sign a consent form—to be tested—and their parents had to give written consent. Athletes then were randomly selected to be tested once a week.

Several years later, in 1991, James Acton signed up to play football, but he refused to sign the consent form. His parents also declined to give their permission. The case went to court and eventually made its way to the U.S. Supreme Court. In its decision under *Vernonia v. Acton* (1995), the court ruled that drug testing was constitutional since the school had acted as a "guardian and tutor of children entrusted to its care" (*Veronia v. Acton* 1995—www.law.cornell.edu).

The Vernonia decision emboldened other communities across the country to initiate drug-testing policies. In 1998 for example, Tecumseh, Oklahoma, began a program that would test all students engaged in extracurricular activities. Lindsay and Lacy Earls and their parents challenged this policy, arguing that drug testing was a violation of their rights under the Fourth Amendment. They also claimed that there was little evidence of a drug problem at the school.

The case made its way to the Supreme Court, and in its 2002 decision it declared that drug testing of students in extracurricular activities was indeed constitutional. Conservative justice Clarence Thomas, writing for the majority, noted that schools have a "custodial and tutelary responsibility for children," and as a result, this form of testing was legal. He also noted that even a potential drug problem in the schools was justification for this kind of program. Clearly, the influence of authoritarian reformers had informed these policies (*Board of Education v. Earls* 2002—www.law.cornell.edu).

Students Rights—Conclusion

Since the democratic progressive era of the 1970s, the issue of students' individual rights has been controversial to say the least. The courts have essentially given states the right to establish policies to use corporal punishment on students who misbehave. However, students now have the right to sue members of school boards, and they also have access to their personal records under the Buckley Amendment. Moreover, students and their parents are now allowed to attend disciplinary hearings and explain their side of the case.

Free speech is a bit more complex. The court has ruled that expression of political beliefs by students is protected under the First Amendment of the U.S. Constitution, but that vulgarity is not protected. In the latter case, schools can suspend or discipline students who violate this principle.

Finally, the broad issue of search and seizure under the Fourth Amendment to the U.S. Constitution is complex. The court has consistently argued that strip searches are unconstitutional but that searches of a student's personal property such as backpacks, lockers, and vehicles are acceptable under certain circumstances.

A higher standard is imposed, however, with regard to "personal searches." Only when there is a reasonable likelihood that a student is carrying a weapon or that he or she is a drug dealer can a student be searched. Finally, drug testing of students has been seen by the courts as constitutional. The Supreme Court essentially argued that since schools have a "custodial responsibility" to students, they are allowed to take this sort of action.

TEACHER RIGHTS

Many of the constitutional issues discussed above affected both students and teachers. And yet there are specific issues that apply only to teachers. These include academic freedom, personal lifestyle, collective bargaining, and legal liability.

As we have seen, Title IX legislation has provided a great deal of protection for the rights of women in general and female teachers specifically. Under this legislation, pregnant students were allowed to remain in school to continue their education, but teachers often were required to take a maternity leave. A number of teachers protested this policy and eventually, in *Cleveland Board of Education v. LaFleur* (1974), the court declared this action was a violation of Title IX legislation (*Cleveland Board of Education v. LaFleur* 1974—www.law.cornell.edu).

With regard to equal pay, we have seen that women teachers have traditionally been paid less than their male counterparts. Under the Supreme Court decision *Burkey v. Marshall County Board of Education* (1981), this policy was declared unconstitutional and a violation of the Civil Rights Act of 1964 (*Burkey v. Marshall County Board of Education* 1981—www.law.cornell.edu).

Due Process

Teachers also have some due process protection under the *Goss v. Lopez* decision (1975). For example, teaching licenses cannot be denied without due process, teachers have the right to tell their side of the story in a disciplinary hearing, and they cannot be fired on the spot by an angry administrator.

Free speech is another matter and is as complex for teachers as it is for students. Generally free speech is guaranteed for teachers—even criticism of school board policies! This particular issue was resolved when Marvin Pickering, a teacher in the DeKalb public schools criticized the board of education in a letter to the editor of a local newspaper for its allocation of school funds. For this action, he was fired, allegedly because his letter was "detrimental to the efficient operation and administrations of the schools" (*Pickering v. Board of Education* 1968—www.law.cornell.edu).

Pickering challenged this action and presented the issue to the courts. The Supreme Court eventually ruled in *Pickering v. Board of Education* (1968) that the school board had acted illegally and had violated Pickering's constitutional rights under the First and Fourteenth Amendments. Essentially, this case established the precedent that unless a teacher makes reckless claims, school boards cannot fire you because it does not like or does not agree with your stated position (*Pickering v. Board of Education* 1968—www.law.cornell.edu).

Collective Bargaining

The issue of collective bargaining for teachers, however, is somewhat controversial. Over the years, teachers have organized to protect their rights and achieve a living wage. As we have seen, teachers have been fired or not rehired for offenses that may seem trivial today. Benjamin

Gue, for example, was fired because he "didn't whip [his students] enough," while Mary Augusta Roper was not rehired because she "don't lick them at all" (Parkerson and Parkerson 2001, 155).

Other teachers were fired for violating the dress code (such as wearing a dress that was more than three inches from the ground!) or riding in a carriage on a Sunday with a young man. And, of course, as we have just seen, Marvin Pickering was suspended because he criticized decisions made by the board of education regarding their funding priorities.

While teachers have fought against these kinds of arbitrary firings, they also have struggled to achieve higher wages and better facilities for their students. They now have the right to join labor organizations such as the NEA or the AFT (American Federation of Teachers) and engage in collective bargaining. But they are limited in most states from actually striking to achieve higher wages.

The landmark Supreme Court decision *Hortonville Joint School District v. Hortonville Education Association* (1976) set the precedent of declaring strikes illegal, and this action has become commonplace throughout the nation. In fact, teacher strikes are legal in only eleven states today (*Hortonville Joint School District v. Hortonville Educational Association* 1976—www.law.cornell.edu).

Academic Freedom

While the issues of collective bargaining rights and the right to strike have been settled—at least for the moment—issues of academic freedom are also important for teachers. What can we teach in the classroom? Can we be fired for addressing controversial subjects such as American foreign policy or HIV/AIDS?

The Supreme Court has not made a definitive ruling on these matters, but lower courts certainly have made their positions clear. The guiding principle over the last half-century is that the classroom is a "marketplace of ideas," and if teachers avoid propagandizing their students, they have considerable freedom. And yet, many states have attempted to impose strict guidelines on curriculum content. North Carolina, for example, currently forbids teachers to discuss birth control, abortion, or the prevention of sexually transmitted diseases (www.dpi.State.nc.us).

Moreover, some communities in the past have attempted to control the curriculum by forcing teachers to adhere to a script of lessons. This idea was challenged in the important Federal Appellate Court decision—*Cary v. Board of Education* (1977). In this case, the judge ruled that teachers "cannot be made to simply read from a script prepared or approved by the [school] board" (*Cary v. Board of Education* 1977—www.law.cornell.edu).

RELIGION IN THE CLASSROOM

While these issues seem to be settled, the role of religion in the classroom continues to be controversial. Since the emergence of the common school in the early nineteenth century, democratic educators have argued for a clear separation of church and state in the classroom. Throughout most of American history, however, there has been some inclusion of religion in the schools. For example, common school teachers often led a pan-Protestant-oriented prayer at the beginning and end of the school day. This tradition appealed to many Americans, but as we have seen, as the nation became more multicultural, it alienated millions of children and their parents.

The landmark *Engle v. Vitale* decision essentially ended that tradition in 1962. Justice Hugo Black wrote in his majority opinion that "prayer [in the classroom] was wholly inconsistent with the establishment clause [of the First Amendment to the U.S. Constitution]." Two decades later, in 1985, the court ruled in *Wallace v. Jaffree* that silent prayers or moments of silence led by a teacher also were unconstitutional. And in 1992, the court ruled in *Lee v. Weisman* that prayers as part of a graduation ceremony also were unconstitutional (*Engle v. Vitale* 1962; *Wallace v. Jaffree* 1985; *Lee v. Weisman* 1992; www.law.cornell.edu).

But while prayers in schools led by teachers or administrators have been ruled unconstitutional, student religious clubs and organizations can use school facilities during and after school hours. *Board of Education of the Westside Community Schools v. Mergens* (1990) and *Lamb's Chapel v. Center Moriches Union Free School* (1993).

Finally, it also should be remembered that students and teachers clearly have the right to personal silent prayer, meditation, or a moment of silence as long as others are not coerced to participate (*Board of Education v. Mergens* 1990; *Lambs Chapel v. Center Moniches Union Free School* 1993; www.law.cornell.edu).

LEGAL LIABILITY

One final part of our discussion of rights and responsibilities has to do with legal liability of teachers. Generally speaking, the courts have made a distinction between four types of liability: misfeasance, nonfeasance, malfeasance, and educational malpractice.

Misfeasance is a failure to act appropriately with students. Nonfeasance is a failure to perform assigned teaching duties. Malfeasance is breaking the law directly and malpractice is not providing students with an adequate education. Although the court protects teachers for the most part (especially from educational malpractice), breaking the law, injuring a student or colleague, or being negligent in the performance of teaching duties will have consequences (Fischer, Schimmel, and Kelly 1973).

The legal and constitutional history of American education is complex. It involves a dramatic rethinking of the pernicious policies, laws, and culture of that "dog in the manger," local control. And like the changes in the larger society, some progress has been made.

Nevertheless, we want more. We demand greater protection from discrimination as our society becomes more culturally, ethnically, and racially diverse. We want our teachers and students to be protected under the law just like all other citizens. And we want teachers to be funded and paid in a fair and equitable way. Only then will this longstanding struggle come to an end.

CONCLUSION

The Complexity of Change in American Education

Our journey is nearly complete. We have traveled the long and perilous road through our educational history. We have explored the religious schools of the colonial era, the common schools of the nineteenth century, the graded schools of the early twentieth century, and the large consolidated schools of today. It has been an incredible journey, and we hope that you now have a better understanding of the history of education.

AUTHORITARIAN AND DEMOCRATIC SCHOOLS OF EDUCATION

In chapter 1, we introduced the two great educational schools of thought—the authoritarian and the democratic. As we have seen, these two schools have embraced very different positions on education; they perceived students differently; they differed as to the proper way to instruct and discipline children as well as the kinds of values that they should develop. The vision of the school curriculum also was very different as was their preferred method of assessment of both students and teachers.

But while each of these schools has a very different vision of the future of education, they also have one thing in common—advocates of each want a better education for American children coupled with a stronger society and economy. This can be the basis of compromise and consensus as we move forward into the twenty-first century.

THE STRUCTURE AND ORGANIZATION OF SCHOOLS

In chapter 2, we turned to the changing structure and organization of American schools. We have seen schools move from the small, colonial, religious schools and locally controlled common schools of young America to the larger graded schools of the late nineteenth century controlled by states and larger municipalities, to the consolidated mega-schools of today.

This transformation from the local intimacy of smaller neighborhood schools typically favored by democratic educators to the regional isolation and bureaucracy of today's schools has fundamentally altered the educational experience of American children. Moreover, it has tended to alienate parents and members of the community from the schools themselves and has weakened the fabric of the educational village.

Local control of education with all its flaws has, in effect, been transferred to states, larger municipalities, and to a degree, the federal government. There have, of course been some improvements in education as a result. Schools now offer a more diverse curriculum, teachers are better educated, and the parochial policies of local schools have been limited.

Nevertheless, the isolation of a large school clearly has consequences for some students. African American and immigrant children, lower achieving students, and the poor do not have the role models and personal attention of caring teachers that are necessary to succeed in school. These are problems that we must understand as we enter the classrooms of the twenty-first century.

SCHOOL CONSOLIDATION

In chapter 3, we built on our understanding of the process of change in American public schools by turning to the process of school consolidation vigorously promoted by authoritarian reformers. In this chapter, we described the three phases of school consolidation. The first was the high school movement of the late nineteenth century where the template of consolidated schools was developed. This included a centralized regional location, departmentalized learning environment, a specialized teaching staff, and a complex administrative bureaucracy.

The second and third phases involved the rural and urban consolidation movements of the twentieth century where both the administrative structure and schools themselves were combined into more "efficient" organizations. Here, a new corporate model of administration favored by authoritarians gradually replaced the locally controlled boards of education of the past. Within that system, moreover, teachers gradually lost their academic independence and essentially were relegated to positions of employees within the larger educational enterprise.

The final stage of school consolidation was the process of desegregation/consolidation of the late twentieth century. While not a planned consolidation process, it involved the closing of black schools, the reduction in the number of black administrators and teachers, and the transfer of black students to all-white schools.

This process led to the virtual collapse of the black educational village, the removal of role models from their schools, and the alienation of black students, who found themselves to be strangers in previously all-white schools.

In short, while the desegregation movement was seen as a positive for both the black community and society in general, for African American teachers, administrators, the black educational village, and especially black students, there was a high price to pay for this historic change.

By the end of our "consolidation century" in the early 1980s, everyday Americans and reformers of all sorts were pleased. Brand new buses moved students to new, "productive" schools throughout the nation. These schools boasted of expanded curriculums, specialized teachers, and more facilities, with potential cost savings for the community as an added bonus. As we have seen, however, many of these promises faded as the reality of consolidated schools began to shatter our collective dreams of educational improvement.

THE STRUGGLE FOR DIVERSITY

In chapter 4, we turn to the ongoing struggle for diversity in American schools. We have seen that as with other aspects of American history, the struggle for diversity in schools paralleled that of other groups for recognition as well as collective and individual rights. We focused on the monumental struggles of women, African Americans, and immigrants to achieve simple justice.

Throughout much of our early history, American schools typically were reserved for white boys. Women were seen as intellectually inferior—a view that was a commonly held throughout much of world history. Some girls received an education in church schools or with the help of a home tutor, but for the most part, they were not admitted to the schools of colonial America.

New attitudes of equality, however, developed because of the American Revolution and the market revolution of the nineteenth century. Slowly, under the influence of democratic reformers, we saw the emergence of the common school in the early to middle decades of the nineteenth century with primary school education slowly offered to young girls.

And yet, beyond the basic common school education, women had few opportunities. Only with the establishment of a number of female seminaries such as Emma Willard's Troy Academy and Mary Lyons's Mount Holyoke College was more advanced education seen as plausible by a very socially conservative nation. Nevertheless, by the eve of the Civil War, boys and girls were attending school at about the same rate.

Today, women attend schools at all levels at rates comparable to men, and in the case of college or university study, women actually outnumber men! Women now dominate teaching at the elementary level and, depending on the subject, are well represented in secondary education. At the college level, however, they remain woefully underrepresented. And yet, fundamental change is in the air.

African Americans also have struggled to receive an education since the first slaves were brought to this country in the early 1600s. Slaves, of course, were not allowed to attend school and were seen as intellectually inferior. A handful of slaves was able to receive a basic education from a kindly mistress of the plantation, and some free blacks attended charity schools—especially in the North.

Then, in the early years of the nineteenth century, many states throughout the South imposed punitive laws that made it illegal either to teach a slave or for slaves to receive an education. These laws sought to

CONCLUSION

slow the process of enlightenment of black slaves who might then challenge the plantation system.

By the end of the American Civil War in 1865, however, the door to education was opened slightly for both freedmen and poor whites in the South, creating what one African American scholar called "a veritable fever" for education.

This excitement was nearly extinguished during the dark days of Jim Crow—beginning in the late 1870s and lasting for well over half a century. Blacks, once again struggled to receive an education to improve their lives. Some philanthropists established black schools, such as the Jeanes schools, and there was some progress in the North, integrating a handful of African Americans into city schools.

Much of this slow progress, however, ended abruptly with the infamous 1896 *Plessy v. Ferguson* "separate but equal" decision of the Supreme Court. Nevertheless, the renewed struggle of African Americans to achieve equality in society and equal access to educational facilities for their children eventually reached a crescendo in 1954 with the *Brown v. Board of Education* decision that signaled the official end of segregation in American schools.

While progress has been made since then, there is still a great deal to do. Poor black communities often must contend with substandard educational facilities, and while dedicated teachers do their best, it remains a monumental task.

Moreover, the destruction of the black educational village and the dramatic reduction in the number of both black teachers and administrators in the late 1960s and 1970s has taken its toll on African American education. And as we have noted, the large, consolidated, mega-schools of today, along with a persistent standardized testing agenda, has fostered dangerous alienation among many young black men and women.

Finally, immigrants to this nation also have experienced their share of exclusion, prejudice, and violence. Like other oppressed groups, immigrants have traditionally been barred from the schools of America. In some cases, this exclusion was imposed by law, in others it was through ridicule and or violence against immigrant children and their families.

Because of this hostile environment, some immigrant groups turned inward, creating their own institutions—including schools. Church schools provided important educational opportunities for many immigrants from the colonial period into the nineteenth century.

The common school offered hope for some immigrant groups, but hope turned to disappointment as these public schools embraced a pan-Protestant curriculum that often ignored and even ridiculed people of other cultures and religious orientations.

Roman Catholics, for their part, created an entire educational system during this period to combat this injustice, and other religious groups did the same. And while there has been progress in this area, people of different cultures continue to struggle to enter the public schools of America.

Today, because of the work of democratic progressive activists and groups such as the National Coalition of Advocates for Students (NCAS), the doors of American public schools have opened slightly. And despite persistent calls for English-only instruction and immigrant restriction, we are making some progress.

CURRICULUM AND INSTRUCTION

In chapters 5 and 6, we turn our attention to the dramatic changes in the curriculum and instruction in American schools. We have seen that changes in society, the economy, politics, and culture, as well as the work of educational philosophers have informed these changes.

The American Revolution and market revolution that followed transformed our ideas regarding education in this country. The Revolution brought about a new sense of egalitarianism unheard of in modern world history. Democratic statesmen such as Thomas Jefferson, Benjamin Franklin, and many others called for some form of universal education to secure our "blessings of liberty." The market revolution, on the other hand, extended that vision of equality and promoted a new idea of individual freedom.

America's schools responded to these new ideas, and many church schools of the colonial era gradually were eclipsed by the powerful common school movement of the early Republic. Common schools were theoretically designed to provide an education for all—through they fell short of this lofty goal. The curriculum of these schools, however, shifted from an exclusive religious focus to one that emphasized nationalism and patriotism. It also centered on the new values of the marketplace, such as hard work, persistence, and punctuality.

Instruction also changed during this period—though progress was slow. The standard form of instruction during the colonial era and well into the nineteenth century was memorization of material and then recitation of passages to the teacher. Slowly, as the McGuffey *Readers* and other standardized materials were introduced into the classrooms of the nation, we made gradual progress toward the goal of comprehension of material rather than simple memorization.

By the end of the nineteenth century, the nation was growing rapidly due to immigration from Europe, and cities were growing from the movement of Americans from farms to cities. The economy also was booming, and young America had matured into a modern industrial state. Once again, the curriculum of America's schools was transformed in the wake of these changes.

High schools were the first to experience these changes. Authoritarian businessmen reformers demanded that education move toward vocational training for a broad segment of society. Democratic progressives, on the other hand, maintained their support of a broad-based classical approach that would prepare students for college or university study.

As we have seen, the bitter struggle between these two approaches led to an important compromise report—*The Cardinal Principles of Secondary Education* published by the NEA in 1918. This report recognized the importance of vocational training as part of the curriculum, but it also promoted new methods of instruction including group work.

Meanwhile, a powerful intellectual transformation within education itself was taking place. Democratic progressives had begun to reconsider the role of education in American society. Visionaries such as John Dewey, William Kilpatrick, and many others saw education as the primary means of reestablishing connections between members of our fragmented society.

Innovative instructional approaches such as the open classroom, cooperative learning, and later, whole-language instruction slowly were introduced into the classroom. Moreover, with the introduction of the basal reader, our shift from memorization to understanding was complete.

And yet, the tension between authoritarian reformers and democratic progressives continued. During the 1980s and until quite recently, both curriculum and instruction moved frenetically toward a more standardized, vocational, "no frills" approach to education. The Common Core curriculum briefly fascinated these reformers, and we plunged forward with its implementation.

Today, however, the promise of a diversified, comprehensive curriculum built around established instructional techniques has once again taken hold of American educators. As we write these words, the future appears brighter.

CLASSROOM DISCIPLINE

In chapters 7 and 8 we turned from the curriculum and instruction techniques to discipline and moral education in the classroom. And once again, each of these important topics can be seen through the historical lens of social, economic, political, and cultural change.

Discipline, for example, has been one of the most contentious and controversial features of American education throughout our history, and today it continues to be divisive. Nevertheless, there has been a steady change in our attitudes regarding discipline over the years that can be summarized as a transition from corporal punishment to preventative discipline.

Our traditional attitudes toward the disciplining of children have their roots in the Bible. Imperatives such as "Spare the rod and spoil the child" and other passages in Proverbs had a dramatic effect regarding the control of children and persisted well into the nineteenth century in this country.

And yet, we have seen that four powerful developments, beginning in the eighteenth century, began to challenge these ideas. New secular ideas of John Locke and Jean-Jacques Rousseau, Johann Pestalozzi and others had a dramatic effect on our ideas regarding discipline. Each of these philosophers called for change and argued that children were not evil at birth and corrupted by original sin.

The First Great Awakening of the eighteenth century also was important in this regard. Evangelical preachers at camp meetings in frontier settlements challenged the fundamental notion of the basic depravity of humankind. Rather, they promoted a vision of personal salvation and redemption. These ideas gradually had an impact on attitudes toward children and their discipline.

The two great revolutions of the late eighteenth century and early nineteenth century also helped to change our attitudes toward the discipline of children both inside and outside the classroom. The American Revolution promoted a vision of equality as well as a new perspective on human dignity and individual freedom. The market revolution that followed embraced the merit-based society that demanded a new rationale for discipline.

The effect of new philosophical ideas, a transformation of religious beliefs, a powerful social and political revolution, and a market revolution together helped to change our world. Common school readers—notably the McGuffey *Readers*, moreover, helped to shape these new ideas. Selections in these *Readers* typically emphasized rational reasons for children to subordinate their individual interests to a higher secular authority—namely their parents, family and community. Later *Readers* focused on the importance of nationalism.

By the end of the nineteenth century, however, young America had matured into a modern industrial state, and thousands of immigrants from all over the world were making their way to this country. Their children flocked to America's public schools, and educators sought new forms of discipline to "keep order" in this new seemingly chaotic environment.

New forms of "industrial discipline" were introduced by authoritarian reformers that focused on the regimentation of children through military-like formations and standardized school architecture. These measures were successful in "quieting" classrooms, but as we have seen, democratic progressives argued that this new disciplinary focus was crushing the individuality and creativity of students.

During the early twentieth century, new scientific approaches to discipline—namely behaviorism—also were introduced into the classrooms of the nation. Here, the work of John Watson, B. F. Skinner, and others promoted ideas of positive reinforcement to encourage good behavior. Here the focus was on the use of praise for achievement and outstanding conduct with such rewards as silver and gold stars, smiley faces, and student certificates of success.

While behavior modification techniques continue to have an effect on discipline, democratic progressives argued that these approaches were simply another form of indoctrination and regimentation. Rather, they promoted what has been called the "democratic classroom," where mutual respect and trust is developed between the teacher and students.

Clearly we have made dramatic strides from the days of vicious corporal punishment of children for poor achievement and unruly behavior.

And while some communities continue to condone these forms of discipline, over the last several hundred years, we have learned that positive reinforcement, democratic classrooms, and mutual respect are more appropriate ways to handle misbehavior. We have come a long way, but as with other aspects of American education, we have a long way to go.

MORAL EDUCATION

Changes in our attitudes toward moral education—the focus of chapter 8—parallel the struggle to adopt more humane and effective forms of discipline in the classroom. As we have seen, during the colonial period and well into the nineteenth century, morality was seen as the exclusive province of the church and the family. The community as well as the artisan guilds also played an important role.

Church schools typically promoted their sectarian religious values through the memorization of a catechism. Parents reinforced these values through regular church attendance and strict adherence to a moral code. The community monitored the behavior of children outside the household, and artisan guilds demanded a set of moral principles in the workplace.

As America matured into a more complex nation, we collectively embraced the common schools to both educate and help provide a moral structure for the children of the nation. The church, the family, the community, and the workplace would continue their important roles, but gradually public schools became the centerpiece of a new moral order.

The common schools typically promoted a moral vision of respect for God and country through what was called the "virtuous balanced curriculum." Here the idea was to integrate basic academic instruction with what Noah Webster referred to as schools' "moral and social duties." Becoming a useful citizen by balancing individual desires and achievement with a sense of community and nation became the moral focus of these schools.

While the virtuous balanced curriculum was successful and seemed appropriate for children of America, democratic progressive reformers at the turn of the twentieth century offered a different approach. Visionaries like John Dewey argued that the social and political issues facing young

CONCLUSION

Americans in the new century required that they be able to deal with a wide range of complex moral dilemmas.

Dewey and other progressives recommended that teachers help students develop a "social intelligence" through group discussion, scientific reasoning, and cooperative learning. Above all, these approaches should encourage students to recognize the relative nature of morality—especially in our new emerging multicultural world.

The clash between authoritarian moral advocates and democratic progressives has raged over the years. The debate has centered on whether moral education should focus on a more traditional rigid code of absolute and inelastic values or whether students should adopt a civic approach to morality that will allow them to respond to the ambiguities and moral dilemmas they will face throughout their lives.

The bitter conflicts between these two very different approaches have become the central focus of our ongoing "culture wars." Thus, teachers and administrators are caught in the middle of political crossfire and typically have "sanitized" the curriculum to avoid further conflict and fallout from angry parents and members of the community on both sides of the debate.

Moreover, our developing obsession with competitive standardized tests and preparation for them has left little room in the day for memorizing moral codes, much less solving moral dilemmas through cooperative learning and group discussion.

As we gradually move toward a more rational appreciation of the importance of "morality"—however we define it—we can make some progress. There is room for compromise here as we end the culture wars and replace conflict with consensus.

TESTING

In chapter 9, we turn to yet another central theme in education today—testing. As we have seen, American educators have always embraced some form of testing, whether it was the recitation, the written in-class exam, or the standardized tests of today. But controversy over the correct form of testing has surrounded this "hot button" educational issue.

From the early colonial period through the first half of the nineteenth century, recitation of memorized passages was the mainstay of assessment. In New England and throughout most religious-based schools in the middle colonies and elsewhere, students sat on hard benches and prepared for the gut-wrenching experience of facing the stern schoolmaster and reciting their lessons to him.

In addition to this age-old method, a new form of assessment emerged on the American frontier and in remote rural areas—the bee! As we have seen, the bees were as much entertainment as they were important methods of assessment. Frontier folk who had few opportunities for entertainment saw these contests as community events and often traveled miles in wagons and by horseback to see the students compete.

Contests might last all day as one student after another struggled to spell a word or recite the "times tables." But those who succeeded often became local heroes of a sort, and some went on to careers as politicians and businessmen. A poor performance by the class, however, often led to ridicule of students and dismissal of teachers. This was a very serious form of assessment.

By the middle of the nineteenth century, a new form of testing—the written exam—emerged in America. As we have seen, it was first introduced by Horace Mann in 1845 as a sort of "wager" with independent schoolmasters of Massachusetts who resented any interference with their curricular or instructional techniques from the newly created educational bureaucracy.

Mann had criticized the "uneven" quality of teaching in the state and sought to prove his point with a written exam. The schoolmasters agreed, the test was administered, and Mann's predictions were confirmed and widely publicized in the October issue of *The Common School Journal*. The age of written exams had arrived.

By the end of the nineteenth century, recitation was still used in some areas, but the written appraisal of student progress became more common. Graded schoolteachers throughout the country now routinely assessed their student's achievement through spelling tests, math quizzes, and writing exercises.

Meanwhile, a new form of examination was beginning to take hold in this country—the standardized test. The turning point in this movement was the widespread administration of the Alpha test to millions of recruits during World War I. Its "success" stunned the educational establishment, and within just a few years following the end of the war in 1918, standardized tests were being distributed to millions of young children throughout the nation.

Our embrace of standardized exams had many supporters. Some authoritarian educators argued that these instruments provided an accurate measure of educational progress by using reliable scientific methods. Others saw them as a way to "sort" students and then track them into vocational or college preparatory programs.

Democratic progressives also accepted these exams. Some saw them as a way to "level the playing field" and provide gifted students with an opportunity to enter colleges or universities. And still others perceived these exams as a diagnostic tool to identify learning problems in students that could be addressed and corrected at an early age.

Whatever their reasons, the standardized exam quickly became a central part of the educational experience. Standardized entrance exams were developed for college admissions; they were used as a measure of educational progress and as the basis of certification in various fields. By the end of the twentieth century, standardized exams were routinely administered as high-stakes end-of-year assessments used to evaluate the "success" of schools, teachers, and students.

The testing movement reached a crescendo in 2001 with the passage of the No Child Left Behind Act. This law mandated the use of standardized tests throughout America's public schools. These exams were expected to motivate students and teachers to achieve at a higher level. Those schools that did not perform well on these exams were subjected to punitive measures including possible closure with their students transferring to better, higher performing schools.

Today, however, many Americans are reconsidering this reckless use of standardized exams in the schools. Students and teachers have become alienated, teachers are forced to "teach to the exam," and the confidence in American public education has been severely damaged.

With the recent passage of the All Children Succeed Act in 2015, there has been an important change in the direction of assessment. We are cautiously optimistic that this new law will signal a shift in policy that will help to empower teachers and return testing to the classroom where it belongs.

RIGHTS AND RESPONSIBILITIES

Our final stop on this long journey through the history of American education centers on the rights and responsibilities of teachers and students. In chapter 10, we revisited the important struggles of women, African Americans, and immigrants in achieving basic human rights both inside and outside the classroom.

We then shifted our attention to the question of individual legal rights of students and teachers, focusing on the turbulent 1960s and 1970s, when we made dramatic progress moving from a mentality of *in loco parentis* to individual rights and responsibilities.

Like other themes in American education history, this struggle centered on the restrictions imposed on teachers and students, especially at the local level. It was in this aspect that women, African Americans, and immigrants were excluded from attending public schools for decades. Women eventually could attend common schools during the nineteenth century—though secondary and postsecondary education would only come much later.

Former African slaves and black freedmen were routinely excluded by law or custom after emancipation and struggled throughout much of the twentieth century to achieve equal rights. Immigrants, on the other hand, were "allowed" to attend school throughout this period but were often ridiculed and subjected to violence because of their appearance, customs, or language.

Very slowly, over the course of the late nineteenth century and into the twentieth century, some progress was made. Rights were not just secured from above but were hard won through individual struggle, organization, and eventually, democratic, progressive legislation and court decisions.

But admittance to schools across the land was one thing—achieving basic legal rights was another. As we have seen, schools typically embraced the authoritarian idea of *in loco parentis* and treated students of all ages, gender, races, and ethnic origins as children.

Corporal punishment remained a constant feature of most school experiences well into the twentieth century and remains legal in some communities today. In fact, about a third of a million students are physically punished each year in American public schools!

Until recently, students did not have basic constitutional rights such as due process and could not sue for damages. They also had no access to their personal records, including test scores, grades, and health and attendance records as well records of teachers' comments and disciplinary actions.

Moreover, students were denied equal protection under the law. Students had no protection from unlawful search and seizure and were not allowed in disciplinary hearings to "tell their side of the story." Finally, students typically were denied the right of free speech or expression and could be suspended and even dismissed if they spoke, wrote, or acted "inappropriately."

Throughout the turbulent 1960s and 1970s, students and democratic progressive reformers began to challenge many of these accepted legal precedents. The right of due process was affirmed by the court in the *Goss Lopez* decision in 1975. Strip searches were forbidden under the *Bellinger* decision in 1977. And, under the *Tinker* decision of 1969, students are now allowed to peacefully protest.

And yet, there also have been setbacks and limitations on student rights. The *Veronia* decision of 1995 granted schools the right to conduct random drug tests on athletes, and the 2002 *Earls* decision expanded a school's legal right to test for drugs.

Many of the constitutional rights of students that have been affirmed by the court affect teachers as well. For example, teachers are now allowed to remain in the classroom even if they become pregnant. The important *LaFleur* decision of 1974 guaranteed that right under Title IX legislation.

Similarly, teachers have some protection from being fired on the spot by provisions of the *Goss* decision of 1975. Moreover, under the *Pickering* decision of 1968, teachers have the right to criticize administrative polices without the threat of being fired.

In other legal matters, however, teachers have not fared as well. They have the right to join labor organization such as the NEA and the AFT and engage in collective bargaining. However, because of the *Hortonville* decision of 1976, the right of the state to declare strikes illegal has been upheld. As a result, teacher strikes are legal in only eleven of the fifty states.

On the other hand, teachers generally have a great deal of academic freedom. The court has ruled again and again that a classroom is a "marketplace of ideas." For example, under the *Cary* decision of 1977, teachers cannot be forced to read a prepared script as part of their instruction of students. And yet, some states strictly forbid the teaching of evolution and about family planning, birth control, abortion, and sexually transmitted diseases.

Finally, the court has typically protected teachers from legal liability, especially in cases of malpractice (not providing a student with an education that allows him or her to get a job). However, teachers will face consequences with regard to misfeasance (failure to act appropriately), nonfeasance (failure to perform assigned teaching duties), and malfeasance (breaking the law).

The legal and constitutional history of American education is complex and ever changing. The struggle for basic human, civil, and legal rights for both students and teachers from the arbitrary whims of local communities and state legislatures remains a constant struggle, and we must remain vigilant.

Our journey is now complete. We have addressed the basic themes in American educational history and have seen the complexities of change. Moreover, we have seen how the struggle between authoritarian and democratic educators and reformers has shaped those changes. And yet, the story of educational history is not over. Each generation of new teachers will face these important issues throughout their careers and struggle to adapt to them.

Nevertheless, we hope this book has helped to equip teachers, parents, and the educational village with the tools necessary to change the world, one child at a time.

REFERENCES

Adler, M. J. (1982). *The Paideia Proposal: An Educational Manifesto*. New York: Macmillan.
Adler, M. J., C. Fadiman, and P. W., Goetz (Eds.). (1990). *Great Books of the Western World* (second edition). Chicago: Britannica.
Alspaugh, J. (1994). The Relationship between School Size, Student Teacher Ratio, and School Efficiency. *Education* 114(4): 593–97.
Arnez, N. (1976, Spring). Desegregation of Public Schools: A Discriminatory Process. *Journal of Afro-American Issues* 4, 274–82.
Astell, M. (1700). *Some Reflections upon Marriage*. London: John Nutt Publisher.
Axtell, J. (1974). *The School upon a Hill: Education and Society in Colonial New England*. New Haven, CT: Yale University Press.
Bagley, W. ([1907] 1925). *Classroom Management*. New York: Macmillan.
Barker, R., and P. Gump. (1964). *Big Schools, Small Schools*. Palo Alto, CA: Stanford University Press.
Bennett, W. J. (1993). *The Book of Virtues: A Treasury of Great Moral Stories*. New York: Simon & Schuster.
Berry, C., and M. West (2010). Growing Pains: The School Consolidation Movement and Student Outcomes. *Journal of Law, Economics, and Organization* 26, 1–29.
Bethel School District v. Fraser. (1986). www.law.cornell.edu.
Binder, F. (1970). *Education in the History of Western Civilization, Selected Readings*. New York: Macmillan.
Blackwell Museum of History of Education, Northern Illinois University, Dekalb, IL. www.cedu.niu.edu/blackwell/books.html.
Board of Education v. Earls. (2002). www.law.cornell.edu.
Board of Education v. Mergens. (1990). www.law.cornell.edu.
Bobbitt, J. F. (1909). Practical Eugenics. *The Pedagogical Seminary* 16(3): 385–94.
Bobbitt, J. F. (1912, February). The Elimination of Waste in Education. *The Elementary School Teacher*.
Bracey, G. W. (2004). *Setting the Record Straight: Responses to Misconceptions about Public Education in the U.S.* Portsmouth, NH: Heinemann.
Brock, J. (1987, July–August). Bigness Is the Problem, Not the Solution. *Challenge* 30.
Bronner, E. (1962). *William Penn's Holy Experiment: The Founding of Pennsylvania, 1681–1701.* New York: Temple University Publication. (Distributed by Columbia University Press.)
Burkey v. Marshall County Board of Education. (1981). www.law.cornell.edu.
Burton, W. (1852). *The District School as It Was*. Boston: T. R. Marvin.

Callahan, R. (1962). *Education and the Cult of Efficiency*. Chicago: University of Chicago Press.
Cardinal Principles of Secondary Education: A Report of the Commission on the Reorganization of Secondary Education. (1918). Appointed by the National Education Association. Bulletin, 1918, No. 35. Washington, DC: Department of the Interior, Bureau of Education.
Cary v. Board of Education (1977). www.law.cornell.edu.
Casement, W. (1984, Winter). Moral Education: Form Without Consent? *Educational Forum* 48, 177–90.
Cattell, J. (1890). Mental Tests and Measurements. *Mind* 15, 373–81.
Cecelski, D. S. (1994). *Along Freedom Road: Hyde County, North Carolina and the Fate of Black Schools in the South.* Chapel Hill, NC: University of North Carolina Press.
Chandler, A. D. (1962). *Strategy and Structure: Chapters in the History of the Industrial Enterprise.* Cambridge, MA: MIT Press.
Chandler, A. D. (1977). *The Visible Hand: The Managerial Revolution in American Business.* Cambridge, MA: Belknap Press.
Chicago Tribune. (1902, October 27) Truant Officers Raid Ghetto.
Child Trends. (2015, December 14). *Huffington Post.*
Clark v. Haworth. (1890). State Supreme Court of Indiana, 23 N.E. at 948.
Clarke, M., G. F. Madaus, C. J. Horn, and M. A. Ramos. (2000). Retrospective on Educational Testing and Assessment in the 20th Century. *Journal of Curriculum Studies* 32(2): 159–81.
Cleveland Board of Education v. LaFleur. (1974) www.law.cornell.edu .
Clinton, W. J. (1996, January 23). *Address before a Joint Session of the Congress on the State of the Union.* www.presidency.UCSB.edu/ws.
Cohen, S. (1974a). *A History of Colonial Education: 1607–1776.* New York: Wiley.
Cohen, S. (1974b). *Education in the United States: A Documentary History* (Vol. 3). New York: Random House.
College Board. (2010). *2010 SAT Trends.* [Electronic version.]
Collins, R. (1979). *The Credential Society: An Historical Sociology of Education and Stratification.* New York: Academic Press.
Committee of Ten on Secondary School Studies: With Reports of the Conferences Arranged by the Committee. (1892). National Education Association of the United States. Washington, DC: American Book Co.
Conant, J. (1940, May). Education for a Classless Society. *The Atlantic.*
Conant, J. (1943, May 3). Wanted American Radicals. *The Atlantic.*
Constitution of the State of Connecticut, 1818. (1818) (Article Eighth).
Cotton, K. (1996). School Size, School Climate, and Student Performance. *School Improvement Research Series, Close-Up #20.* Retrieved March 1, 2012, from http://www.nwrel.org/scpd/sirs/10/cO20.html.
Cuban, L. (1984). *How Teachers Taught: Constancy and Change in American Classrooms, 1890–1980.* New York: Longman.
Cuban, L. (2004). *The Blackboard and the Bottom Line: Why Schools Can't be Businesses.* Cambridge, MA: Harvard University Press.
Cubberley, E. P. (1916). *Public School Administration.* Boston: Houghton Mifflin.
Cubberley, E. P. (1919). *Public Education in the United States.* Boston: Houghton Mifflin.
Cubberley, E. P., and E. C. Elliott. (1915). *State and County School Administration.* New York: Macmillan.
Dee, T., and B. Jacob. (2010, Summer). Evaluating NCLB. *Education Next* 10(3): 1–9.
Demetriou, A., M. Shayer, and A. Efklides. (1992). *Neo Piagetian Theories of Cognitive Development: Implications and Applications to Education.* London: Routledge.
Dewey, J. (1899). *School and Society.* Chicago: University of Chicago Press (21st impression, 1965).
Dewey, J. (1909). *Moral Principles in Education.* Boston: Houghton Mifflin.
Dewey, J. (1916). *Democracy and Education: An Introduction to the Philosophy of Education.* New York: Macmillan.
Dewey, J., and E. Dewey. (1915). *Schools of To-Morrow.* New York: E. P. Dutton & Co.

REFERENCES

Dinwiddy, J. (1982). The Nineteenth Century Campaign against Flogging in the Army. *English Historical Review* 97, 308–33.
Draper, A. S. (1909). *American Education*. Boston, MA: Houghton Mifflin. (Reprinted by ULAN Press, n.d.)
Drucker, P. (1954). *The Practice of Management*. New York: HarperBusiness.
Drug Abuse Resistance Education (DARE). (1995). (Describes the DARE school program.) www.ncjrs.gov/pdffiles/darefs.pdf.
DuBois, W. E. B. (1903). *The Souls of Black Folk*. Cambridge, MA: University Press John Wilson and Son.
Dutton, S. T., and D. Snedden. (1912). *The Administration of Public Education in the United States*. New York: Macmillan.
Educational Testing Service. (1999a). *PRAXIS—Tests at a Glance* (various disciplines). Princeton, NJ: Educational Testing Service.
Educational Testing Service. (1999b). *PRAXIS II—Subject Assessments Study Guide*. Princeton, NJ: Educational Testing Service.
Educational Testing Service. (1999c). *PRAXIS II—Test Preparation Workshop*. Princeton, NJ: Educational Testing Service.
Engle v. Vitale. (1962). www.law.cornell.edu.
Every Student Succeeds Act (ESSA). (2015). www.ed.gov .
Fabricant, M. (2012). *Charter Schools and the Corporate Makeover of Public Education: What's at Stake?* New York: Teachers College Press.
Fairbanks, Mrs. A. W. (1898). *Emma Williard and Her Pupils: Or 50 Years of Troy Female Seminary, 1822–1872*. New York: Mrs. R. Sage.
Fancher, R. E. (1985). *The Intelligence Men, Makers of the I.Q. Controversy*. New York: Norton.
Fischer, L., D. Schimmel, and C. Kelly. (1973). *The Civil Rights of Teachers*. New York: Harper and Row.
Fish, S. (1994). *There's No Such Thing as Free Speech and It's a Good Thing Too*. New York: Oxford University Press.
Ford, P. ([1897] 1962). *The New England Primer: A History of Its Origin and Development*. New York: Teachers College Press.
Forrest, D. W. (1974). *Francis Galton: The Life and Work of a Victorian Genius*. New York: Taplinger Publishing.
Foucault, M. (1977). *Discipline and Punish*. New York: Pantheon.
Fowler, W., and H. Walberg. (1991, Summer). School Size, Characteristics and Outcomes. *Educational Evaluation and Policy Analysis* 13(2): 189–202.
Fox, W. (1981, Winter). Reviewing Economies of Size in Education. *Journal of Education Finance* 60(3): 273–96.
Frank, J. (2013, January 29). McCrory Wants to Revamp Higher Ed Funding—Takes Aim at UNC–Chapel Hill. *News and Observer.com/Under the Dome*. http://projects.newsobserver.com/under_the_dome/mccrory_wants_to_revamp_higher_ed_funding_takes_aim_at_uncchapel_Hill .
Franklin v. Guinnett. (1992). www.law.cornell.edu.
Freeman, F. N. (1939). *Mental Tests, Their History, Principles and Applications*. Boston, MA: Houghton Mifflin.
Friedkin, N., and J. Necochea. (1988). School Systems Size and Performance: A Contingency Perspective. *Educational Evaluation and Policy Analysis* 10(3): 237–49.
Galton, F. (1869). *Hereditary Genius: An Inquiry into Its Laws and Consequences*. London: Macmillan.
Galton, F. (1874). *English Men of Science: Their Nature and Nurture*. London: MacMillan.
Galton, F. (1875). Short Notes on Heredity in Twins. *Journal of the Royal Anthropological Institute*.
Galton, F. (1908). *Inquiries into Human Faculty and Its Development*. London: J. M. Dent & Co.
Galton, F. (1909). *Essays in Eugenics*. London: Eugenics Education Society.

Gardner, H. (2000). *The Disciplined Mind: Beyond Facts and Standardized Tests, The K–12 Education That Every Child Deserves.* New York: Penguin Putnam.
Gerwig, G. W. (1918). *Schools with a Perfect Score, Democracy's Hope and Safeguard.* New York: Macmillan.
Gladden, R. (1998). The Small School Movement: A Review of the Literature. In *Small Schools, Big Imaginations: A Creative Look at Urban Public Schools.* Edited by M. Fine and J. Sommerville. Chicago: Cross City Campaign for Urban School Reform.
Glasser, W. (1965). *Reality Therapy: A New Approach to Psychiatry.* New York: Harper & Row.
Glasser, W. (1969). *Schools Without Failure.* New York: Harper & Row.
Glasser, W. (1977). Ten Steps to Good Discipline. *Today's Education* 6(1): 23–24.
Goddard, H. H. (1912). *The Kallikak Family: A Study in the Heredity of Feeble-Mindedness.* New York: Macmillan.
Goddard, H. H. (1917). Mental Tests and the Immigrant. *Journal of Delinquency* 2, 243–77.
Goddard, H. H. (1926). *Feeble-Mindedness, Its Causes and Consequences.* New York: Macmillan.
Goldin, C. D., and L. Katz. (2008). *The Race between Education and Technology.* Boston: Harvard University Press.
Goodlad, J. L. (1984). *A Place Called School: Prospects for the Future.* New York: McGraw-Hill.
Goss v. Lopez. (1975). www.cornell.law.edu.
Gould, S. J. (1991). *The Mismeasure of Man.* New York: W. W. Norton & Co.
Green, J., and D. Barnes. (1993). *Discipline in Secondary Schools: How Administrators Deal with Misconduct* (Tech. Rep. No. ERIC Document Reproduction Service No. ED 357 507).
Greenwald, R., L. Hedges, and R. Laine. (1996). The Effect of School Resources on Student Achievement. *Review of Educational Research* 66(3): 361–96.
Gregory, T. (1992). Small Is Too Big: Achieving a Critical Anti-Mass in the High School. Hubert H. Humphrey Institute of Public Affairs. File: Report No RC 019 319. Minnesota University, Minneapolis, MN.
Gue, B. (1962) *Diary of Benjamin F. Gue in Rural New York and Pioneer Iowa, 1847–1856.* Edited by Earle D. Ross. Ames: Iowa State University Press.
Haller, E. (1992). High School Size and Student Discipline: Another Aspect of the School Consolidation Issue? *Education Evaluation and Policy Analysis* 14(2): 145–56.
Hanson, F. (1994). *Testing Testing: Social Consequences of the Examined Life.* Berkeley and Los Angeles: University of California Press.
Heatwole, C. (1916). *A History of Education in Virginia.* New York: Macmillan.
Herbart, J. (1904). *An Introduction to Herbart's Science and Practice of Education.* Translated by H. M. Felkin and E. Felkin. Boston: D. C. Heath.
Hewett, E. (1884). *A Treatise on Pedagogy for Young Teachers.* Cincinnati: Van Antwerp.
Higham, J. ([1970] 1988). *Strangers in the Land, Patterns of American Nativism, 1860–1925.* New Brunswick, NJ: Rutgers University Press.
Hillway, T. (1964). *American Education: An Introduction through Readings.* Boston: Houghton Mifflin.
Holy Bible: Containing the Old and New Testaments, King James Version. (1975). Nashville, TN: National Publishing.
Horner, H. H. (1934). *The Life and Work of Andrew Sloan Draper.* Urbana: University of Illinois Press.
Hortonville Joint School District v. Hortonville Education Association. (1976). www.cornell.law.edu.
Howley, C. (1994). The Academic Effectiveness of Small-Scale Schooling: An Update (ERIC—Document Reproductive Service No. 372 897) [Abstract]. ERIC Clearinghouse of Rural Education and Small Schools.
Jacobs, J. (1961). *Death and Life of Great American Cities.* New York: Random House.
James, W. ([1890] 1950). *Principles of Psychology.* New York: Dover.
Johnson, C. (1963). *Old-Time Schools and School Books.* New York: Dover.

REFERENCES

Johnson, D. W. (1994). *Learning Together and Alone: Cooperative, Competitive and Individualistic Learning.* Needham Heights, MA: Allyn and Bacon.
Johnson, D. W., and R. Johnson. (1989). *Cooperation and Competition: Theory and Research.* Edina, MN: Interaction Books.
Johnson, D. W., and R. Johnson. (1991). Classroom Instruction and Cooperative Learning. In *Effective Teaching: Current Research.* Edited by H. Waxman and H. Walberg, 277–93. Berkeley, CA: McCutchan.
Johnson, R. (1985, Winter). Schoolman among Scholars: Andrew S. Draper at the University of Illinois, 1894–1904. *Illinois Historical Journal* 78(4): 257–72.
Joncich, G. M. (1968). *The Sane Positivist: A Biography of Edward L. Thorndike.* Middletown, CT: Wesleyan University Press.
Justia, Inc. (2006). *Louisiana Laws Title 17—Education: RS17:416.12—Section B.*
Kaestle, C. (Ed.). (1973). *Joseph Lancaster and the Monitorial School Movement: A Documentary History.* New York: Teachers College Press.
Kaufman, P. (1984). *Women on the Frontier.* New Haven, CT: Yale University Press.
Kennedy, D. (1980). *Over Here: The First World War in American Society.* New York: Oxford University Press.
Kevles, D. (1968, December). Testing the Army's Intelligence: Psychologists and the Military in the First World War. *Journal of American History*, 565–81.
Kevles, D. (1985). *In the Name of Eugenics: Genetics and the Uses of Human Heredity.* NY: Alfred A. Knopf.
Kidd, T. (2009). *The Great Awakening: The Roots of Evangelical Christianity in Colonial America.* New Haven, CT: Yale University Press.
Kilpatrick, W. (1918). *The Project Method.* New York: Teachers College Press.
Kliebard, H. (1987). *The Struggle for the American Curriculum, 1893–1958.* Boston: Routledge & Kegan Paul.
Kohlberg, L. (1975). Moral Education for a Society in Moral Transition. *Educational Leadership* 33, 46–54.
Kohn, A. (2007, May 31). Too Destructive to Salvage. *USA Today.*
Kozol, J. (1992, September). Whittle and the Privateers. *The Nation*, 272–78.
Krug, E. A. (1972). *The Shaping of the American High School, 1880–1920* (Vol. 1). New York: Praeger.
Lambs Chapel v. Center Moriches Union Free School. (1993). www.law.cornell.edu.
Larabee, D. (1986, January). Curriculum, Credentials, and the Middle Class: A Case Study of a Nineteenth Century High School. *Sociology of Education* 59(1): 42–57.
Lawrence, I., G. W. Rigol, T. VanEssen, and C. A. Jackson. (2002). A Historical Perspective on the SAT: 1926–2001. Research Report No. 2002-7: College Entrance Examination Board.
Lee v. Weisman. (1992). www.law.cornell.edu.
Lee, V. E., and J. B. Smith. (1997). High School Size: Which Works Best and for Whom? *Educational Evaluation and Policy Analysis* 19(3): 205–27.
Locke, J. ([1705] 1968). Some Thoughts Concerning Education. In *The Educational Writings of John Locke.* Edited by James Axtell. Cambridge: Cambridge University Press.
Lumsdaine, A. (1947). Experimental Research and the Improvement of Teaching Films. *Educational Screen* 26, 254–55.
Luther, S. (1836). *An Address to the Workingmen of New England on the State of Education.* Boston: Author.
Maddison, A. The World Economy: A Millennial Perspective. (2001). File: Tables A-1-c; A-1d. Paris: OECD.
Mann, H. (1841, January). Education. *The North American Review* 52(110), 148–91.
Marcus, J. (2014, February 6). New Analysis Shows Problematic Boom in Higher Ed Administrators. *New England Center for Investigative Reporting.*
Marland, S. (1971, April). The Condition of Education in the Nation. *American Education* 7.
McClellan, B. (1992). *Schools and the Shaping of Character: Moral Education in America, 1607 – Present.* Bloomington, IN: Educational Resources Clearing House.

McCluskey, N. (Ed.). (1964). *Catholic Education in America: A Documentary History*. New York: Bureau of Publications, Teachers College Press.
McGuffey, W. (1836/1982a). *The Eclectic First Reader*. Cincinnati: Mott Media.
McGuffey, W. (1836/1982b). *The Eclectic Second Reader*. Milford, MI: Mott Media.
McGuffey, W. (1879/1962). *Fifth Eclectic Reader*. New York: Signet Classics.
McKenzie, F. A. (1901). *The American Invaders: Their Plans, Tactics and Progress*. New York: Street and Smith, Publishers.
Meier, D. (1996, September). The Big Benefits of Smallness. *Educational Leadership* 54, 12–15.
Michigan Supreme Court. (1875). *Charles E. Stuart and Others v. School District no. 1 of the Village of Kalamazoo and Others*. http://education.stateuniversity.com/pages2579/Appendix III.
Monk, D. (1987). Secondary School Size and Curriculum Comprehensiveness. *Economics of Education Review* 6(2): 187–50.
Monroe, P. (1901). *Source Book of the History of Education*. New York: Macmillan.
Montessori, M. (1912). *The Montessori Method: Scientific Pedagogy*. New York: Fredrick Stokes Co.
Murphy, M. (1990). *Blackboard Unions: The AFT and the NEA, 1900–1980*. Ithaca, NY: Cornell University Press.
Nachtigal, P. M. (1994). High School Size. *Educational Evaluation and Policy Analysis*, 205–27.
National Association of the United States. Dept. of Supervisors and Directors of Instruction. (1931). *The Evaluation of Supervision*. New York: Bureau of Publications, Teachers College, Columbia University.
National Board of Professional Teaching Standards—Survey. (2013). D. H. Parkerson and J. Parkerson. Various Teachers.
National Center for Education Statistics. (1982). *High School and Beyond 1980: Sophomore Cohort* [Data File users' manual]. Washington, DC.
National Commission on Excellence in Education. (1983). *A Nation at Risk: The Imperative for Educational Reform*. Washington, DC: Government Printing Office.
National Education Association. (1895). Report of the Sub-Committee on the Organization of City School Systems. In *Journal of Addresses and Proceedings of the National Education Association, 1895*.
National Education Association. (1911). *Proceedings*. Department of Superintendence, Ed.
National Education Association. (1951). *Moral and Spiritual Values in the Public Schools*. Washington, DC: National Education Association.
National Education Association Papers. (1966, August 19). Minutes of the Meeting between Hyde County Board of Education and the Team from the Office of Education of HEW.
National Education Association Proceedings. (1911). Departments of Superintendents, Ed.
National Education Association Proceedings. (1912). Department of Superintendents, Ed.
Nelson, E. (1995). School Consolidation. *ERIC Digest—Clearinghouse on Educational Management*, *13*(ED282346).
New American Schools Development Corporation. (1991). *Design for a New Generation of American Schools*. Arlington, VA: New American Schools Development Corporation (NASDC).
New Jersey State. (1844). *New Jersey State Constitution of 1844*. http://www.state.nj.us/state/archives/docconst44.html.
New Jersey v. T.L.O. (1985). www.law.cornell.edu.
New York State Education Department. U.S. Department of Education. New York State Archives Educational Policy Research. http://www.NYSED.gov.
New York State Times. (1904). School Reform (series of articles).
New York Times. (1904, April 8). State Education Plan Provides Big Shakeup.
Noble, S. (1955). *A History of Education* (revised edition). New York: Rinehart & Co.
No Child Left Behind Act. (2001). www2.ed.gov/nclb.

Northend, C. (1853). *The Teacher and the Parent: Treatise Upon Common School Education. Containing Practical Suggestions to Teachers and Parents.* Boston: Jenks, Hickling & Swan.
Oliphant, J. (Ed.). (1903). The Educational Writings of Richard Mulcaster. Glasgow: n.p.
Overbury, A. (2003, February). School Size: A Review of the Literature. *Research Watch.*
Page, D. (1867). *Theory and Practice of Teaching.* New York: American Book Company.
Parker, F. (1883). *Notes of Talks on Teaching: Given by Francis W. Parker, at the Martha's Vineyard Summer Institute, July 17 to August 19, 1882.* Translated and reported by Lelia E. Patridge. New York: E. L. Kellogg.
Parkerson, D. H., and J. Parkerson. (1998). *The Emergence of the Common School in the U.S. Countryside.* Lewiston, NY: The Edwin Mellon Press.
Parkerson, D. H., and J. Parkerson. (2001). *Transitions in American Education.* New York: RoutledgeFalmer.
Parkerson, D. H., and J. Parkerson. (2008). *The American Teacher.* New York: Routledge.
Patridge, L. (1885). A Disciple of Francis W. Parker on the Distinguishing Features of the Quincy Schools. In *Education in the United States: A Documentary History. Vol. 3. 1814–15.* Edited by Sol Cohen. New York: Random House.
Pavlov, I. (1923). *Lectures on Conditional Reflexes.*
Pearson, K. (1924). *The Life, Letters and Labours of Francis Galton: Volume 1.* Cambridge: Cambridge University Press.
Pearson, K. (1930a). *The Life, Letters and Labours of Francis Galton: Volume 2.* Cambridge: Cambridge University Press.
Pearson, K. (1930b). *The Life, Letters and Labours of Francis Galton: Volume 3.* Cambridge: Cambridge University Press.
Perkins, L. (1989). The History of Blacks in Teaching: Growth and Decline Within the Profession. In *American Teachers: Histories of a Profession at Work.* Edited by Donald Warren, 344–69. New York: Macmillan.
Pestalozzi, J. (1894). *How Gertrude Teaches Her Children.* Edited by Ebenezer Cooke, translated by Lucy E. Holland and Francis C. Turner. London.
Pestalozzi, J. ([1781] 1901). *Leonard and Gertrude.* Edited and translated by Eva Channing. Lexington, MA: D. C. Heath.
Piaget, J. (1926). *The Language and Thought of the Child.* London: Routledge and Kegan Paul.
Pickering v. Board of Education. (1968). www.law.cornell.edu.
Potter, A. (1842). *The School and the Schoolmaster: A Manual for the Use of Teachers, Employers, Trustees, Inspectors, Etc., of Common Schools, Pt. 1.* New York: Harper & Brothers.
Ramirez, A. (1992). Size, Cost and Quality of Schools and School Districts: A Question of Context. [Abstract]. In *Source Book on School and District Size, Cost and Quality.* Report No. RC 019 318): ERIC Document Reproduction Service No. ED 361 162.
Randall, S. S. (1871). *History of the Common School System of the State of New York.* Chicago: Ivison, Blakeman, Taylor Co.
Raths, L., M. Harmin, and S. Simon. (1966). *Values and Teaching.* Columbus, OH: Charles E. Merrill.
Ravitch, D. (1978). A Wasted Decade for Urban Educators. *Education Digest* 43(5): 2–4.
Reese, W. J. (2005). *America's Public Schools: From the Common School to "No Child Left Behind."* Baltimore: Johns Hopkins University Press.
Regents of the University of California v. Bakke. http://www.law.umkc.edu/faculty/projects/ftrials/conlaw/bakke.html.
Reiner, J. (1982). The Republican Child: Attitudes and Practices in Post-Revolutionary Philadelphia. *William & Mary Quarterly* 39(3): 150–63.
Report on Violence in Public Schools. (2000, April). Justice Policy Institute.
Reynolds, D. R. (1999). *There Goes the Neighborhood: Rural School Consolidation at the Grass Roots in Early Twentieth-Century Iowa.* Iowa City: University of Iowa Press.
Rickover, H. (1959). *Education and Freedom.* London: Dutton.
Rickover, H. (1963). *American Education, a National Failure: The Problem of Our Schools and What We Can Learn from England.* London: Dutton.

Rousmaniere, K. (1997). *City Teachers: Teaching and School Reform in Historical Perspective*. New York: Teachers College Press.
Rousseau, J. (1974). *Emile*. Translated by Barbara Foxley. London: Everyman's Library.
Rudolph, F. (1962). *The American College and University: A History*. New York: Alfred A. Knopf.
Schmooker, J. (1972). *Patents, Invention and Economic Change: Data and Selected Essays*. Cambridge, MA: Harvard University Press.
Schubert, W. (1986). *Curriculum: Perspective, Paradigm and Possibility*. New York: Macmillan.
Schumacker, E. (1989). *Small Is Beautiful: Economics As If People Mattered*. New York: HarperCollins.
Scott, C. (1908). *Social Education*. Boston: n.p.
Selden, S. (1999). *Inheriting Shame: The Story of Eugenics and Racism in America*. New York: Teachers College Press.
Sizer, T. (1984). *Horace's Compromise*. New York: Houghton Mifflin.
Skinner, B. F. (1951). *Science and Human Behavior*. Boston: Houghton Mifflin.
Skinner, B. F. (1954). The Science of Learning and the Art of Teaching. *Harvard Educational Review* 24, 86.
Skinner, B. F. (1971). *Beyond Freedom and Dignity*. New York: Alfred A. Knopf.
Slate, J. R., and C. H. Jones. (2012). Effects of School Size: A Review of the Literature with Recommendations. www.usca.edu.essays/vol132005/state.pdf.
Slavin, R. (1988). Cooperative Revolution Catches Fire. *School Administration* 45(9–13).
Small, W. (1969). *Early New England Schools*. New York: Arno Press and the *New York Times*.
Smith, A. (1976a). *An Inquiry into the Wealth of Nations: Vol 1*. Edited by R. Campbell and A. Skinner. Oxford: Oxford University Press.
Smith, A. (1976b). *An Inquiry into the Wealth of Nations: Vol 2*. Edited by R. Campbell and A. Skinner. Oxford: Oxford University Press.
Smith, J. (1860, June 30). The Huxley-Wilberforce Debate on Evolution. *BRANCH: Britain, Representation and Nineteenth Century History*. Retrieved on December 13, 2013, from http://www.branchcollective.org.
Social Welfare History Project. (2013). Elementary and Secondary Education Act of 1965.
Sprinthall, N. (1979). Learning Psychology by Doing Psychology: A High School Curriculum in the Psychology of Counseling. In *Adolescents' Development and Education*. Edited by R. Mosher. Berkeley, CA: McCutchan.
State Control of Schools—Principle Established by a Decision in the Watervilet Case. (1897, December 5). *New York Times*.
State of Indiana—Constitution (1851) (1). http://www.law.indiana.edu/uslawdocs/inconst.html.
Stowe, S. (1887). *History of Mount Hollyoke Seminary, South Hadley, Massachuetts During the First Half-Century*. South Hadley, MA: n.p.
Strober, M., and A. Langford. (1986, Winter). The Feminization of Public School Teaching: A Cross-Sectional Analysis. *Signs* 11(2): 212–35.
Strober, M., and D. Tyack. (1980, Spring). Why Do Women Teach and Men Manage?: A Report on Research on Schools. *Signs* 5(3): 494–503.
Swanson, A. (1988). The Matter of Size: A Review of the Research on Relationships between School and District Size, Pupil Achievement and Cost. *Research in Rural Education* 5(2): 1–8.
Swift, F. H. (1911). *A History of Public Permanent Common School Funds in the United States, 1795–1905*. New York: Henry Holt and Company.
Taylor, F. W. (1911). *The Principles of Scientific Management*. New York: Harper.
Taylor, F. W. (1972). *Scientific Management: Comprising Shop Management, the Principles of Scientific Management [and] Testimony before the Special House Committee*. Westport, CT: Greenwood Press.

REFERENCES

Terman, L. M. (1916). *Measurement of Intelligence: An Explanation of and a Complete Guide for the use of the Stanford Revision of the Binet Simon Intelligence Scale.* Boston: Houghton Mifflin.
Thompson, E. P. (1967, December). Time, Work, Discipline and Industrial Capitalism. *Past and Present* 38, 56–97.
Thomson, K. (2000, May–June). Huxley, Wilberforce and the Oxford Museum. *American Scientist* 88(3): 210–13.
Thorndike, E. (1898, June 2). Animal Intelligence: An Experimental Study of the Associative Processes of Animals. *Psychological Review—Monograph Supplements.*
Tinker v. Des Moines. (1969). www.law.cornell.edu.
Tocqueville, A. de. ([1835] 1838). *Democracy in America.* Translated by H. Reeve, Esq. New York: George Dearborn & Company.
Tomlinson, S. (2005). *Head Masters: Phrenology, Secular Education, and Nineteenth-Century Social Thought.* Tuscaloosa: University of Alabama Press.
Tyack, D. (1974). *The One Best System.* Cambridge, MA: Harvard University Press.
U.S. Census (Government Printing Office). (1862). *Preliminary Report of the Eighth Census* (p. 19). Washington, DC: Government Printing Office.
U.S. Department of Education, Office for Civil Rights. (2002) 2002 Elementary and Secondary School Civil Rights Compliance Report. www.stophitting.com/disatschool/statesBanning.php.
Veronia v. Acton. (1995). www.law.cornell.edu.
Walberg, H. J. (1992). On Local Control: Is Bigger Better? In *Source Book on School and District Size, Cost and Quality.* Report No RC 019 324 No. Report No. RC 019 318. Minneapolis: Hubert H. Humphrey Institute of Public Affairs.
Walberg, H. J., and H. J. Walberg III. (1994). Losing Local Control. *Educational Researcher* 23(5): 19–26.
Wallace v. Jaffree, (1985). www.law.cornell.edu.
Ward, L. (1935). *Young Ward's Diary.* Edited by Vernhard J. Stern. New York: Macmillan.
Washington, B. T. (1974). *Booker T. Washington Papers: Volume 3.* Edited by L. R. Harland, 583–87. Urbana: University of Illinois Press.
Watson, J. (1924). *Behaviorism.* New York: W. W. Norton.
Webster, N. (1790). *A Collection of Essays and Fugitiv Writings on Moral, Historical, Political and Literaty Subjects.* Boston: Delmar; New York: Scholars Facsimiles and Reprints 1977.
Wechsler, D. (1940). Non-Intellective Factors in General Intelligence. *Psychological Bulletin,* 37, 444–45.
Whipple, G. M. (1921, June). The National Intelligence Tests. *The Journal of Educational Research* 43(1): 16031.
White, K. (1999). Girls' Sports: The Best of Times, the Worst of Times. *Education Week* 19(7): 6.
Wood v. Strickland. (1975). www.law.cornell.edu .
Woodson, C. (1968). *The African Background Outlined: Or the Handbook for the Study of the Negro.* New York: Negro Universities Press.
Woody, T. (1929). *A History of Women's Education in the United States* (Vol. 1). New York: The Science Press.
Yerkes, R. (1921). Psychological Examining in the United States Army. In *Memoirs of the National Academy of Sciences.* Edited by R. Yerkes, 1–890.
Yudof, M., D. Kirp, and B. Levin. (1992). *Education, Policy and the Law* (third edition). St. Paul, MN: West.
Zenderland, L. (1998). *Measuring Minds: Henry Herbert Goddard and the Origins of American Intelligence Testing.* Cambridge: Cambridge University Press.
Zenger, T. (1994). Explaining Organizational Diseconomies of Scale in Rano D: Agency Problems and the Allocation of Engineering Talent, Ideas and Effort by Firm Size. *Management Science* 40(6), 708–29.

INDEX

Accelerated Christian Education (ACE) program, 125
Acton, James, 155
Adams, Lewis, 69
Adler, Mortimer, 3, 5
African Americans, xiv, xvii, 45, 54, 148, 177, 179; attending school percentages of, 57; basic education received by, 46, 178; busing of, xvi, 56, 148; in colonial period schools, 16; discrimination against, 47, 147; Freedman Bureau schools for, xviii, 23, 46, 55–56, 147; Jeanes Schools for, 147, 178; Jim Crow and *Plessy v. Ferguson* education impact on, xviii, 46, 56, 147, 178; laws prohibiting education of, 55, 147, 178, 180; NAACP involvement with, 56; NATCS work for, 56; racial prejudice in schools against, 54–55; religious schools for, 54, 147; "resegregation" of, 148; segregation of, xviii, 147; "separate but equal" doctrine impacting, 39, 56, 147, 178; student and teacher struggles of, 46–47; teacher and administrator decline of, 39–40, 57, 178; underground schools of, 55; Washington and DuBois high school direction debate of, 34, 69–70. *See also Brown v. Board of Education*; "desegregation consolidation"
African Free School, 54

AICE. *See* American Institute of Character Education
America 2000 project, 138; comprehensive accountability package of, 139; Edison Project of, 139; NASDC in, 139; voluntary national exam of, 139
American Association of School Supervisors, 119
American Civil War, xviii, 23, 32, 46, 55, 147, 178
American Institute of Character Education (AICE), 124
American Psychological Association (APA), 133
American Revolution, xiv, 95, 111–112, 112–113, 178
APA. *See* American Psychological Association
Assertive Discipline (Canter, L., and Canter, M.), 100
assessment, xxv; "bee" as raw form of, xxv, 129, 179; in-class written examination as, xxv; memorization as, xxv, 127; "report card" as, xxv, 130; standardized exam as, xxv–xxvi; of teachers, 140. *See also* testing
Astell, Mary, 3
Austen, Jane, 73
authoritarian educators, xvi, xxvii; "back to basics" curriculum of, xx; corporate-business model of organization by, xvi;

moral absolutism of, xxiv; physical consolidation of schools by, xvi; *Report of the Committee of Ten* response of, 33; standardized exams view of, 136; vocational curriculum of, xix–xx, xx, 33

authoritarian school, xx, 77, 116–117, 119; American educational history influences of, xiii; "back to basics" as component of, 4; behaviorism element in, 4–5; blank slate belief of, 3, 8, 93–94; businessmen reformers of, 5, 5–6, 31, 33, 37, 38; conservative perennialists perspective in, 3; corporate business model component of, 8, 31; "credential-based society" in, 5; democratic school struggle with, 1–2, 2, 180; democratic school versus, 12, 63; educational philosophies of, 2; educational policies influence of, 8; essential schools movement approach of, 4; NCLB and STEM support of, 8; productivity improvement in, 7; scientific management promotion in, 6–7; subject-centered teacher-focused approach of, 7–8; vocational and manual-skills training preference of, 68, 69, 71, 178

Bagley, William, 33, 98
Baldwin, James, 72–73
basal readers, xxi, 178; children's interests and experiences basis of, 84; "controlled vocabulary" use in, 84; "Dick and Jane" series as, 84, 85; difficulty grading of, 85; instructional materials in, 85; lesson plan and illustrations in, 85; multicultural perspective transformation of, 87–88; reading achievement tests in, 85; reading comprehension in, 84, 85; subject-centered approach of, 85; traditional family values in, 85
Beaman, Hannah, 51
Bell, Terrell, 73
Bennett, William, xxiv, 73, 117, 125
Bernard, John, 93
Beyond Freedom and Dignity (Skinner), 99
Binet, Alfred, 131, 132

Binet-Simon Scale, 131, 132
Black, Hugo, 159
Black Lives Matter movement, 148
Bobbitt, John Franklin: "platoon system" of, 7; "productive school" of, 7; as scientific management advocate, 5
Bolton, Thaddeus L., 131
The Book of Virtues (Bennett), xxiv, 125
Boy Scouts of America, 118
Brown v. Board of Education, 45, 178; in "desegregation consolidation," 39; desegregation directive of, 56
Buckley Amendment, 151–152, 155
Burton, Warren, 66, 78, 127
Bush, George H. W., 73, 138–139, 139
Bush, George W., 24
businessmen reformers, 5, 5–6, 31, 33, 37, 38
Butler, Nicholas Murray, 37; as businessmen reformer, 5, 33; business model reorganization and consolidation of, 6; school consolidation movement template of, 6

Campbell, George, 69
Canter, Lee, 100
Canter, Marlene, 100
Cardinal Principles of Secondary Education report, 33, 34, 68, 69, 70, 82; students' health emphasis in, 35; unification promotion in, 118; vocational and democratic educational approaches compromise in, xx, 34–35; vocational training and teaching methods recommendation in, 35, 178
Carver, George Washington, 69, 73, 87
Casement, William, 123
Cattell, James, 131
Cavazos, Lauro, 73
character education: absolute moral code promotion of, 117–118; ACE program use in, 125; authoritarian view of, 119; civic approach use in, xxiv, 115, 117, 119, 179; club success influence of, 118, 119; in colonial period schools, xxiii; compromises in, 119–120; debate over, 119; democratic vision of, 119; McGuffey *Readers* use in, xxiv, 114, 115; as moral education alternative,

INDEX

117; NEA involvement in, 118, 119; pledge use in, 118, 124; unification promotion in, 118; virtue-centered approach in, 124–125. *See also* moral education

Character Education Association, 117, 118

Cheever, Ezekiel, 48–49, 93

Civil Rights Act, 39, 56, 121, 148, 157

classroom discipline, 48, 53; active intervention in, 105; American Revolution and market revolution changing, 95, 178; Bagley student regimentation in, 98–99, 106; behaviorists influence of, 100, 178; behavior modification in, 99, 179; biblical imperative in, xxii, 91–92, 178; changing attitudes in, 93, 94; competency-based packaged programs in, 100; consequences of actions experience in, 94; constant supervision of students approach in, 96; as contentious and controversial, 91, 178; corporal punishment as, 92, 93, 106, 178; "deference" decline in, 95; democratic progressives view of, 101; dunce cap use in, 97; First Great Awakening challenging, 94, 106, 178; Freudian psychology in, 104; "industrial discipline" as, xxii, 100, 106, 178; McGuffey *Readers* approach to, 96, 106, 169; misbehavior prevention in, xxii; mutual respect in, 95, 103, 106, 179; new classroom design in, 98, 99, 106, 178; nonverbal methods of communication in, 100; "original sin" idea in, 91, 106; peer pressure and persuasion in, 103; Pestalozzi influence on, 101–102, 178; praise and humiliation use in, 93–94, 105, 106, 178; preventative approaches in, 104, 107, 178; principals as disciplinarians in, 98; Proverbs influence on, 91–92, 178; "Quincy Methods" in, 102; "reality therapy" use in, 104–105; "reinforcement" concept of, 99; severe problem causes in, 105; social cooperation development in, 102–103, 107, 179; society changing norms reflected in, xxii, xxiii; "stimulus-response" experiments in, 99; student little need of, 103; teachers losing jobs due to, 96–97

classroom instruction, xx, 3, 71, 145, 178; authoritarian and democratic favoring of, 77; authoritarian shift to democratic approach in, xx; basal readers use in, xxi, 84–85; basal reader transformation in, 87–88; bee as form of, 80; ciphering emphasis in, 81; comprehension in, xxi–xxii, 178; copybook use in, 79; desegregation of schools affecting, 86–87; extracurricular activities promotion in, 70, 82–83; flexible scheduling in, 86; hands-on experiences and group learning in, 75, 81–82; handwriting or penmanship component of, 79; Herbart's lesson plan use in, 83–84; immigrants tension in, 60, 148, 178; inquiry-based, 86; Kilpatrick's Project Method use in, xxi, 71, 83, 116; "learn by doing" concept in, xxi, 83; McGuffey *Readers* on reading comprehension in, 80–81; McGuffey *Readers* use in, 79–80; memorization and recitation as primary method in, xxi, 79–80; *A Nation at Risk* report changing, 88; open classroom and team teaching as, 86; progressive instructional ideas in, 86, 89; public education transformation of, xviii, xix; slates and pencils as aid in, 79; spelling story in, 78–79; teachers as role models in, 87; textbooks multicultural perspective in, 64, 73, 88; three-stage process of memorization as, 77–78

Classroom Management (Bagley), 98

Clinton, Bill, 24, 140

colonial period schools, xiv; African Americans and poor whites in, 16; apprenticeship and testing in, xxv, 16–17, 58, 111, 127–128; catechism primary schools in, 15; charity types of, 16, 178; church officials as teachers in, 49; church reliance of, xiv, 178; classic "hornbook" use in, 63–64; as community entertainment, xxi; compulsory primary schooling of, 16; corporal punishment in, xxvi, 93, 106,

109; dame schools in, 16, 50; discipline instruments used in, 48; exclusion and discrimination in, 30–31; federal government interest in, xiv; "Holy Experiment" in, 15; in-home and private types of, 16; local communities and private source funding of, 25, 27; as locally controlled, xiv, 13, 29; male teacher domination in, 48; memorization and recitation as primary method in, xxi, 77–78, 127, 178; memorization as assessment in, xxv, 127; middle colonies ethnic and religious heritage in, 15–16; moral-character education in, xxiii; *New England Primer* use in, xxiii, 64, 77, 109; New England schoolmasters in, 48–49; "Old Deluder Law" in, 14, 63; one-room schoolhouses of, 14, 41, 68; parochial nature of, xvii, 15, 30–31; parsimony towards, 29–30; private schools and tutors use in, xiv, 50, 177; Puritan educational measures in, 13–14; religion as centerpiece in, xix, 13, 63, 65, 109; as small and intimate, 29; southern colonies two-tiered educational approach in, 16–17; "sum books" use in, 64–65

Comenius, John Amos, 49, 58

common school, xiv, xv, 12, 78, 178; basic education in, 112; centralized public school system of, 20–21; civic responsibility and patriotism developed in, 17; commercial farmers' support of, 19; community-level funding commitment of, 25–26; court decisions concerning state control of, 22; Department of Education creation and, 23; early state funding of, 19–20; federal government funding of, 27, 28; fees collected to support, 19; God and country curriculum in, 65–66, 178; idealistic goal of, xvii; Kalamazoo Decision in, 22; local communities funding of, 25, 28; local communities state control opposition in, 21, 28; market revolution affecting, 17, 18; moral education in, xxiii, 111–112; Northwest Ordinance regarding, xiv, 17, 23; "Old Pike" use in, 65, 81; patriotism and individual achievement in, 112; religious education elimination in, 59; rich and poor communities funding difference in, 27; secular values promotion in, xix; slow change in, 17; spelling and arithmetic in, 112; state and property tax funding of, 26–27; *State ex rel. Clark v. Haworth* in, 22; state legislators ignoring of, 18; state mandates for, 20, 27; state oversight and administrative control of, 20–21, 22, 27–28, 31, 67, 177; success of, 67; teacher demand in, 52; Tenth Amendment concerning education in, xv, 18, 23; virtuous balanced curriculum in, xxiii, 113, 114, 115, 179; women admittance of, 46, 177; written exam use in, 130. *See also* public education

The Common School Journal (Mann), 21, 130, 179

Conant, James Bryant, 135–136

consolidated schools, xiv, xvi, xviii, 30; corporate model basis of, 31, 43, 177; cost and curricular offerings in, 42, 43; democratic progressives embracing of, 31; desegregation consolidation in, 39–40; high school movement of, 32–35; phases of, 31–32; regional isolation of, 29, 177; rural movement of, 35–37; urban movement in, 37–38

"Consolidation Century," 41, 177; black school closures in, 41, 177; Butler plan in, 6; educational landscape altered in, xvii; educational researchers findings on, 42; high schools as template in, 32, 40, 177; physical result of, 41; rural and urban school administration centralization in, 40–41; school districts decline in, xvii, 41; school size increase in, 41; smaller local school benefit instead of, 43; social integration decline in, 42; three distinct components of, xvi; two central arguments of, 41–42

Constitution, U. S., 143; First Amendment of, 153, 156; Fourteenth Amendment of, 152, 157; Fourth Amendment of, 156; Tenth Amendment concerning

education in, xv, 18, 23; Thirteenth Amendment of, xviii
corporal punishment, 150, 180; as classroom discipline, 92, 93, 106, 178; in colonial period schools, xxvi, 93, 106, 109
corporate-business model, xvi, 8, 31, 43, 177
Crandall, Prudence, 54–55
Cubberley, Elwood, 29, 143; as businessmen reformer, 5; state control of education favored by, 6, 22
Curie, Marie, 73
curriculum, xx, 3, 61, 70, 120, 178; authoritarian educators "back to basics" in, xx; authoritarian educators vocational promotion of, xix–xx, xx, 33; authoritarian vocational and manual-skills training preference in, 68, 69, 71, 178; classic "hornbook" use in, 63–64; Common Core regulations in, 75, 178; democratic educators classically oriented preference in, 68–69, 69; democratic educators transformation of, xix, 178; Dick and Jane series in, 72; diversified and comprehensive, 178; ESEA changing, 75; extracurricular activities in, 70, 82–83; fundamental transformation of, 63, 178; funding cuts in, 74; God and country in, 65–66, 178; group instruction in, 71; "hidden", 72–73, 87; integration of schools response in, 72–73; McGuffey *Readers* use in, 66–67; national unity promotion in, xix; *A Nation at Risk* report changing, 73; NCLB testing domination of, 74–75, 141, 179; new American, 67–68; *New England Primer* use in, 64; "Old Deluder Law" in, 14, 63; "Old Pike" use in, 65, 81; open classroom example in, 72; public education transformation of, xviii, xix; religion as, 65; science and foreign language courses in, 70; scientific education advocacy in, 73–74; single topic focus in, 71; student-centered, 11; "sum books" use in, 64–65; textbooks multicultural perspective in, 64, 73, 88; virtuous balanced in, xxiii, 113, 114, 115, 179; Washington and DuBois high school direction debate in, 34, 69–70; wave of conservatism in, 73; whole language theme in, 72. See also Cardinal Principles of Secondary Education report; Report of the Committee of Ten

Darwin, Charles, 130
DECA. See Distributive Education Clubs of America
democratic educators, xvi, xvii, xxvii, 178; classical form of education by, xix, 33; classically oriented curriculum preference of, 68–69, 69, 178; creative methods of instruction by, xx; curriculum transformation of, xix; memorization use rejected by, xxi; moral relativism of, xxiv; *Report of the Committee of Ten* support of, 33; standardized exams view of, 136; "virtuous balanced curriculum" of, xxiii, 113, 114, 115, 179
democratic school, xv, xx, 34–35, 77, 119; American educational history influences of, xiii; authoritarian school struggle with, 1–2, 2, 180; authoritarian school versus, 12, 63; constructivism in, 10; contemporary philosophies of, 8; different positions on education of, 177; humanist principle of, 9–10; moral education views of, 116–117; new postmodernist perspective in, 11; oppositions of, 12; "outside the box" thinking promotion in, 12; pragmatists and progressives of, 10–11, 31, 101; Rousseau association with, 8–9; student-centered curriculum in, 11
Department of Education: common school and, 23; educational policies promotion of, 24; educational research of, 24; regional resource centers of, 24; specific purpose funding of, 24
Department of Education's Office of Civil Rights, 146
Department of Health, Education, and Welfare, U. S., 39
Department of Justice, U. S., 39

"desegregation consolidation", xvi, 32, 86–87, 177; black educational village damage in, 39, 40, 177, 178; black principals and teachers number decline in, 39–40, 57, 178; black students transfer to white schools in, 39, 40, 41, 177; *Brown v. Board of Education* in, 39, 56; Civil Rights Law of 1964 in, 39; court initiation of, 39; as desegregation movement consequence, 39, 45; student dislike of, 40

Dewey, Alice Chipman, 10, 83, 102

Dewey, John, xxi, 8, 71, 102, 178; cooperative-learning environment of, 10–11; "learn by doing" concept of, 54, 83; moral-character education civic approach of, xxiv, 115, 179; "open classroom" of, 10, 178; on role of school, 10; social cooperation development of, 102–103, 179. *See also* Lab School, University of Chicago

Dick and Jane series (Foresman), xxi, 72, 84, 85

discrimination, 150; against African Americans, 47, 147; AIDS crisis impacting, 149; in colonial period schools, 30–31; against immigrants, xxvi, 47, 57, 148; against LGBTQ students, 149; P.L. 94-142 and IDEA protection of handicapped against, 149; regressive legislation about, 150; of women, 47, 147

Distributive Education Clubs of America (DECA), 82

The District School as It Was (Burton), 78

Dock, Christopher, 49, 58, 65

Draper, Andrew, 5, 6, 33, 37, 38

Dreikers, Rudolph, 104

DuBois, W. E. B., 34, 69–70

Educational Testing Service (ETS), 140

Elementary and Secondary Education Act (ESEA), 74, 75, 141

Emile (Rousseau), 9

ESEA. *See* Elementary and Secondary Education Act

ETS. *See* Educational Testing Service

European Enlightenment, xiii, 51

Every Student Succeeds Act, 24, 75, 89, 179

Experimental Studies of Intelligence (Binet), 131

FFA. *See* Future Farmers of America

First Great Awakening, xxii, 94, 106, 178

Fish, Stanley, 11

Fisher, Ronald, 130, 131

Foresman, Scott, xxi, 72, 84, 87

Foucault, Michel, 8, 11

Franklin, Benjamin, xiv, 17, 178

Frasier, Matthew, 153

Freedman Bureau schools, xviii, 23, 46, 55–56, 147

Freud, Sigmund, 104

Froebel, Fredrick, 9, 102

Future Farmers of America (FFA), 82

Galton, Francis, 130, 130–131

Gerwig, George, 33

Ginott, Haim, 104

Glasser, William, 104–105

Goddard, Henry H., 132

graded schools, xiv, 68, 177, 179

Granson, Milla, 55

Griscom, John, 101

Gue, Benjamin, 96, 157

Hackley, Delos, 26, 30

Haley, Margaret, 38

Harper, William Rainey, 5, 6, 37, 38

Head Start, 24, 27, 71–72

Herbart, Johann, 83–84, 84, 85

Hewitt, Edwin, 129

high school movement, xvi, 31; all student education in, 35; authoritarian vocational and manual-skills training preference in, 68, 69, 71, 178; as consolidated school prototype, 32, 40, 177; democratic educators classically oriented curriculum in, 68–69, 69, 178; extracurricular activities in, 70, 82–83; hands-on experiences and group learning in, 75, 81–82; Kilpatrick's Project Method use in, xxi, 71, 83, 116; "learn by doing" concept in, 54, 83; market revolution necessity of, 32; as "Peoples College," xix; proper direction

of education debate in, 32–33, 34, 68; science and foreign language courses in, 70; secondary education importance of, 32; "terminal degree" in, 32; Washington and DuBois direction debate in, 34, 69–70. *See also Cardinal Principles of Secondary Education* report; *Report of the Committee of Ten*
Horace's Compromise (Sizer), 4
Hutchins, William, 118

IDEA. *See* Individuals with Disabilities Education Act
immigrants, xvii, xviii, xix, 5, 12, 45, 179; anti-Catholic riots against, 59; assimilation of, 6; bilingual instruction of, 148; church schools for, 178; common school low tolerance for, 59, 178; culture conflict of, 60, 180; discrimination against, xxvi, 47, 57, 148; "English only" instruction tension among, 60, 148, 178; inclusion struggle of, 61; isolation and exclusion of, 60, 177, 178, 180; latent prejudice against, 47; nativism against, 149; NCAS work for, 60; promise of freedom draw of, 47; public education exclusion of, 31; as religious school teachers, 58
Individuals with Disabilities Education Act (IDEA), 149
"infant schools," 9, 102
in loco parentis, xxvi, 150, 151, 153, 180

James, William, 2, 4, 5
Jastrow, Joseph, 131
Jefferson, Thomas, xiv, 17, 18, 178
Jim Crow, xviii, 46, 56, 147, 178
Johnson, Marietta, 103
Jones, Fredric, 99–100

The Kallikak Family: A Study of the Heredity of Feeblemindedness (Goddard), 132
Kilpatrick, William Heard, xxi, 71, 83, 84, 116, 178
Kohlberg, Lawrence, 124
Kounin, Jacob, 104

Lab School, University of Chicago, 10, 83, 102, 103
Leonard and Gertrude (Pestalozzi), 101
Lilly Ledbetter Fair Pay Act, 147
Locke, John, xxii, 2, 5, 53, 178; blank slate belief of, 3, 8, 93–94; conservative perennialists perspective of, 3; method of instruction by, 3; middle-class education beginning of, 3
Lopez, Dwight, 152
Lumsdaine, A. A., 5
Lyon, Mary, 52, 146, 177

Mann, Horace, 20–21, 129–130, 179
Marland, Sidney, 137
Massachusetts Board of Education, 20
Mayo, Charles, 9, 102
McCarthy, Joseph, 121
McGuffey *Readers*, 60, 84, 178; classroom discipline approach of, 96, 106, 169; classroom instruction use of, 79–80; curriculum use of, 66–67; hard work emphasis in, 67; market values in, 66; moral-character education use of, xxiv, 114, 115; perseverance values in, 66–67; reading comprehension in, 80–81; secular values in, 66
Mennonites, 58, 65, 109
Meriam, J. L., 103
Montessori, Maria, 9
Moral and Spiritual Values in the Public Schools report, 119
moral education, 101, 110, 117, 117–118; American Revolution and market revolution changing, 111–112, 112–113; authoritarian and democratic views on, 116–117; cognitive moral development as, 124; in colonial era, xxiii; in common schools, xxiii, 111–112; communism fear changing, 120–121; community members involvement in, 111; compromises in, 119–120; culture wars and polarized political climate affecting, 121–122, 179; debate challenges over, 120; Dewey, J., civic approach to, xxiv, 115, 179; family and tradesmen responsibility in, 111, 179; illegal drug use issue and DARE program in, 122;

McGuffey *Readers* use in, xxiv, 114, 115; *New England Primer* use in, 110–111; patriotism and individual achievement in, 112; politics web in, 125–126; project method approach in, 116; proper form debate in, xxiv–xxv; religion in, xxiv, 114; school administrators distancing of, 122; SEC involvement in, 116; "Shorter Catechism" use in, 109–110, 179; STEM curriculum expansion over, 120; Ten Commandments use in, 109–110; values clarification movement in, 123; virtuous balanced curriculum affecting, xxiii, 113, 114, 115, 179

Moral Principles in Education (Dewey, J.), 115

Mount Holyoke Female Seminary, 52, 146, 177

Mulcaster, Richard, 92

NAACP. *See* National Association for the Advancement of Colored People

NAEP. *See* National Assessment of Educational Progress

NASDC. *See* New American Schools Development Corporation

NATCS. *See* National Association of Teachers of Colored Schools

National Achievement Test, 135

National Assessment of Educational Progress (NAEP), 75

National Association for the Advancement of Colored People (NAACP), 56

National Association of Teachers of Colored Schools (NATCS), 56

National Coalition of Advocates for Students (NCAS), 60

National Commission on Excellence in Education, 137–138

National Education Association (NEA), xx, 118, 119, 158, 178

National Research Council, 135

National Teachers Exam, 140

A Nation at Risk: The Imperative for Educational Reform report, xx, 4, 24, 73, 88, 137–138

NCAS. *See* National Coalition of Advocates for Students

NEA. *See* National Education Association

New American Schools Development Corporation (NASDC), 139

New England Primer, xxiii, 64; moral lessons in, 110–111; "Shorter Catechism" use of, 109–110, 179; three-stage process of memorization in, 77–78

No Child Left Behind Act, xx, 8, 12, 24, 75, 88–89; testing domination of curriculum by, 74–75, 141, 179

Northend, Charles, 113, 114, 129

Northwest Ordinance, xiv, 17, 23

Obama, Barack, 24

"Old Deluder Law," 14, 63

On the Origin of Species (Darwin), 130

open classroom, 10, 72, 86, 178

Page, D. P., 59

Paideia Proposal (Adler), 3

Parker, Francis, 102

Pearson, Karl, 130, 131

Penn, William, 15

Pestalozzi, Johann, xxi, 8, 80, 83, 84, 85; child-centered approach of, 101; classroom discipline influence of, 101–102, 178; humanist principle of, 9; love element of, 101; on mental and moral order, 101

Piaget, Jean, 8, 10

Pickering, Marvin, 157, 158, 180

Positive Classroom Discipline (Jones), 100

Potter, Alonzo, 52, 53, 113, 114

Principles of Psychology (James), 4

The Project Method (Kilpatrick), 116

Psychological Examination of Recruits Committee, 133

public education (schools), 45; authoritarian and democratic educators struggles in, xxvii; bilingual education opposition in, xviii; changing structure and organization of, xiv, 177; commercial farmers' support of, 19; curriculum and classroom instruction transformation in, xviii, xix; curriculum debate in, xx; diversity in, xvii; "dog in the manger" local control of, 6, 29, 143, 160; federal government role in, 23; human and civil rights in, xviii, xxvi–xxvii; immigrant and race exclusion from, 31; local control dark side in, 143–144; local control versus state control of, xiii–xiv; local intimacy to regional isolation in, 29, 177; national unity curriculum in, xix; "original sin" of, xvii; promotion of, xv; religion controversy in, 159; small-business support for, 19; states' authority over, xv, 31; structural transformation of, 29; student's constitutional rights in, xxvi–xxvii, 150, 155; workingmen's support for, 18

Quakers, 15, 54, 58, 65, 109

Raths, Louis, 123
Reagan, Ronald, 24, 73, 137
Reality Therapy: A New Approach to Psychiatry (Glasser), 104
Report of the Committee of Ten, 33, 68; authoritarian businessmen reformers against, 33; backlash over, 33; democratic educators support of, 33; educational ladder importance in, 33
Rickover, Hyman, 136
Robinson, John, 93
Roman Catholics, xix, 58, 60, 109, 178
Roper, Mary Augusta, 97, 157
Rousseau, Jean-Jacque, xxi, xxii, 8, 80, 83, 93, 102; child centered education belief of, 9, 101; consequences of actions discipline view of, 94, 178; democratic school association of, 8–9; learning based on experiences view of, 9
rural consolidation movement, xvi, 32, 40–41, 177; bitter struggles in, 36; local control at stake in, 36; political and social issue of, 35; reformers strategy in, 36–37
Rush, Benjamin, xiv, 17

Scholastic Aptitude Test (SAT), 135–136
The School and the School Master (Potter), 52
Schools with a Perfect Score (Gerwig), 33

Schools without Failure (Glasser), 104
Schulordnung (School Order) (Dock), 49, 58, 65
science, technology, engineering and math (STEM), 8, 73, 120
scientific management, 5, 6–7, 73–74
Scientific Management (Taylor), 6
SEC. *See* Social Education Association
Sheldon, Edward, 102
Short Introduction to the Latin Tongue (Cheever), 49
Simon, Theodore, 131, 132
Sizer, Theodore, 2, 4, 5
Skinner, B. F., 2, 4, 5, 99, 178; "programmed learning" of, 4–5; "reinforcement" concept of, 99
Snyder, C. B. J., 98
Social Education Association (SEC), 116
Society for the Propagation of the Gospel in Foreign Parts, 54
Some Thoughts Concerning Education (Locke), 3, 53, 93
Stanford-Binet exam, 132
STEM. *See* science, technology, engineering and math
"stimulus-response," 4, 5, 99, 100, 101
students, xxvii, 35, 46–47, 149, 180; access to personal records right of, 151–152, 180; -centered curriculum, 11; classroom discipline of, 96, 98–99, 103, 106; constitutional rights of, xxvi–xxvii, 150, 155; corporal punishment of, 150, 180; "desegregation consolidation" impacting black, 39, 40, 41, 177; drug testing controversy about, 154–155, 156, 180; due process rights of, 152, 180; freedom of speech concerning, 153, 156, 180; right to sue of, 151, 180; search and seizure specifications towards, 154, 156, 180
Succeeding with Difficult Students (Canter, L., and Canter, M.), 100
Supreme Court, U. S., 144; *Bellnier v. Lund*, 154, 180; *Bethel School District v. Frasier*, 153; *Brown v. Board of Education*, 39, 45, 56, 178; *Burkey v. Marshall County Board of Education*, 157; *Cleveland Board of Education v.*

LaFleur, 156, 180; *Engle v. Vitale*, 121, 159; *Franklin v. Gwinnet County Schools*, 146; *Goss v. Lopez*, 152, 157, 180; *Hortonville Joint School District v. Hortonville Education Association*, 158, 180; *Ingraham v. Wright*, 150; *Lee v. Weisman*, 159; *Pickering v. Board of Education*, 157, 180; *Plessey v. Ferguson*, xviii, 46, 56, 147, 178; *Roe v. Wade*, 121; *Swan v. Charlotte-Mecklenburg*, 56, 148; *Tinker v. Des Moines*, 153, 180; *Vernonia v. Acton*, 155, 180; *Wallace v. Jaffree*, 159; *Wood v. Strickland*, 151

Taylor, Fredrick Winslow, 5, 6–7
teachers, xxvii, 7–8, 46, 52, 177, 180; academic freedom of, 158, 180; African American struggles and decline of, 39–40, 46–47, 57, 178; assessment of, 140; collective bargaining of, 157–158, 180; in colonial period schools, 48, 49; due process regarding, 157; equal pay for women as, 157; free speech complex issue for, 157, 180; immigrants as, 58; legal liability of, 160, 180; losing jobs due to classroom discipline of, 96–97; PRAXIS series exams for, 140; as role models, 87; strikes illegal for, 158, 180; Title IX legislation protection for, 156, 180; urban consolidation movement worker position of, 38, 53–54, 177
Terman, Lewis, 132
testing, xxv, 85, 129, 179; Alpha and Beta educational levels in, 134; Alpha test in, 134, 179; America 2000 project regarding, 138–139; "bee" as raw form of, xxv, 129, 179; Binet and Simon influence on, 131–132; Clinton on, 140; in colonial period schools, xxv, 16–17, 58, 111, 127–128; diagnosis to sorting use of, 132–133, 139, 179; Galton colleagues and students work on, 131; Galton human intelligence variations study in, 130–131; General Order no. 74 for, 134; Goddard's work major impact on, 132; Mann struggle for written examination as, 129–130, 179;

memorization and recitation as, 127, 128–129, 179; National Achievement Test implementation in, 135; *A Nation at Risk* effect on, 137–138; NCLB pressure on, 74–75, 141, 179; new attitudes toward, 130; politics and, 136; progressive renaissance in, 137; rigor in education call regarding, 137; SAT for college admission, 135–136; standardized, 128, 134–135, 138, 178, 179; Stanford-Binet exam in, 132; Yerkes promotion of military, 133; of young women, 128
Thomas, Clarence, 155
Training up of Children (Mulcaster), 92
Troy Female Seminary, 52, 145, 177
Tubman, Harriet, 87
Tuskegee Institute, 34, 69

Uncle Sam's Boys and Girls Clubs, 118
universal education, 18, 21, 49, 178
urban consolidation movement, xvi, 32; administrative structure change in, 38, 40–41; board members and principals position in, 37–38; Butler plan use in, 37–38; reactions to, 38; superintendent of schools position in, 37; teachers as "workers" in, 38, 53–54, 177

Values and Teaching (Raths), 123
Voting Rights Act, 56, 121, 148

Ward, Lester, 97
Washington, Booker T., 34, 55, 69–70, 73
Watson, John, 4, 5, 99, 178; environmental importance in learning of, 4; "stimulus-response" experiments of, 99
Webster, Noah, 113, 114, 179
Whittle, Christopher, 139
Willard, Emma, 52, 145, 177
Wirt, William, 67
women, xvii, 45, 128, 147, 157, 179; changing attitudes towards, 51; classroom discipline change of, 53; common school admittance of, 46, 177; discrimination of, 47, 147; educational environment transformed by, 52; "female academies" for, 51–52, 145–146, 177; lower wages of, 52–53;

in patriarchal world, 47–48, 144; "Republican Motherhood" regarding, 51; right to vote of, 146; school limitations on, xviii, 46, 48, 51, 177, 180; school sports participation of, 146; segregated classes and inferior education of, 145; teacher preference of, 52; as teachers in urbanization, 38, 53–54, 177; teaching profession domination of, 46, 177; Title IX of Higher Education Act impact on, 146

A Year in Europe (Griscom), 101
Yerkes, Robert, 133
Young Ladies Academy of Philadelphia, 51, 145

ABOUT THE AUTHORS

Donald Parkerson is the Distinguished Professor of Teaching in the History Department at East Carolina University. He has published six books on the history of education with his coauthor, Jo Ann Parkerson. Their previous book with Rowman & Littlefield focused on the background of issues facing schools today—assessment, bureaucracy, and consolidation.

Jo Ann Parkerson is professor emerita of education at Methodist University. Previously she taught in the public schools and she draws on her educational experiences and research in her writing.

www.ingramcontent.com/pod-product-compliance
Lightning Source LLC
Chambersburg PA
CBHW031550300426
44111CB00006BA/243